"This outstanding work offers clinicians a sophisticated yet accessible [approach to integrating] mindfulness into trauma treatment. What sets this book apart is its [emphasis on flexibility over] protocol—teaching therapists not just what to do, but how to thoughtfully select and adapt mindfulness practices for trauma survivors. The authors' careful attention to safety, empowerment, and the therapeutic relationship demonstrates a deep understanding of trauma-sensitive mindfulness. Their focus on the four key mechanisms—attention regulation, body awareness, emotion regulation, and changes in perspective—provides a clear road map for clinicians while honoring the complexity of trauma recovery. This is the resource I wish I had when I first brought mindfulness into my trauma work."

—**David Treleaven, PhD**, author of *Trauma-Sensitive Mindfulness*

"This brilliant book makes mindfulness shine in therapy, and helps therapists shine when working with trauma. The authors' approach to clients is warm, curious, and nonjudgmental. Their vision is inclusive, flexible, and balanced. Mindfulness-based therapists will learn how to bring compassionate awareness more deeply into their work, and trauma-based therapists will be able to expand their clinical repertoire in safe and effective new ways. Highly recommended for clinicians of all persuasions!"

—**Christopher Germer, PhD**, Harvard Medical School lecturer, author of *The Mindful Path to Self-Compassion*, and coauthor of *The Mindful Self-Compassion Workbook* and *Teaching the Mindful Self-Compassion Program*

"In *Integrating Mindfulness into Psychotherapy for Trauma*, Zerubavel and Messman provide clinicians with insightful, nuanced, actionable guidance that will be of great benefit to their clients who are recovering from trauma. By focusing on the *why* and *how* of incorporating mindfulness, the authors provide flexible guidance that clinicians can readily adapt to their specific clients. This evidence-based, clinically informed book will be an essential resource for all clinicians."

—**Lizabeth Roemer, PhD**, professor of psychology at the University of Massachusetts Boston, and coauthor of *Acceptance-Based Behavioral Therapy*

"While mindfulness practices have much to offer in treating trauma, their use requires careful formulation. This detailed and accessible book provides exactly that! In combining theoretical observations with in-session transcripts, clinicians are amply supported in guiding their patients back to trusting their bodies, thoughts, and feelings in a restorative arc of healing from trauma."

—**Zindel Segal, PhD**, distinguished professor of psychology in mood disorders, and coauthor of *Better in Every Sense*

"Messman and Zerubavel have written a wonderful, hands-on guide to the integration of mindfulness and psychotherapy in the treatment of trauma survivors. Mindfulness can be a boon for people affected by adversity, and yet the nature of trauma symptoms can mean that trauma-related material intrudes during mindfulness meditation. This book does an outstanding job of addressing safety issues, and provides a safe and wise approach to mindfulness-based trauma therapy."

—**John Briere, PhD**, professor emeritus of psychiatry at the University of Southern California; author of numerous books, including *Principles of Trauma Therapy* and *Treating Risky and Compulsive Behavior in Trauma Survivors*; and long-time student of Buddhist psychology

"There is much to commend in this book. Zerubavel and Messman provide a highly informative guide for clinicians in the application of mindfulness practice into trauma treatment. Their trauma-informed foundation and attention to safety, individualization, and context—along with a clear articulation of mindfulness steps and procedures—is a gift to clinicians and clients alike. This book makes a distinct and state-of-the-art contribution to the literature on trauma treatment."

—**Christine A. Courtois, PhD, ABPP**, Delaware-licensed psychologist, board certified counseling psychologist, and author of *Healing the Incest Wound*

"Clinicians using process-based therapies for people with a wide range of clinical presentations will love this book. Grounded in scientific support and useful for clinicians at all levels, this is an anchoring resource and transdiagnostic light that brilliantly illuminates the many different reasons and ways to use mindfulness when treating people with traumatic stress."

—**M. Zachary Rosenthal, PhD**, associate professor and director of the Center for Misophonia and Emotion Regulation at Duke University

Integrating Mindfulness into Psychotherapy for Trauma

A Clinician's Guide to Using
Mindfulness Processes to Facilitate
Healing and Reduce Suffering

NOGA ZERUBAVEL, PHD | TERRI MESSMAN, PHD

CONTEXT PRESS
An Imprint of New Harbinger Publications, Inc.

Publisher's Note

This publication is designed to provide accurate and authoritative information in regard to the subject matter covered. It is sold with the understanding that the publisher is not engaged in rendering psychological, financial, legal, or other professional services. If expert assistance or counseling is needed, the services of a competent professional should be sought.

Authors' Note

The case material presented in this book is fictional or a composite of many cases. We use gender-neutral pronouns (they/them/their) throughout the book. Any exceptions are examples that refer to specific individuals.

NEW HARBINGER PUBLICATIONS is a registered trademark of New Harbinger Publications, Inc.

New Harbinger Publications is an employee-owned company.

Copyright © 2025 by Noga Zerubavel and Terri Messman
Context Press
An imprint of New Harbinger Publications, Inc.
5720 Shattuck Avenue
Oakland, CA 94609
www.newharbinger.com

All Rights Reserved

Cover design and illustration by Sara Christian

Acquired by Jess O'Brien

Edited by Iris van de Pavert

Library of Congress Cataloging-in-Publication Data on file

Printed in the United States of America

27   26   25

10   9   8   7   6   5   4   3   2   1   First Printing

For Dave, with gratitude for your kindness, grounded steadiness, and peaceful ways.

—Noga Zerubavel

For my parents, who gave me wings, and for Carol, who reminded me I could fly.

—Terri Messman

Contents

Foreword		vii
Acknowledgments		xi
Introduction: How Mindfulness Can Help Trauma Survivors		1

Part 1: Working with Trauma Survivors

1	Understanding Trauma and Its Effects	6
2	Mindfulness and Trauma in Case Conceptualization	24
3	Treatment Planning Based on Client Needs, Preferences, and Readiness	35

Part 2: Integrating Mindfulness into Treatment for Trauma Survivors

4	Expanding the Window of Tolerance	50
5	Safety-Enhancing Strategies for Mindfulness and Trauma-Related Overwhelm	60
6	How to Use Mindfulness in Session	85

Part 3: Techniques for Implementing Mindfulness Using a Process-Based Approach

7	Mindfulness, Attention Regulation, and Trauma	100
8	Mindfulness, Body Awareness, and Trauma	116
9	Mindfulness, Emotion Regulation, and Trauma	135
10	Mindfulness, Changes in Perspective, and Trauma	159

Part 4: Additional Considerations for the Mindful Trauma Therapist

11	Therapists' Reactions to Working with Trauma	182
	Conclusion	193
	References	195
	Index	203

Foreword

In this moment, in any moment, what relationship are you taking to the outer and the inner experience of your life as it is constantly unfolding? For example, do you feel trapped by painful memories or unpleasant bodily sensations? Are you being beset and pummeled by unwanted thoughts and worries? Lost in memories or planning the future? Feeling driven by relentless desires, cravings, or addiction, or mired in feelings of anger, sadness, or grief, do you feel trapped with no place to turn?

Who does not know these moments? Who has not learned how easily such moments, when loudly commanding the inner life, can shape and direct one's ongoing sense of who they are, their relationships with others, how they act, and how they answer for themselves the question: "who am I?"

Trauma can impress new, horrific, and disturbing memories into the mind and body, but it can also multiply, amplify, and distort the impact of common, everyday emotional and psychological challenges and stressors. In the presence of trauma or a history of trauma, a victim's life can become an unrelenting prison, filled with torment and despair. As the authors point out in comprehensive detail in this book, for people who have known or are experiencing trauma, the impact of that trauma on their body, emotions, thoughts, memories, self-concept, and relationships is extensive and long lasting.

The good news is that in this innovative and insightful book, the authors present a powerful model for understanding in thorough detail, aided by informative clinical examples, how trauma survivors can develop a "change in perspective" regarding themselves and their lives. In practical, concrete terms, the model and associated examples illustrate how a person can transform and move beyond trauma. They can discover and utilize new ways to relate, understand, and respond to the experience of this or any moment, and live richer, happier lives. This change in perspective, with the resultant healing, occurs using a combination of mindfulness practices and therapeutic psychological methods tailored carefully and specifically to each person's needs.

Ones's moment by moment subjective experience, the sense of "I, me, mine," is often called by terms like "the self," or "the experience of oneself," or one's "personality." While we may have heard about our "personality" or referred to "our self" for as long as we knew those words, what most of us have not noticed is that the elements of inner experience, things like thoughts, memories, emotions, and felt sensations—elements you could think of as building blocks of this subjective sense of "self"—are actually not permanent. They are constantly changing. Indeed, recognizing the fluid nature of the inner life experience, it may be more accurate to think of "self/myself" not as an unchanging noun, but rather as a verb—"selfing," you might say—instead of "self." Observing one's moment by moment inner life experience mindfully, anyone can immediately see for themselves the impermanent character of their inner life. Mindful observing reveals the process by which our "self" arises, is unfolding, and is not fixed.

Problems arise for anyone who cannot "unstick" from, over identifies with, clings to, or tries to own any of these various and changing inner conditions by calling it "me." If a person regards the times they are reliving a traumatic memory, or repeatedly experiencing a painful emotion like anxiety or depression, as something permanent or as an identity, or considers such conditions as character defining rather than momentary, their life can become painfully contracted and oppressive. How one thinks about these experiences—and the beliefs one holds about them—shapes one's very experience. The path to freedom from entrapment in these wrong views and beliefs about inner conditions lies in seeing and understanding their true nature. This clarity can come in many ways when the inner life is observed directly through mindful observation partnered with expert description and explanation of the world of memory, emotion, sensation, and perspective.

Mindfulness is the part that notices what is happening in and around us in each moment. Like a good mirror, mindfulness reflects/knows what is before it—but does not *become* that thing. Noticing the heat sensation in a coffee cup just as you touch it before lifting, or noticing the smell of toast before the name of it arises in your mind, or noticing the thought stream of busy planning unfolding as you sit stopped in traffic—these examples are glimpses of your natural mindfulness operating and noticing sensations, smells, or thoughts happening here and now, in the present moment. What attention notices, mindfulness knows, and no matter how disturbing, or sweet the object of attention, mindfulness is not attached. Like a mirror can reflect beauty or ugliness, mindfulness does not cling, but meets the next thing to come before it with fresh eyes.

As the authors point out, a well-known definition of mindfulness is provided by Jon Kabat-Zinn, the father of mindfulness-based stress reduction (MBSR). He defines mindfulness as "The awareness that emerges through paying attention on purpose, in the present moment, and non-judgmentally to the unfolding of experience moment by moment." (Kabat-Zinn 2003 pg. 145). With these elements of *intention* and *attention* in mind, it may also be helpful to consider a bit more about mindfulness. These considerations may be critical in appreciating the unique role of mindfulness, especially as it applies to healing trauma.

Practicing mindfulness in any form or method, consider the possibility that you already have all the mindfulness you need and you do not have to get more, or "deepen" your mindfulness, or change who you are. Whatever the trauma, it can be mindfully observed with the mindfulness one already has, especially with sensitivity to the needs and tolerance of the individual.

Also, it could be helpful to consider the possibility that, when practicing mindfulness, if you are thinking you cannot be mindful, or seem to be struggling with sleepiness, impatience, or a busy mind, for example, what is happening is that your mindfulness is fine, but your attention is bouncing somewhere else, which it is trained and prone to do reactively. Attentional training is needed, not more mindfulness. When this happens, perhaps experiment by looking with more attention, taking a sharper focus, at the experience of the moment *just as it is*.

The authors of this book have presented a powerful and insightful model and a detailed instruction manual for helping people heal and thrive after their sense of self has been distorted by trauma. While trauma has been understood and traditionally thought of as caused by any of a variety of severe stressors including violence, abuse, and exposure to horrific situations, the authors of this book take an innovative and powerful step forward as they say: "We recognize a broader spectrum of traumatic experiences. Events that do not involve physical injury or bodily threat can still cause severe psychological harm. Emotional or psychological abuse chips away at the victim's identity, shaping personality and general coping responses, even if it does not involve life threat." In today's world with so much disturbance impacting everyone, this is likely a timely perspective, possibly with wide applicability.

Trauma's effect and expression can be seen when the body is triggered into a stress reaction by something in the present that evokes the memory of trauma. The traumatic memories, thoughts, and emotions that arise are then reexperienced as threatening. The stress reaction is also called the "freeze, fight, or flight response." It involves one's entire mind and body. From this formation/combination of mental, emotional, and bodily experience unfolding repeatedly and chronically, one can find oneself living with a wide array of signs and symptoms resulting in a condition defined as post-traumatic stress disorder (PTSD).

Years ago, a war veteran came to one of my MBSR classes referred by their psychiatrist. Despite a powerful array of medication and talk therapies, they were still beset with flashbacks and severe anxiety, sleep disturbance, and other issues. Over the weeks of practicing mindfulness, there was pain and they struggled at times. We talked in detail about how to use the mindfulness practice to understand, and meet the experiences of a wartime flashback, and the resulting emotions and bodily sensations bound up in those memories. Over time, the person became much more relaxed and even cheerful in the class. At the end, I remarked about their dramatic change in appearance and energy. "What do you think happened?" I asked.

They replied: "I told myself for years that if I let myself remember the war, it would kill me. So, I did everything not to remember. In this class, by practicing mindfulness, I have learned that those memories will not kill me! I can let them come and go and know they are only memories. As I hold each of those memories mindfully, I know what it is. I know the memories are only something in the past. Those things are not actually happening right now. I don't have to be afraid of them anymore. I can live my life now, in the present moment."

Trauma's impact can live in us long after the actual event is past, and we may well carry that impact and the suffering it causes forward in each moment we live. In writing this book, the authors have given therapists and people suffering from trauma's blows a way forward to healing, to better health, and to greater peace and well-being.

Who among us has not felt the gravitational pull of life's pain, losses, and disappointments? Could this book also be a model and provide some very helpful perspectives and ideas for understanding and dealing with the basic human experience of suffering, even when it does not meet the diagnostic criteria of PTSD? Possibly.

For many reasons, I like and strongly endorse this book. Others are encouraged to read and reflect upon it. I wish to thank the authors, and believe that their efforts stand as another example of the possibility of human endeavor to give cause for immeasurable good to arise in this world. May immeasurable good and healing come to all associated with this work.

Jeffrey Brantley, MD
Sunset Beach, N.C. November, 2024

Acknowledgments

We would like to acknowledge the encouragement and enthusiasm at New Harbinger Publications for supporting this book. In particular, thank you to Jess O'Brien, Madison Davis, and Iris van de Pavert, and a special thanks to Matthew McKay, who attended our clinical institute, encouraged us to submit a book proposal, and shepherded us through initial stages of this process. We are deeply grateful to Jeffrey Brantley for his support and for offering his perspective as an opening to our book.

Thank you to our colleagues in the field who provided a foundation for our work: Judith Herman, Christine Courtois, Julian Ford, David Treleaven, Babette Rothschild, Pat Odgen, Tara Brach, Christopher Germer, John Briere, Britta Hölzel, Melanie Harned, Marsha Linehan, Patti Resick, Marylene Cloitre, Jennifer Freyd, Daniel Siegel, Kristin Neff, Thema Bryant, and many more.

From Noga: I am deeply grateful to the people who helped me learn and expand my thinking about trauma and its sequelae and recovery processes: Terri Messman, Margaret Wright, Laura Weisberg, Julia Kaplinska, Seamus Bhatt-Mackin, Raven Cuellar, Dana E. Crawford, Rebecca Ezechukwu, Hygge Schielke, Patricia Kerig, Kristin Wyatt, Elizabeth Reese, Kelly LeMaire, Gabriela Nagy, Dane Whicker, Kristen Reinhardt, Tyler Beach, and Françoise Mathieu.

I am also thankful to those who guided my journey of cultivating mindfulness and integrating it into therapy: Clive Robins, Zindel Segal, Nancy Zucker, Zach Rosenthal, Jessica West, Hani Elwafi, Sophie Lazarus, Rachel Watersong, Sara Lewis, Loren Mahar, Roger Knudson, Moria Smoski, and Marcus Rodriguez.

I absolutely could not have done this without the support of my beloved family: Yael and Eviatar Zerubavel, who dedicated themselves to disrupting and healing intergenerational trauma, and David Waller, Noam Zerubavel, Kristin Nothwehr, John Waller, Jennifer Waller, Tim Lippert, and Nira Fox. I have endless gratitude for my wonderful friends, along with cherished friends already named: Adam Carmel, Brandon Leishman, Melissa Miller, Max McNally, Marissa Howard, Colleen Cowperthwait, Sara Boeding, Alexandra Adame, Erin Walsh, Tory Eisenlohr-Moul, and a special thank you to Jeff Sapyta for thoughtful feedback on a prior chapter draft.

Finally, thank you to each of the courageous and dedicated clients who gave me the honor of participating in their recovery processes and guided me through their feedback in refining my clinical skills.

From Terri: Thank you to those who were so deeply involved in my development as a trauma therapist and who I carry with me daily: Trish Long and Patti Resick, Noga Zerubavel, Margaret Wright, Sue Orsillo, James DeLeppo, Lisa Fisher, Erika Sharkansky, Stephen Quinn, Phillip Kleespies, John Chaney, Gayle Iwamasa, Maureen Sullivan, Mindy Mechanic, Chebon Porter, Laurel Alexander, Gretchen Clum, Deborah Wise, and Debra Kaysen, and my many students. Thank you to my teachers and friends who supported my mindfulness journey: Noga Zerubavel, Cassie Wilson, Anne Minter, Bernadette Unger, Pat Ryan, Suzanne Klatt, Tim Raine, Patricia Sullivan, Andrea Ciafardini, and Darshan Kaur Khalsa.

Thank you to my family and friends: Larry and Lavonne Messman, Mick and Janet Messman, Randy and Jessica Messman, Nathan and Daniel Moore, Daniel Thomasson, Melissa Thomasson, Laurie Traveline Neyer, Stephanie King, Janie Schuppie, and Cindi Bixler.

I want to express gratitude to the many clients and trauma survivors I have had the privilege to work with over the years—I admire your courage and resilience. I am grateful and humbled to have had the opportunity to walk with you on your journey to recovery.

Lastly, Carol Brady, much gratitude—you are the ultimate trauma therapist.

INTRODUCTION

How Mindfulness Can Help Trauma Survivors

In this book, we advocate for a process-based approach when integrating mindfulness interventions to support trauma recovery. We can incorporate mindfulness into psychotherapy with trauma survivors in many different ways. Our approach emphasizes the intentional, thoughtful selection of mindfulness practices that we integrate with cognitive, behavioral, experiential, and relational strategies.

Much of the literature focuses on technique, often in a prescriptive fashion. While mindfulness-based treatment protocols can be useful guides to clinicians, we must attend to context when working with trauma survivors to enhance client empowerment and recovery as well as maintain safety. Technique is the response to the question, *What shall we do?* Context relates to questions such as, *Who is my client and why might mindfulness benefit them? How would this client's trauma history and current symptoms influence mindfulness practices?* And, *What exercises would be helpful, and when?*

Mindfulness processes are uniquely suited to help trauma survivors manage their distressing symptoms, build capacities that traumagenic contexts may have inhibited—or perhaps even actively suppressed or prohibited—and recover from traumatic stress responses. There are four processes (mechanisms of mindfulness) cultivated through mindfulness practice that we focus on in this book: *attention regulation*, *body awareness*, *emotion regulation (appraisal and exposure)*, and *changes in perspective*. Each of these processes influences the client's relationship to their difficulties and painful experiences (historical and current) in distinct and interconnected ways.

When integrating mindfulness into therapy with trauma survivors, we consider the degree to which the therapy centers around mindfulness practice. Informal mindfulness practices involve applying principles of mindfulness to daily living outside (*off the cushion practice*), such as eating mindfully; these applied practices can be easier for clients to understand and engage in than meditation. Before we provide active treatment, we consider how we will integrate mindfulness-related deficits or strengths into the case conceptualization and mindfulness practices into the treatment plan, tailored to each individual client. We believe this intentional approach is far more therapeutic and appropriate to psychotherapy than choosing a mindfulness practice based on whatever comes to mind in the moment.

We have organized the book in a way we hope will enhance the therapist's thoughtful and intentional approach to integrating mindfulness into psychotherapy so they can clearly articulate the planned purpose (or function) of including mindfulness. This can provide the client a clear understanding of what mindfulness entails, the rationale, and their ability to choose to engage in it or not (informed consent).

We focus on building the client's understanding, willingness, and capacity for tolerating painful emotions and information, all of which are mutually reinforcing and support the client's ability to engage in mindfulness practices and trauma processing. We emphasize that the therapist's mindful choice of practices combined with the deliberate application of safety-enhancing strategies can enhance the client's sense of safety, their building of capacities, and the promotion of their resilience and well-being.

Safety and Trauma-Sensitive Mindfulness

We know mindfulness can bring many benefits to those who experience suffering, which translates into our work with people who have experienced traumatic events and those enduring ongoing abuse and living within systems of oppression. The heart of the mindful trauma therapist's case conceptualization is recognizing that many of the presenting problems clinicians help to address are adaptations developed to cope in a traumagenic context. This viewpoint promotes both understanding and compassion.

The widespread availability and empirical support for mindfulness-related interventions represents an opportunity for trauma therapists to broaden the way we relate to our clients. We prioritize trauma-sensitive principles, such as client safety, autonomy, empowerment, and collaboration. These values that are inherent to the trauma framework supersede all others, including theoretical models of intervention. Mindfulness approaches cultivate qualities that are relevant to trauma recovery. Learning about mindfulness creates opportunities for the trauma survivor to develop skills to regain control and trust their experiences.

Our approach emphasizes safety. Mindfulness functions as a highly effective approach for building safety as it allows for collaborative tracking, therapist support, and intervention as needed to build capacities in the service of distress tolerance. Safety is a fundamental principle of trauma-sensitive intervention, and the integration of mindfulness gives us an opportunity to practice implementing self-regulating strategies that directly address physiological and neurobiological trauma adaptations.

Organization of the Book

In "Part 1: Working with Trauma Survivors," we provide an overview of the impact of trauma and considerations for working with trauma survivors. In chapter 1, we discuss the spectrum of trauma, emphasizing developmental and interpersonal trauma across the lifespan and patterns of traumatic stress, and introduce the trauma-adaptation framework to explain how trauma disrupts human experience. In chapter 2, we discuss mindfulness and trauma in case conceptualization. We introduce the framework put forth by Britta Hölzel and colleagues (2011), whose description of the four previously mentioned overarching mechanisms provides the organizational structure of our process-based approach. The part concludes with chapter 3, which delves into key considerations for treatment planning with trauma survivors. We introduce the principles of trauma-sensitive care, with an emphasis on safety, empowerment, and collaboration.

In "Part 2: Integrating Mindfulness into Treatment for Trauma Survivors," we delve deeper into treatment considerations to integrate mindfulness into psychotherapy with trauma survivors. In chapter 4, we review physiological dysregulation and discuss how the therapist can leverage mindfulness skills to expand the window of tolerance and why doing so increases the client's capacity to process trauma in a manner that safely avoids overwhelm. Chapter 5 focuses on enhancing safety in the integration of mindfulness and therapy. Finally, chapter 6 provides guidance for using mindfulness in session. This framework focuses on essential therapeutic tasks that follow each mindfulness practice: culling knowledge gleaned from the practice, consolidating learning, and generalizing learning. This process emphasizes and privileges experiential learning facilitated by the therapist's inquiry.

In "Part 3: Techniques for Implementing Mindfulness Using a Process-Based Approach," we focus on how we can integrate mindfulness into psychotherapy with the organizing framework of the four mechanisms. We dedicate a chapter to how each of these—attention regulation, body awareness, emotion regulation, and change in perspective—is cultivated through the integration of mindfulness practices and informal applications. We divide each chapter into two parts. The first part discusses each mechanism as it relates to mindfulness and the relevance of it to traumagenic contexts and trauma adaptation. The second part discusses how we can utilize mindfulness practices to enhance the development of that specific mechanism for specific types of trauma-related adaptations in clients. We provide case examples and sample dialogue and explain the online therapist materials (for instance, scripts for specific mindfulness exercises; see http://www.newharbinger.com/54650).

Attention regulation is the focus of chapter 7. We discuss the importance of attention regulation for shifting out of autopilot, as a precursor to mindful awareness. Body awareness is the focus of chapter 8. Here, we discuss how mindfulness enhances body awareness through interoception and somatic awareness, which contributes to a sense of attunement with our body and the capacity for responsiveness. Chapter 9 focuses on emotion regulation. We discuss how mindfulness can promote emotion regulation by enhancing the capacity to tolerate emotional distress (widening the window of tolerance), nonreactivity, and shifting habitual responses (such as decreasing avoidance). Finally, we focus on changes in perspective (of the self and others) in chapter 10. In this chapter, we discuss how mindfulness relates to changes in perspective in three domains—the experience of our thoughts, our mindset, and the relation to our self and others—and the emergent quality of these changes.

We conclude the book with chapter 11, which focuses on therapist reactions to working with trauma, including how difficulties can manifest, such as secondary traumatic stress (STS), empathic strain, and burnout. We encourage therapists to utilize the mindfulness practices discussed in the book to address the impact of trauma exposure. Therapist self-compassion is foundational in our stance toward ourselves.

We have written this book for clinicians who want to incorporate mindfulness practices into psychotherapy with trauma survivors. To make optimal choices that enhance client empowerment and maximize safety, we believe clinicians should understand the processes that explain mindfulness practices (the *why*) and factors that influence the selection of specific mindfulness practices chosen to enhance their current approach (the *how*). We believe that intervention *is* the intervention—teaching our clients about mindfulness is empowering. Engaging in mindfulness practices and participating in the process of inquiry teaches trauma survivors that they can trust their experiences, paving the road to recovery. We created this book with these values in mind. Thank you for joining us on this journey.

Part 1

Working with Trauma Survivors

CHAPTER 1

Understanding Trauma and Its Effects

As clinicians, we are more effective when we understand the nature of trauma and its potential impact on our clients. Knowledge of the different types of trauma and how people adapt to traumatic experiences, including adaptations such as mental disorders and relational difficulties, is crucial for a therapist. In this chapter, we will discuss definitions and types of trauma, patterns of traumatic stress, developmental considerations related to the psychological adaptation to trauma, and patterns of adaptation among trauma survivors. Next, we focus on trauma adaptation and meaning-making among trauma survivors, particularly how different types or patterns of trauma exposure are associated with patterns of beliefs or schemas. Finally, we will briefly discuss how experiences of trauma affect the capacity for mindfulness.

The Spectrum of Trauma

Over 70 percent of people experience trauma during their lifetime (Benjet et al., 2016), making it almost guaranteed that mental health professionals who work with clients will encounter trauma survivors. Trauma can mean several different things, depending upon the context. In some cases, we refer to trauma as an event, such as, *She experienced the trauma of rape*, but often trauma refers to the experience or aftermath of an event, such as, *He was traumatized witnessing the shooting on the bus*. Within the *Diagnostic and Statistical Manual of Mental Disorders* (DSM-5; American Psychiatric Association [APA], 2013), trauma as an event is labeled a potentially traumatic event because it is not always experienced as traumatic. Although the experience of trauma is unique to each individual, traumatic outcomes, such as post-traumatic stress disorder (PTSD) or depression, are connected to aspects of the traumatic event, prior trauma history, prior psychological functioning, and levels of social support.

Our framework encompasses a spectrum of trauma and severe stressors, including childhood or developmental trauma, intimate partner violence, psychological aggression, moral injury, secondary traumatic stress (STS), discrimination, and harassment. Within the *DSM-5* (APA, 2013) diagnostic criteria for PTSD, Criterion A defines trauma as the presence of life threat, serious injury, or sexual violence.

We recognize a broader spectrum of traumatic experiences. Events that do not involve physical injury or bodily threat can still cause severe psychological harm. Emotional or psychological abuse chips away at the victim's identity, shaping personality and general coping responses, even if it does not involve life threat. Traumatic experiences that involve social betrayal, such as child abuse, bullying, workplace harassment, discrimination, or racism, are very damaging, yet the impact may be insidious and thus overlooked or minimized. In this case, there may not be recognition of such experiences as trauma or abuse—either by the victim, witnesses, or institutions in which such experiences occur—leading to a failure to intervene to stop the abuse. Within this context, there can be a compounding effect when trauma such as racism is not recognized or acknowledged, which further invalidates the victim's experience. Thus, we attend to the roles of perpetrators, colluders, enablers, and bystanders in the trauma. This trauma within a trauma exacerbates the original trauma's deleterious impact because discriminatory or abusive actions are not addressed, which can embolden abusers. Ultimately, chronic trauma often leads to cumulative effects (symptoms).

In the next section, we focus on the phenomenon of interpersonal trauma and its deleterious effects. In most cases, interpersonal trauma occurs as childhood abuse or neglect, often within foundational relationships, such as between a caregiver and a child, or significant adult relationships, such as with intimate partners. We will discuss the complexities of interpersonal trauma, including dynamic effects on development and the effects of betrayal. Finally, we discuss more insidious and covert patterns of interpersonal trauma often overlooked by clinicians and clients.

> Interpersonal trauma, such as abuse, is associated with more severe and long-lasting consequences compared to impersonal trauma, such as a car accident.

Interpersonal Trauma

Interpersonal trauma is distressing precisely because it is trauma inflicted by people against people. When the traumatic experience is *interpersonal, relational, and intentional*, PTSD and other forms of psychological distress such as depression are more severe. Interpersonal trauma includes interpersonal violence (such as physical assault, rape, stalking), intimate partner aggression (such as psychological, physical, or sexual abuse), child maltreatment (such as neglect or sexual, physical, or psychological abuse), and witnessing violence within the family, neighborhood, or community. Exposure to war or genocide, combat, or acts of terrorism contains elements that may bridge between the two categories of interpersonal and impersonal trauma. Grief due to the loss of a comrade is interpersonal in nature, whereas other combat trauma can be impersonal. Common impersonal traumas include motor vehicle accidents, natural disasters, or manmade disasters (such as chemical or hazardous material spills).

Interpersonal trauma often leaves behind a more lasting footprint for several reasons. First, it occurs in the context of relationships with caregivers, romantic partners, or authority figures. Second, it is typically intentional, meaning that the trauma survivor lives with the horror that the acts perpetrated against a specific person or group of people were not accidental but purposeful. Third, trauma experienced in isolation (for example, being raped or abused) is associated with greater traumatic stress compared to trauma experienced by a group or community (for example, a natural disaster or terrorist attack). Importantly, the relational context in which trauma occurs is a key factor in predicting how individuals adapt to trauma.

Interpersonal trauma, such as abuse, especially during childhood, is associated with more severe and long-lasting consequences compared to impersonal trauma, such as a car accident. The age at which an individual experiences trauma affects its developmental influence and the trajectory of recovery. For these reasons, childhood maltreatment or other types of childhood trauma, particularly when they occur within a trusting relationship, are especially detrimental.

The context of an abusive relationship predicts the likelihood that abuse is disclosed, which affects the likelihood that trauma will continue. Fear, attachment, and trauma bonding facilitate cycles that involve multiple types of abuse among different family members, making disclosure and help-seeking difficult. In many cases, individuals have a strong attachment to their abuser that affects their adaptation to trauma. In this relational context, abuse can lead to surprise or confusion. When one depends on the abuser, trauma can involve high levels of betrayal, creating additional traumatic stress that can have long-standing effects.

Although other family members may witness trauma, in most cases family violence occurs in relative isolation because others outside this context may not be aware of the trauma being experienced. We should be sensitive to the deleterious impact of trauma occurring within an interpersonal context, particularly experiences of abuse or maltreatment by important figures, such as parents, partners, or close friends.

Betrayal Trauma

Many trauma models emphasize the peritraumatic experience of threat, fear, or terror, whether due to an interpersonal or impersonal event. However, it has been argued that social betrayal is relevant to meaning-making and the impact of trauma beyond fear. In the case of interpersonal trauma, the social context and level of attachment to the abuser will play a critical role in its impact. Betrayal trauma theory (Freyd & Birrell, 2013) argues that the impact of trauma and subsequent effects vary by two dimensions: fear and social betrayal. High levels of betrayal can happen when trauma occurs within a social relationship. Betrayal is more likely when the person experiencing trauma is dependent upon the perpetrator in some way, as in child maltreatment by a caregiver or intimate partner aggression.

The level of dependence intensifies attachment to the abuser and complicates the response to traumatic events. Traumas that involve high levels of betrayal may affect the fight-or-flight response so individuals may not be able to, nor want to, confront the abuser when attachment needs are strong, yet they are also unable to flee. As such, betrayal trauma may be associated with an increased likelihood of a freeze response. Betrayal trauma is also related to problems with memory retrieval of the event (traumatic amnesia), as well as higher levels of psychological distress compared to nonbetrayal traumas (Freyd & Birrell, 2013).

When present, betrayal significantly affects an individual's awareness, comprehension, or understanding of the traumatic experience. According to betrayal trauma theory (Freyd & Birrell, 2013), confronting a perpetrator risks negatively affecting the relationship by potentially alienating a caregiver or partner, which, in some cases, can be dangerous. This creates a bind for the victim, who must navigate the traumatic experience while striving to maintain attachment to the abuser, resulting in cognitive dissonance. One outcome of this dilemma is betrayal blindness. Here, the victim is not aware of the abuse as such, either by denying its occurrence, minimizing it, or shifting meanings to maintain attachment, such as blaming oneself (rather than the abuser) for what has happened. Betrayal blindness is linked to a simultaneous experience of *knowing but not knowing* or *seeing but not seeing*, which may decrease levels of cognitive dissonance when abuse or infidelity occurs in a romantic relationship.

Betrayal trauma and betrayal blindness are associated with disruptions in attention and memory, forgetting, an increased likelihood of dissociation, a risk of revictimization, and a decreased likelihood of disclosing abuse (Freyd & Birrell, 2013). Importantly, betrayal blindness can occur among witnesses to betrayal trauma, such as individuals in an abusive family or those who refuse to acknowledge racism, sexism, or other "isms," atrocities against humanity, or institutional betrayal. Finally, not all experiences of traumatic betrayal are associated with betrayal blindness; it is more common when betrayals are repeated, occur in an attachment bond, or when the victim depends on the abuser in some way.

Complex Trauma

Complex trauma refers to chronic, repetitive, and sustained exposure to multiple types of traumatic events, such as different forms of childhood maltreatment (for instance, sexual, physical, or emotional abuse) or maltreatment by multiple perpetrators (such as parents, siblings, or coaches). Adverse childhood experiences, such as having a substance-dependent parent or an absent parent due to divorce or separation, can be traumatic and affect development. Complex trauma in childhood disrupts and shifts developmental processes, shaping and influencing identity, attachment, and emotion regulation.

> Complex trauma involves chronic, repetitive, and sustained exposure to multiple types of trauma, such as different forms of child maltreatment or maltreatment by different perpetrators.

Complex trauma in childhood, in particular abuse and neglect from caregivers, disrupts the development of attachment and emotional bonds, which serve as a template for future relationships. Insecure attachment can form when the caregiver is relatively intrusive or anxious, which promotes anxious or preoccupied attachment in the child. A neglectful, detached, or nonresponsive caregiver can promote a detached, dismissive, or avoidant attachment.

> Complex trauma may affect development of insecure attachment—anxious-preoccupied, dismissive-avoidant, or disorganized attachment styles—with caregivers and, later, with romantic partners.

In some cases, caregivers are sought out by the child but are an unavailable or an unpredictable source of comfort or security *and* a source of danger (abusive) to the child. This confuses the child and activates physiological dysregulation, often resulting in disorganized attachment. Children with a disorganized attachment style (also called fearful-avoidant) seek closeness and protection while withdrawing due to fear of abandonment or physical threat. Disorganized attachment is a risk factor for significant emotion dysregulation and development of complex PTSD (CPTSD) or borderline personality disorder (BPD). When this pattern of attachment persists into adulthood, we will see emotion dysregulation related to CPTSD (such as withdrawal, rumination, and difficulty self-soothing) and BPD (such as idealization and devaluation, instability, and hostility) that is more severe than patterns seen in adults with secure, anxious, or avoidant attachment (Ford & Courtois, 2021).

Repetitive trauma in the context of significant interpersonal relationships (for instance, between a child and caregiver or between romantic partners) is more likely to disrupt processes related to well-being, such as attachment and self-regulation. Complex trauma can occur in adulthood, most commonly in the form of intimate partner violence; other examples include sex trafficking or being a prisoner of war. In the adulthood context, complex trauma can alter the identity of those who experience it.

Complex trauma fundamentally affects one's understanding of others and the world, assumptions about relationships, and the interpretation of life experiences. Traumatic experiences, beliefs, and identity become inextricably entwined because they can define one's life story, and they are carried forward into relationships, affecting expectations and shaping responses to later abuse or neglect.

Insidious or Covert Trauma

Some forms of trauma are subtle, difficult to perceive or identify, and not easily understood. Insidious or covert trauma is not usually a single discrete act readily identified as verbal or physical abuse. Rather, it is a series of acts identified as problematic but often erroneously not considered traumatic (for instance, relational aggression, racial microaggression, or gaslighting). The importance of these insidious and subtle forms of trauma cannot be underestimated.

> Insidious trauma is subtle, difficult to perceive or identify by the victim, and easily overlooked by many clinicians.

The Criterion A definition used for the diagnosis of PTSD (APA, 2013) is often interpreted to be the default definition of trauma. We believe this is an *incomplete conceptualization* that overemphasizes overt trauma. Traumatic events consistent with Criterion A, such as war, natural disaster, rape, or physical assault, are more overt and, thus, referred to as traumas. In contrast, subtler or covert traumatic experiences do not include life threat or witnessing traumatic death, thus do not rise to the level of Criterion A. These experiences include covert traumas such as relational aggression, bullying, psychological abuse, or infidelity.

Overt and covert traumas are both linked to traumatic stress, including PTSD symptoms. The vast majority of trauma survivors—over 75 percent—experience symptoms consistent with the PTSD syndrome regardless of whether their trauma experience met *DSM-4* Criterion A (Bodkin et al., 2007). Consistent with this research, we advocate for a broad definition of trauma that encompasses experiences reflecting both overt traumas and insidious or covert traumas.

Insidious or Covert Interpersonal Traumas		
Belittling, berating	Infidelity	Caregiver with:
Bullying	Invalidation	Mental illness
Coercive control	Isolation	Substance use disorder
Death of loved one or pet	Job loss	Chronic physical illness
Divorce	Mocking, humiliation	Terminal illness
Emotional abuse or neglect	Parentification	Criminal or legal problems
Estrangement from family	Physical neglect	
	Psychological maltreatment	
Excessive demands	Relational aggression	
Financial abuse	Sibling with terminal illness	
Gaslighting		
Ignoring	Social deprivation	
Inconsistent or unreliable parenting	Verbal abuse	

PSYCHOLOGICAL MALTREATMENT

Psychological maltreatment is an insidious form of interpersonal trauma that occurs in close relationships, typically with caregivers, partners, or authority figures (such as coaches or teachers). This form of maltreatment includes emotional abuse, emotional neglect, and parentification. Emotional abuse can take many forms, including belittling, mocking or humiliating in public, intentionally trying to scare, ignore, or isolate, or having unrealistic or rigid expectations accompanied by threats or intimidation. Emotional neglect involves failures to provide adequate nurturance, praise, affection, soothing, or protection from stressors. It can also involve being detached or uninvolved and restricting social interactions in the community, which, depending upon function and extent, may be better described as coercive control. Finally, intentional physical neglect, verbal abuse, and deprivation of social interactions are part of psychological maltreatment.

Psychological maltreatment fosters shame, and interferes with a child's ability to develop self-regulation and self-soothing. Victims of emotional abuse or neglect may invalidate or minimize their own distress due to beliefs that their experiences are not traumatic or are less severe or significant than other forms of trauma such as physical or sexual abuse (Spinazzola et al., 2014). Psychological maltreatment is associated with elevated risk for a multitude of psychological difficulties, including adult depression, anxiety, substance abuse, suicidal ideation and attempts, dissociation, and self-harm.

TRAUMATIC INVALIDATION

Traumatic invalidation occurs when a person's environment repeatedly or intensely communicates that their characteristics, behaviors, or emotional reactions are unacceptable (Harned, 2022). Intimate partner violence and childhood maltreatment involve traumatic invalidation. Also, racism, sexism, and other "isms," and transphobia, xenophobia, and others are forms of traumatic invalidation, which involves unequal treatment such as discrimination, or being excluded from or denied entry to valued groups. Traumatic invalidation is consequential because the people, groups, or institutions who commit it are those that the victim is dependent on or feels close to. It occurs at the cultural level for people from marginalized groups.

Moreover, traumatic invalidation includes psychological maltreatment behaviors, such as criticizing, ignoring, controlling, blaming, unequal treatment, and excluding. When it is occurring, the abuser is likely to minimize or deny abusive behavior and may go so far to suggest that the victim remembered incorrectly (gaslighting). One pattern of traumatic invalidation is the tendency for abusers to turn things around, claiming they are the victim instead. This pattern of behavior is called DARVO, an acronym for Denial, Attack, Reverse Victim and Offender (Freyd & Birrell, 2013). DARVO is present in relationships characterized by coercive control—in childhood with caregivers, or in adulthood with romantic partners or systemic oppression. When the abuser engages in traumatic invalidation and DARVO, collusion may occur with members of one's family, community, or institutional system such as media coverage of sexual harassment trials. Invalidating behaviors can take many forms; these experiences often cause the development of negative beliefs about oneself.

Patterns of Traumatic Stress

Our key message here is that trauma is not synonymous with PTSD. Overlapping and unique patterns of traumatic stress are associated with the experience of single traumatic events as well as sustained, chronic exposure. Traumatic stress tends to be more severe when it follows complex, chronic, or prolonged trauma, developmental trauma, repetitive trauma exposure across the lifetime, and trauma perceived as intentional. Further, individual characteristics are associated with increased risk for more severe traumatic stress, including female gender, a history of mental disorder, and minority status (ethnic, racial, cultural, sexual, or gender identity minorities).

We think about trauma transdiagnostically, using trauma-informed case conceptualization to formulate mindfulness-related interventions not only for clients with PTSD, but also for clients with depression, anxiety, obsessive-compulsive disorder, binge eating disorder, and so forth, when applicable. Features of traumatic stress include panic attacks, rumination, and fear-based avoidance that span a spectrum of conditions, including phobias, separation anxiety, and generalized anxiety disorder. Ultimately, trauma can be a profound, relational experience that affects perceptions of safety, trust, power or control, and the benevolence of others.

Post-Traumatic Stress Disorder

PTSD is perhaps the most easily recognized form of traumatic stress, characterized by intrusive symptoms such as nightmares and flashbacks, avoidance of reminders of the trauma, shifts in cognition (such as self-blame) and mood (such as detachment) related to the trauma, and physiological arousal (such as irritability, or an exaggerated startle response). The PTSD syndrome can be present in individuals regardless of whether their traumatic experience meets *DSM* Criterion A (Bodkin et al., 2007), although we only provide the diagnosis if Criterion A is met.

> **Patterns of Traumatic Stress**
> - Post-traumatic stress disorder (PTSD)
> - Complex PTSD
> - Dissociation/dissociative disorders
> - Borderline personality disorder

In the *DSM*, PTSD was originally classified as an anxiety disorder, given the emphasis on fear and network models as the basis for the disorder. In the *DSM-5*, it was moved to a new category given the recognition that other trauma responses occur alongside fear, including shame, disgust, hostility, sadness/loss/grief, and moral injury. Externalizing symptoms or behaviors such as rage, anger, aggression, risky behavior, and substance misuse are frequently comorbid or prominent features of PTSD. Variants of PTSD include a dissociative subtype (PTSD-D), CPTSD, and DESNOS (Disorders of Extreme Stress Not Otherwise Specified).

Complex PTSD

Providers who serve traumatized clients generally acknowledge that the diagnosis of PTSD does not adequately describe the distress of many trauma survivors, especially those who experienced complex trauma in childhood. Over thirty years ago, Judith Herman argued for a diagnostic conceptualization that accounts for complex trauma. First called complex PTSD, Herman (2015) formulated a new diagnosis that describes the effects of inescapable, complex trauma occurring within a relational context. With this, Herman was seeking to replace other diagnoses that do not fully reflect the role of trauma adaptations, such as BPD.

As portrayed in the *International Statistical Classification of Diseases and Related Health Problems* (11th ed. [ICD-11], World Health Organization, 2019), CPTSD includes three symptoms of PTSD: fear-related intrusive memories, avoidance, and hypervigilance. In addition, the ICD-11 includes disturbances of self-organization, namely: emotional dysregulation (such as emotional numbing and emptiness), relational detachment, and stable, negative self-perception (such as feeling damaged). According to Ford and Courtois (2021), the disturbances of self-organization are consistent with the flight response, characterized by unmodulated distress (for example, difficulty self-soothing and feeling guilt) and conscious (and unconscious) attempts to escape further harm (for instance, emotional numbing and relational detachment). Dissociation was originally included in the CPTSD concept developed by Herman but was not included as part of the *ICD-11* formulation (Ford & Courtois, 2021).

Dissociation

Trauma survivors often experience overwhelm as they seek to process and integrate the experience of trauma. This can result in dissociation, which is present in flashbacks and relates to other intrusive symptoms, amnesia, and altered states of consciousness (Fung et al., 2023). Dissociation is common among trauma survivors and can occur in the context of PTSD. Of those diagnosed with PTSD, approximately 20–33 percent have the dissociative subtype (PTSD-D), with heightened depersonalization, derealization, and prominent autonomic hypoarousal. Research suggests PTSD-D is associated with a more chronic and complex trauma history and is more common among survivors of early childhood maltreatment (Schiavone et al., 2018).

Across diverse traumatic stress syndromes such as PTSD, CPTSD, and BPD, dissociation reflects a state of physical or behavioral disorientation and shutdown that may result from the final stage of the stress response when freeze, flight, and fight responses have failed to restore safety and homeostasis (Ford & Courtois, 2021). Between 28.6 percent and 76.9 percent of people with CPTSD experience clinically significant dissociation (Fung et al., 2023). People with CPTSD or DESNOS have higher rates of dissociation than those with PTSD alone (Fung et al., 2023). Dissociation may be a mechanism that leads to the development of CPTSD among individuals with a history of childhood maltreatment. However, the nature of dissociation appears to be somewhat distinct depending on the disorder. In the case of PTSD, dissociation appears to reflect chronic adaptation to fear resulting from polyvictimization, whereas with BPD, dissociation is a transient reaction to extreme interpersonal stress.

Borderline Personality Disorder

BPD is similar to, but distinct from, CPTSD. Key features of BPD include an unstable identity or sense of self, attachment-related disruption that leads to frantic efforts to avoid abandonment, cycles of idealization and devaluation of others in relationships, and severe emotion dysregulation. In the context of pervasive difficulties with emotion regulation, episodes of severe dysregulation include bouts of rage, self-injurious behavior, and behaviors indicative of emotional dysregulation (for example, binge eating, reckless driving, or addictive behaviors such as shopping).

Transient, stress-related dissociation is also part of BPD and is especially prevalent among those with a history of childhood abuse. The rates of trauma exposure are very high in this population. Individuals diagnosed with BPD are three times more likely to have experienced childhood maltreatment compared to individuals with other personality disorders or psychiatric diagnoses (Ford & Courtois, 2021). It is noteworthy that rates of BPD are elevated among people who have experienced complex interpersonal trauma in adulthood (for instance, sex trafficking or torture). Other pathways to BPD include traumatic invalidation (Harned, 2022).

Because of the high prevalence of interpersonal trauma in the lives of patients with BPD, there has been increasing attention focused on the connection between BPD, PTSD, and CPTSD. This resulted in the conclusion that BPD is a distinct diagnostic entity, although frequently comorbid with traumatic stress. Ford and Courtois (2021) conceptualize BPD as a fight response that occurs when the trauma survivor is unable to sustain the hypervigilance associated with PTSD or the flight response associated with CPTSD. In the case of BPD, the fight mode involves impulsive, disorganized, and hostile behavior in relationships, in the context of low levels of self-awareness and self-efficacy.

Distinguishing PTSD, CPTSD, and BPD

Emerging research suggests distinct traumatic stress syndromes evolve with the increasing complexity and accumulation of trauma across the lifetime. Common variants of traumatic stress may include PTSD, CPTSD, or the combination of CPTSD and BPD. There is evidence that BPD and CPTSD involve distinct symptom profiles, each overlapping to a lesser degree with PTSD (Ford & Courtois, 2021). Further, there appears to be a dose-response pattern regarding trauma exposure and traumatic stress syndromes. Those with CPTSD have higher levels of and more severe emotional, sexual, and physical abuse and emotional and physical neglect in childhood compared to individuals diagnosed with PTSD. Comorbid CPTSD and BPD, associated with higher prevalence and more severe childhood emotional abuse and physical neglect compared to individuals with only CPTSD, is the most severe end of the spectrum.

Despite similarities, we can ascertain nuanced differences in emotion dysregulation, self-perceptions, and relational patterns among those with CPTSD versus BPD. Key differences (see the table in this section) include both the nature and intensity of the symptoms present. For example, emotion dysregulation in CPTSD involves chronic difficulty with self-soothing when distressed and chronic emotional numbing. However, in BPD, emotion dysregulation involves intense emotional lability, extreme uncontrolled anger, and profound emotional dysregulation (Ford & Courtois, 2021). Related, the negative self-perceptions in CPTSD involve a stable and chronic sense of guilt, shame, and worthlessness compared to the more unstable and fragmented sense of self in BPD.

Central Features of PTSD, CPTSD, and CPTSD+BPD		
PTSD	**CPTSD**	**CPTSD + BPD**

Central features:
 	
    Fear-related intrusive memories
 	
    Hyperarousal
 	
    Avoidance
 	
    Persistent fear
 	
    Dissociative amnesia, flashbacks
	Central features:
	
	    Emotional numbing & emptiness
	
	    Intense, diffuse emotional distress
	
	    Worthlessness, shame, & guilt
	
	    Stable perception of self as damaged
	
	    Sense of betrayal
	
	    Fear of closeness, relational detachment
		Central features:
		
		    Fragmented & unstable sense of self
		
		    Alternating enmeshment or disengagement
		
		    Intense, volatile relational hostility
		
		    Terror of abandonment
		
		    Chronic emptiness
		
		    Relational dysregulation
		
		    Transient, stress-related dissociation

Relative Likelihood of Trauma Type:		
Impersonal adult trauma Recent (< 6 months) trauma	Childhood emotional abuse Childhood sexual abuse Childhood physical abuse Childhood polyvictimization	Childhood emotional abuse Childhood sexual abuse Childhood physical abuse Childhood neglect Adult sexual victimization Lifetime polyvictimization Lifetime revictimization

The relational problems seen in CPTSD are characterized by avoidance and detachment related to a fear of closeness, whereas BPD is characterized by intense volatile relational instability, with alternating enmeshment and disengagement to avoid real or imaged abandonment (Ford & Courtois, 2021). It is important to note that CPTSD may better explain some symptoms typically attributed to BPD. This is especially relevant if negative self-perceptions are stable rather than unstable.

Psychological Adaptation to Trauma

The impact of trauma is far-reaching. Because of this, it is necessary that clinicians identify the imprint of trauma in present-day difficulties outside a diagnostic framework. Psychological adaptation to trauma cannot be adequately described by a single diagnostic category (or even multiple disorders). Instead, our clients and their problems are best understood within an ecological model that explains how trauma disrupts the human experience. We encourage clinicians to develop a case conceptualization that emphasizes how trauma uniquely affects an individual and their capacity for self-regulation—including distress tolerance, emotion regulation, and the experience of self and identity—as well as interpersonal functioning. A transdiagnostic lens allows us to have a more complete understanding through an inclusive trauma framework that sets the foundation for working with numerous populations affected by traumatic stress.

Domains of Psychological Adaptation

Individuals adapt to stressors in order to survive. Adaptation to trauma is no different. We base our trauma-informed case conceptualization on the assumption that the origin of symptoms lies within the desire to survive pain by developing strategies to cope with or adapt to a traumagenic environment.

A central tenet of this book is that many of the problems clients struggle with develop out of their adaptations to trauma. In this case, we can expect to witness behaviors (or symptoms) that developed initially within a traumagenic context and that persist outside this context or become maladaptive. These behaviors occur within several domains: biological, emotional, cognitive, behavioral, and interpersonal. Difficulties within each of these domains may present as symptoms of psychological conditions but may also exist outside this framework.

> Symptoms originate as adaptation strategies in a traumagenic environment.

We can organize our understanding of psychological adaptation to trauma by focusing on patterns of symptoms within each of the domains (McCann et al., 1988). Each one includes a range of responses, of which only some will be present for each client. This framework provides a guide for us as we identify the unique set of adaptations that relate to our clients' traumatic experiences, including the specific circumstances and the context of trauma, their temperament, and relational factors, such as receiving adequate support.

Domains of Trauma Adaptation: Symptoms & Sequelae

Biological	Emotional	Cognitive	Behavioral	Interpersonal
Physiological hyperarousal	Fear and anxiety	Shifts in belief systems	Aggression	Insecure attachment
Physiological hypoarousal	Anger and rage	Self-blame	Self-injurious behavior	Submissiveness or subjugation
Immune dysfunction	Irritability	Self-hatred	Suicidal behavior	Fawning response
High blood pressure	Guilt and regret	Disturbances in self	Avoidance	Assertiveness difficulties
Digestive disturbances	Shame	Dissociation	Overworking	Abandonment fears
Hypervigilance	Sadness, grief, or loss	Flashbacks	Eating disorder	Mistrust and paranoia
Sleep difficulties	Disgust	Perceptual disturbances	Impulsivity	Dominance and control
Pain disorders	Emotion dysregulation	Amnesia	Substance abuse	Hostility and aggression
Physical impairment	Feelings of emptiness	Attention problems	Compulsive behavior	Sexual problems
	Emotional numbing	Rumination		Revictimization
	Detachment	Worrying		
		Intrusions		
		Obsessions		

Our goal is to identify how we can integrate mindfulness into therapy to help our clients address problems within each domain. To do so, we start by observing and assessing the psychological adaptations our client developed to cope with prior traumatic experiences. Many of these adaptations are aspects of resilience and are not inherently problematic. The mindful therapist assists their client in observing and identifying patterns of adaptation and then determines whether those responses are helpful or maladaptive in the current context. These patterns of trauma adaptation can be stable or trait-like, episodic when associated with particular trauma-related cues (such as mistrust or abandonment), or vacillating, which involves shifting from one extreme to another in a predictable manner (for instance, from hyperarousal to immobilized hypoarousal). In the context of complex trauma, we are likely to see an oscillation between hyper- and hypoaroused states.

Clients will experience both common and unique psychological adaptations to trauma. Those common patterns resemble traumatic stress syndromes or related conditions. For example, many trauma survivors experience PTSD, which involves disruption in all of these domains: biological (such as hyperarousal), cognitive (such as mistrust, dissociation), emotional (such as reactivity to trauma cues), behavioral (such as avoidance, aggression), and interpersonal (such as detachment) (see table "Domains of Trauma Adaptation" for additional examples). A common cognitive adaptation is difficulty with concentration, a symptom of PTSD as well as depression. The mindful therapist may select specific mindfulness exercises, such as focusing on the breath or an external object, to help the client learn to improve concentration by enhancing their capacity for attentional control.

In addition to common adaptations, trauma survivors will each have their own unique constellation of psychological adaptations related to their trauma history. For example, individuals who experience chronic abuse in childhood are more likely to experience high levels of dissociation in contrast to those who experience a single traumatic event or an impersonal form of trauma. Mindfulness can help trauma survivors modulate arousal and dissociative responses, particularly by focusing on deepening interoceptive awareness. Mindfulness practices enable trauma survivors to detect dissociation when it is happening and to shift their attention in a way to reduce this response and bring themselves back to present awareness.

Trauma Adaptation and Meaning-Making

Our work is based on the Psychological Adaptation Model (McCann et al., 1988), which states that trauma survivors actively create their reality through processing the meaning of traumatic experiences. This model explains psychological adaptation to trauma by focusing on the construction of meaning through the development and maintenance of cognitive schemas. In this case, trauma influences the development of schemas, which affect the interpretation of traumatic events and psychological adaptation. Schemas affect how psychological adaptation is expressed across numerous domains, and psychological adaptation influences the cognitive processing of later life experiences, which then serve to strengthen or challenge schemas in a cyclical manner. The process of adaptation involves the revision of schemas, which is a continual process taking place across the life span.

> **Traumatic Schema Domains**
> - Safety
> - Trust
> - Control and power
> - Esteem
> - Intimacy

The schemas of safety, trust, power, esteem, and intimacy are emphasized by numerous trauma theories and in PTSD treatments due to their relevance to trauma survivors. Schemas about the self and others form in the context of developmental trauma and are elaborated or challenged based upon subsequent life experiences and additional exposure to trauma. Although most trauma survivors will experience a traumatic impact across these schemas, the degree and nature of the effects on the belief system will vary for each trauma survivor based upon their unique traumatic experiences (such as the nature of abuse, duration, and identity of the perpetrator), the context of trauma (such as the age of abuse, presence of witnesses or intervention, and disclosure), the presence of multiple forms of trauma (such as complex trauma or multiple forms of childhood maltreatment), and individual characteristics of the trauma survivor (such as personality, mental health, and resources). For example, a trauma survivor physically assaulted by a stranger may experience a greater disruption in the safety and power schemas relative to the other schemas, whereas a survivor of complex trauma may experience greater disruption in the schemas related to trust, esteem, and intimacy.

The relational context and severity of traumatic experiences is directly connected to their impact on beliefs about the self and others. In some cases, traumatic experiences are discrete events that occur in adulthood after a period of normal development marked by an absence of trauma. In this situation, prior schemas related to the self, others, and the world were typically not traumagenic.

When trauma does occur in this context, the survivor may experience shattered assumptions when beliefs regarding their safety, trust in others, and their sense of control are disrupted by the trauma, such as a robbery by a stranger in a parking garage (Janoff-Bulman, 1992). Although the trauma survivor previously recognized the potential risk of parking garages in certain areas or times of day, the trauma survivor assumed their own safety. After being robbed, the trauma survivor is forced to contend with the cognitive dissonance resulting from the conflict between the previously held belief that the world is a safe place and the reality of the assault. Faced with discrepant information, the trauma survivor can modify their belief system to acknowledge the reality of their traumatic experience (schema accommodation) albeit in a moderate fashion (for instance, *some* places are unsafe versus *all* places are unsafe).

When trauma survivors have difficulty accepting or acknowledging the reality of their trauma, such as minimizing or denying its existence (for instance, *It wasn't sexual assault; it was a miscommunication*), we see patterns of self-blame and other problematic beliefs develop as unconscious attempts to retain the previous belief system. This process, called assimilation, involves the failure to change or modify one's belief system to incorporate the reality that an event was traumatic. It is a hallmark feature of unprocessed trauma and related to the presence of traumatic stress.

In contrast, some individuals will dramatically shift their belief system following trauma, a common pattern in the context of shattered assumptions. In this case, beliefs are shifted significantly, reflecting a change in schemas that is extreme. This process, overaccommodation, involves a drastic, extreme, and inaccurate change in beliefs or schemas (for instance, *I will never date again because all men are potential rapists*). Both assimilation and overaccommodation are associated with symptoms of traumatic stress.

Conversely, accommodation involves an acceptance of the traumatic experience and modification of existing schemas to incorporate the experience, but in moderation. In this case, the survivor acknowledges the trauma and its impact while not drastically changing their worldview or beliefs about themselves or others.

For those who experience trauma across their lifetime, or for whom childhood trauma influenced the development of key beliefs about safety, trust, control, esteem, and intimacy, the pattern of meaning-making is slightly different. Instead of shattering assumptions, repeated traumatic experiences are frequently assimilated into existing schemas that the world is unsafe, others are dangerous or untrustworthy, and that the individual is helpless to protect themselves or their loved ones from danger. In this case, additional traumas are processed as confirmatory evidence of these traumatic schemas.

Among child abuse survivors, additional experiences of victimization, or revictimization, strengthen schemas that one is unable to protect oneself (self-safety), that one cannot trust their judgment (self-trust), or that others control their life (other-control). Patterns of revictimization or repeated victimization across the lifespan are more common than isolated traumatic events. Thus, we are more likely to encounter trauma survivors who have experienced polyvictimization and revictimization across the lifespan, resulting in beliefs and schemas more difficult to shift in contrast to trauma survivors whose beliefs have been shattered by isolated, adult-onset, impersonal traumatic experiences.

> **Examples of Psychological Adaptation to Trauma**
>
> - Self-criticism, self-blame
> - Self-doubt or not trusting oneself
> - Questioning perceptions of reality
> - Perfectionism or unrealistic standards
> - People-pleasing, fawning, acquiescing response

Trauma, Identity, and Interpersonal Relatedness

Different types of traumatic events will have distinct impacts on specific schemas and the meanings made by the trauma survivor. Interpersonal traumas are associated with impairment in aspects of social functioning and development of the self. In many cases of interpersonal violence, meaning-making involves schemas that result from the internalization of beliefs transmitted from the perpetrator to the victim. These schemas are the foundation for psychological adaptation. This can look like self-invalidation, for instance judging or criticizing oneself, ignoring one's own needs, or blaming oneself for problems. Interpersonal violence leads survivors to doubt their own perceptions of reality or avoid responsibilities by allowing others to decide for them. Another adaptation involves the setting of unrealistic standards or goals.

Early Maladaptive Schemas Associated with Childhood Maltreatment

- Emotional deprivation
- Social isolation
- Mistrust or abuse
- Abandonment
- Defectiveness or shame
- Subjugation
- Self-sacrifice
- Failure
- Vulnerability to harm

Childhood maltreatment and other adverse childhood experiences are associated with traumagenic beliefs related to interpersonal relatedness, including expectations of disconnection and rejection, emotional deprivation, abandonment, social isolation, defectiveness or shame, and mistrust or abuse. In addition, adults who experience child maltreatment can come to expect specific patterns of relating within adult intimate relationships, such as a need for self-sacrifice or subjugation to maintain relationships.

Many survivors carry within themselves a pervasive insecurity and fear of abandonment (for example, expecting others to reject or hurt them). This results in interpersonal styles of fawning and appeasement, such as trying hard to please others. Trauma adaptation can result in the survivor believing they do not matter or are inherently bad or simply feeling like they do not fit in. At times, the internalization of such beliefs can interfere with the ability of clinicians and traumatized clients to identify or detect the presence of trauma. In many cases, psychological adaptation can resemble personality traits or interpersonal styles rather than clear trauma responses.

Linking Trauma and Mindfulness

Research across types of trauma indicates that individuals with PTSD have lower levels of mindfulness, particularly in accessing mindful awareness and nonjudgment. People who are more mindful report fewer symptoms of PTSD (Harper et al., 2022). Most studies of trauma and mindfulness focus on specific types of traumatic experiences. Relevant to our discussion here, child maltreatment is associated with lower levels of trait mindfulness and self-compassion in adulthood. Moreover, low levels of mindfulness and self-compassion explain the link between numerous forms of childhood maltreatment and psychopathology in adults, suggesting that enhancing mindfulness can improve psychological functioning among survivors, including levels of PTSD, depression, anxiety, dissociation, and sleep problems (Fitzgerald, 2022).

Certain facets of mindfulness are associated with trauma-related schemas and interpersonal conflict (Janovsky et al., 2019). Mindfulness may improve functioning among survivors of child maltreatment by enhancing emotion regulation and adaptive cognitive processes, as well as reducing problematic or avoidant responses, including thought suppression and rumination (Fitzgerald, 2022). The next few chapters will discuss in further detail how the mindful trauma therapist can incorporate mindfulness into psychotherapy with trauma survivors.

Conclusion

The mindful trauma therapist is cognizant of the spectrum of trauma, including experiences not tied to *DSM* conceptualization of traumatic events. Interpersonal trauma versus impersonal experiences and the relational context of trauma, including betrayal, are important factors shaping trauma adaptations. Specific types of trauma, such as complex, developmental trauma, are associated with greater maladjustment related to widespread psychological adaptations, many of which come to resemble aspects of identity or characterological patterns.

Many clients will experience common aspects of psychological adaptation, such as post-traumatic stress syndromes, but shifts in beliefs about the self, others, and the world frequently will be unique given connections to specific aspects of the client's trauma and personal history. Clients often struggle with problems that develop out of their adaptations to trauma. Given this, we can expect to witness behaviors (or symptoms) that developed initially within a traumagenic context and persist outside this context or become maladaptive.

CHAPTER 2

Mindfulness and Trauma in Case Conceptualization

We can use mindfulness in therapy in a variety of ways. It is always a good idea to understand the purpose of mindfulness before introducing it to the client. Having a clear understanding of what mindfulness is and how mindfulness skills can be useful to our clients are important to our decisions of how and when to use it in therapy with trauma survivors. In this chapter, we will discuss mindfulness practices, the why and how of integrating mindfulness into our work with trauma survivors, how the therapist can bring mindful awareness to trauma symptoms and distress, our integration of psychological adaptation to trauma, mindfulness, and physiological arousal, and how to introduce mindfulness to the client.

The Why and How of Mindfulness

Misconceptions about mindfulness abound with plenty of problematic beliefs and myths. For example, the idea that mindfulness is a "cure all" and appropriate for all individuals with all types of difficulties is not accurate. Further, mindfulness is not a form of relaxation or a method to de-stress. Although these practices *can* produce a feeling of relaxation, it is not the primary purpose for inclusion in trauma-focused psychotherapy. Having relaxation as a goal is also inconsistent with mindfulness.

These misconceptions become even more problematic when applied to trauma recovery. Therefore, when choosing a mindfulness exercise for therapy, we must consider the purpose or goal of that intervention. If release of muscle tension is the goal, use evidence-based methods such as progressive muscle relaxation first, and make mindful nonstriving adaptations (for instance, terminology of muscle release in place of muscle relaxation). As part of a more comprehensive self-care plan, mindfulness practices may help lower our clients' levels of stress overall. If the therapist or client believes relaxation *should* result from mindfulness practices, especially immediately, it can lead to frustration and premature abandonment of that strategy.

Importantly, there is a popular myth that all mindfulness practice is benign, despite some research on detrimental outcomes for practitioners (Goldberg et al., 2022). As mindfulness practices become increasingly popular and widespread, especially meditation and yoga, there seems to be little discussion or understanding about the potential problems that can be encountered.

We recommend that the mindful trauma therapist approach the integration of mindfulness into psychotherapy by first identifying what purpose mindfulness can serve and second, how they will integrate it into treatment. We always start with the case conceptualization, which is client-specific (ideographically tailored) and connects presenting problems and contextual factors, in addition to client history, to arrive at a treatment plan. The case conceptualization influences our rationale for using mindfulness and provides the therapist with a roadmap for planning interventions. We refer to this as the *why* and the *how*.

> We recommend that the mindful trauma therapist first identify what purpose mindfulness can serve and second how mindfulness will be integrated into treatment.

Mindfulness is a multifaceted concept that encompasses a way of being. Jon Kabat-Zinn defined mindfulness as "The awareness that emerges through paying attention on purpose, in the present moment, and nonjudgmentally to the unfolding of experience moment by moment" (Kabat-Zinn, 2003, p. 145). Aspects of mindfulness, including nonreactivity, acceptance, and equanimity, emerge over time as individuals engage in mindfulness practice. When introducing mindfulness to our clients, we draw upon their own experiences and practice. As the therapist, we also embody qualities of mindfulness in session. We offer compassion and acceptance of challenges in the context of commitment to caring for oneself effectively.

Our rationale for integrating mindfulness in our work with trauma survivors draws upon the research of Britta Hölzel and colleagues (2011), who describe how mindfulness meditation improves psychological outcomes through four overarching mechanisms: 1) attention regulation, 2) body awareness, 3) emotion regulation, involving reappraisal and informal exposure, extinction, and reconsolidation, and 4) change in perspective. These overarching mechanisms develop sequentially.

Attention regulation is relevant to helping our clients shift out of automatic pilot. We can integrate mindfulness into therapy to improve attention regulation (for instance, with attentional control), teaching clients how to harness and shift their attention. This can be especially useful when the client feels "stuck" in the past through regret or rumination. Body awareness is an essential component of work with trauma survivors, as the body may hold cues associated with, or be part of, the traumatic experience itself. Mindfulness practices such as the body scan or walking meditation can enhance sensitivity to body sensations (interoception), as well as anchor attention in the present moment.

Mindfulness can enhance emotion regulation through appraisal by facilitating awareness of habitual patterns, such as avoidance, as well as discerning what is healthy versus harmful. Focusing on emotion regulation via appraisal can build cognitive flexibility and shift attributions of responsibility among trauma survivors, reducing self-blame. Further, mindfulness can enhance metacognition, promoting changes in perspective about the self and others. Mindfulness promotes cognitive defusion—seeing thoughts as mental events that are not necessarily true—allowing the client to observe their thoughts without getting caught up in the content. In addition, changes in perspective emerge from mindfulness practice, such as the cultivation of radical acceptance (for instance, that the abuser will not change). Although mindfulness may alleviate distress due to any one of these mechanisms, emotion regulation may be the most proximal precursor to such change (Hölzel et al., 2011).

We organize our why and how around these four overarching mechanisms as we consider the goal or focus of introducing mindfulness for a particular issue. We encourage the therapist to keep these primary mechanisms in mind to guide how the case conceptualization relates to relevant treatment options (treatment planning). Once we introduce mindfulness in treatment planning conversations, we discuss this rationale (the why) with clients to facilitate their understanding of the purpose of learning specific concepts and skills, as well as how mindfulness can benefit the trauma-focused therapy. In this process, we also correct misconceptions of what mindfulness entails and what mindfulness-based strategies or skills can do. Keeping in mind the why can increase client willingness to accept ideas related to mindfulness, and understanding the how may increase their willingness to try, engage in, and consistently practice specific mindfulness strategies.

Bringing Mindful Awareness to Trauma Symptoms and Distress

As the case conceptualization synthesizes through collaborative discussion, we begin to introduce treatment options. We can integrate mindfulness into therapy to facilitate our clients' awareness of the difficulties they experience. For example, for clients whose trauma adaptation involves a lack of awareness of internal experiences, mindfulness practices in session can build awareness of physical sensations, emotions, or thoughts tied to trauma. Mindfulness exercises help clients who struggle with emotional awareness and clarity by developing or strengthening those skills, cultivating their ability to tolerate painful emotions, and enhancing meta-awareness of the connections between current-day experiences and their trauma history. Clients can cultivate mindfulness and use it outside of therapy as well; the therapist's use of inquiry (chapter 6) facilitates generalization.

A trauma-informed framework is fundamental to our work with survivors. This means we hold a trauma-informed mindset sensitive to the context of the development and maintenance of the trauma responses. The heart of trauma-informed therapy is recognizing that many of the presenting problems clinicians help to address are adaptations developed to cope in a traumagenic context (Clark et al., 2015). This viewpoint promotes understanding and compassion. We are cognizant of how trauma shapes the human experience and are in touch with the many ways individuals adapt to traumagenic contexts. It is essential that we take a nonpathologizing stance on the trauma-related symptoms of our clients. Adaptation to trauma will often involve what is "normal" or "adaptive" in that particular traumagenic context. Symptoms, rather than a sign of intrinsic pathology, were once an adaptive response to trauma itself. We find it is helpful to discuss this functional framework with the client to help them explore the impact of their traumatic experiences and their response to it, including the purpose and function of symptoms or behaviors in the original traumagenic environment.

> Symptoms, rather than a sign of intrinsic pathology, were once an adaptive response to trauma itself.

Mindfulness provides a lens that promotes the client's ability to explore potential connections between traumatic experiences, symptoms, and coping strategies (adaptive and maladaptive) with curiosity and nonjudgment, which can reduce self-blame and shame. We can discuss how various responses kept the survivor safe and how the danger inherent in traumatic experiences activated physiological automatic processes. We maintain awareness of trauma's impact within relevant domains, explore hypotheses about the historical context of symptom development with the client, and convey clearly to the client that such responses were a way to adapt psychologically to the original (historical) traumagenic context. Symptoms connected to post-traumatic stress disorder (PTSD), for example, are the residual of chronic dysregulation of the activation of the sympathetic nervous system—dysregulation originally activated during trauma and maintained by survival strategies following trauma or between traumatic events. Generally, traumagenic responses cease to be adaptive in the current context, and in some cases, the responses are maladaptive or dysfunctional.

We encourage trauma survivors to use mindfulness to explore the sensations and thoughts associated with their symptoms and behavior (such as habitual patterns) to determine whether they believe changes would be helpful in the current environment. Holding this understanding dialectically, we acknowledge the origin and purpose of the symptom while also acknowledging that such responses are no longer effective in other contexts (or that the cost of such responses is too high).

Transdiagnostic Conceptualization and Diagnostic Considerations

We organize the diversity of client response to trauma in a framework that encompasses five areas (McCann et al., 1988): biological (physiological arousal, somatic complaints), emotional (fear, anger, shame), cognitive (perceptual disturbances, traumagenic beliefs), behavioral (suicidal behavior, aggression, substance use), and interpersonal (relationship problems, vulnerability to revictimization). As we assess client difficulties and determine treatment targets and goals, we recommend this framework to identify and prioritize specific problems and begin to think about relevant mindfulness mechanisms and practices to include in their treatment. Teaching clients the trauma-adaptation model helps to normalize their

> **Domains of Trauma Adaptation**
> - Biological
> - Emotional
> - Cognitive
> - Behavioral
> - Interpersonal

trauma responses and depathologize symptoms and related diagnoses. Mindfulness skills can facilitate client awareness, augmenting traditional cognitive behavioral strategies and exercises (such as ABC sheets) to increase awareness and clarity of thoughts, feelings, and behaviors.

A transdiagnostic framework allows us to notice various manifestations of trauma adaptations. Although PTSD is common among trauma survivors, many clients with significant trauma histories have other presenting problems, including variants of depression. Also common are anxiety disorders, related conditions such as obsessive-compulsive and hoarding disorder, or appetitive disorders such as substance use and eating disorders. When traumagenic in nature, these disorders may have an earlier onset, a more severe presentation, or a chronic, treatment-resistant course. For example, among adult survivors of childhood maltreatment, there is a distinct predominance of anhedonia in depression, and depression related to childhood maltreatment involves more suicidality, greater psychiatric comorbidity, and more severe, entrenched, and nonremitting symptoms (Medeiros et al., 2020).

Symptoms of these disorders emerge during the process of adaptation to the original traumatic experience(s). Diagnostic comorbidity is typical among trauma survivors, who frequently report mood problems, anxiety, and dysregulated behavior. Some problems are directly connected to dysregulated patterns of arousal (such as anxiety or panic), whereas others seem connected to compensatory strategies of coping with that arousal (such as substance use disorders [SUDs] or eating disorders). Trauma survivors also experience clinically significant behavior that does not fit within a specific diagnostic category, including suicidality, self-harm, dissociation, and interpersonal difficulties. Given the broad range of problems that trauma survivors bring into therapy, we embrace a transdiagnostic conceptualization of the presenting problems.

Identifying common underlying mechanisms helps to explain the overlap between PTSD and depression and the presence of behavioral problems, such as suicidality, self-harm, or eating disorders. Later we will layer in mindfulness to build awareness of interoceptive and emotional experiences that cue intense emotions and motivate maladaptive behavior. We target transdiagnostic constructs such as emotion dysregulation, with benefit for clients across diagnostic categories. For example, individuals who experience childhood maltreatment have greater difficulties with emotion regulation, which are associated with problems such as eating disorders or SUDs (Messman-Moore & Bhuptani, 2017). Emotion dysregulation often is treated using mindfulness-based interventions (MBIs).

Across the broad range of presenting problems that trauma survivors bring to therapy, we will hear stories of a client's traumatic experiences and will learn how the client understands their world, their beliefs about others, and how trauma has shaped or disrupted their identity. These stories contain key trauma themes, such as safety, trust, control, esteem, and intimacy. We can explore each in connection to the client's beliefs about self, others, and the world, helping our clients observe, describe, and integrate these themes within the context of the diagnosis. These observations contribute to our client's increased trust in their beliefs, perceptions, and experiences.

Noting the traumagenic origins of prevalent processes is a key feature of trauma-informed case conceptualization. For example, cognitive rumination is a common marker of the traumatic response. Individuals often engage in rumination in an unattainable effort to understand why they experienced abuse or what the abuser was thinking when it occurred. However, in this context, rumination can be a sign of cognitive avoidance or nonacceptance (for example, the failure to accept that the trauma [or some aspect of it] occurred). In cognitive processing therapy (CPT), we call this a *stuck point* (Resick et al., 2016).

Observing these thought processes and identifying their function aids the client in the processing and resolution of trauma themes, which often can bring about symptom resolution. For instance, the client may become aware that their negative self-talk is actually the internalized critical voice of an abusive, harsh parent. Making such an observation can create an opportunity for the therapist to introduce self-compassion and invite shifts in the client's beliefs around self-worth. Here, mindfulness is useful because it promotes a greater awareness of the connection between the client's traumatic experiences, their beliefs about what happened to them, and the present-day difficulties for which they are seeking treatment.

Mindfulness promotes attention regulation, body awareness, emotion regulation, and changes in the perception of the self and others. We will have numerous opportunities to integrate mindfulness exercises to facilitate the client's mindfulness skills in observing and describing their thoughts and emotional experiences. Throughout therapy, choice points will arise during which the therapist will decide which approach to take and which goal to privilege. Ultimately, where to focus the therapy is a decision for the therapist and the client. Our process-based approach (see chapter 3) allows great flexibility in this regard. In cases where trauma processing is the focus, we may utilize evidence-based practice with empirically supported therapies, such as CPT or exposure-based cognitive behavioral therapy (CBT) approaches.

Trauma and Physiological Dysregulation

Dysregulated physiological arousal is a hallmark feature of trauma (Herman, 2015). Hypervigilance, exaggerated startle response, and sleeping problems are key symptoms of PTSD and typically present for many trauma survivors. We aim to facilitate the client's understanding of how our bodies are equipped to protect us from danger and yet our bodies can set off false alarms.

We can introduce mindfulness to help our clients recognize physiological shifts in their body related to arousal, identifying changes that may be markers of specific emotional states. This means mindfulness can help trauma survivors be more in touch with their body and the information that it offers. We teach our clients safety-enhancing strategies that shift levels of arousal in their bodies—skills that reduce arousal directly, such as breathing exercises, or strategies that shift attention from internal to external stimuli to reduce distress.

Most trauma survivors who experience active symptoms have difficulty maintaining and rapidly returning to an optimal level of arousal. Instead, they frequently experience involuntary overcompensation, shifting between states of over and underarousal. Trauma-related difficulties relate directly to the disruption of the arousal system, including dysregulation of the sympathetic and parasympathetic branches of the autonomic nervous system (ANS). David Treleaven (2018) identified how mindfulness is relevant to patterns of disruption to the ANS in trauma survivors, which results in chronic dysregulated arousal, including vacillating hyperarousal and hypoarousal. The former includes increased sensation, emotional reactivity, hypervigilance, intrusive imagery, and disorganized cognitive processing. Conversely, the latter includes an absence of sensation, emotional numbing, dissociation, reduced physical movement, and disabled cognitive processing.

Window of Tolerance

Trauma survivors often present with either intense emotional suffering or emotional suppression (or dissociation) to avoid emotions that they deem unbearable; in such cases, the client must build the capacity to tolerate very painful emotions. In parallel, the client may experience their trauma memories as overwhelming, horrifying, shame inducing, destabilizing, or unbearable, signifying that they must build capacity to tolerate the memories and the associated emotions. A basic tenet of trauma-focused therapy is the importance of processing trauma-related experiences or themes, which occurs through participating in painful discussions. To do so, the client must have the capacity for emotion regulation to effectively process information (or new experiences) and integrate new meaning that occurs. If the client is dysregulated, they may not encode the experience fully, may not consolidate the meaning of the experience, and may struggle to generalize new learning.

Mindfulness can increase the client's capacity to do this difficult work in several ways. First, mindful awareness of one's thoughts, feelings, and bodily sensations provides information to the client about their emotional state and their current capacity to process trauma material. Second, mindful awareness facilitates the capacity for clients to notice, attend to, and label cognitive, physiological, and emotional experiences, increasing clarity of experience. It allows clients to notice any desire to avoid or ward off painful emotions. Third, mindfulness provides clients access to strategies to maintain a presence and engagement in the face of distressing memories or other difficult content in the therapy session. It facilitates awareness, emotional clarity, and distress tolerance. The mindful trauma therapist's process of engaging in inquiry (detailed in chapter 6) scaffolds and develops the client's ability to investigate, consolidate, and generalize new learning.

Clients can use mindfulness strategies to reduce their intensity of responses to trauma cues and broaden the window of tolerance. The window of tolerance describes the optimal zone of arousal for a person to function in everyday life (Siegel, 1999). When we are in the optimal zone, we feel grounded, open, curious, and present; we can effectively regulate our emotions, tolerate life stress, and engage in flexible strategies for coping and self-regulation.

According to Daniel Siegel (1999), the window of tolerance differs from person to person. Such differences are influenced by temperament, genetic factors, life experiences, and the current circumstances, such as hunger or fatigue. Experiencing trauma, particularly interpersonal violence, abuse, or neglect—especially in childhood—can negatively affect (narrow) the window of tolerance. For our purposes, we refer to the window of tolerance as the space in which optimal arousal exists, given the limits of a client's capacity to engage actively in therapy, or in our case, trauma-focused therapy. The therapeutic window represents the psychological midpoint between inadequate and overwhelming activation of trauma-related arousal during treatment, which is the hypothetical space where trauma-focused interventions are likely to be most beneficial (Briere & Scott, 2015).

Mindfulness can broaden or widen this therapeutic window, which increases the client's capacity for distress tolerance and decreases vulnerability to trauma-related cues. The window is a continuum, with client overwhelm marking the limit of both ends of the window of tolerance. Activation of the fight-flight system sends the client into the hyperarousal side of overwhelm. When the client's sympathetic nervous system becomes triggered and activated in session, signs of hyperarousal may include flushing, excessive crying, or difficulty calming themselves. Clients may describe feeling hyperarousal, fear, panic, and an increased heart rate and respiration. Clients might report being overly reactive, feeling distressed, having racing thoughts, or having difficulty processing information when they are in states of hyperarousal.

At the other end of the window of tolerance, the client is nearing a state of shutting down when they move into hypoarousal. This state involves the inhibition of normal reactions or a deactivation of the system. This may look like a client who is spacing out or dissociated, failing to initiate dialogue for long periods (or not responding to therapist comments), or showing drowsiness. Clients may report feeling numb, lethargic, or unmotivated. At extreme levels, the hypoarousal can manifest as a state of freeze where the client is immobilized.

The window of tolerance defines the parameters within which optimal therapeutic impact occurs, simultaneously maintaining the trauma survivor's sense of safety and leveraging the capacity to effectively deal with difficult emotions that arise during the therapeutic process. We can target the window of tolerance as we guide the session, observing the client response to know when to shift the focus as needed, organizing the session to titrate client arousal. We support the client so they remain within the window of tolerance while engaging with difficult stimuli (emotions, memories, or thoughts), guiding them in safety-enhancing strategies to help the client modulate emotional and physiological responses.

Once the client is able to use strategies to return to physiological equilibrium, we teach the client to expand the window of tolerance (Ogden, 2010). To do so, the client must find a willingness to maintain contact with high levels of distress when discussing trauma-related events or experiencing trauma-related emotions during therapy sessions. At this point, clients are experiencing significant distress but not an overwhelmed feeling, working on the edge or in the margins of the window of tolerance, which is safe but not too safe (Bromberg, 2006). We aim to work *near the farthest edges*, or margins, within the window of tolerance.

The goal is to gradually increase the client's capacity and thus gently expand the window of tolerance. The goal is not to eliminate distress; instead, the goal is for the client to allow themselves to experience distress as being within their capacity for self-regulation. Importantly, *staying in the middle of the window of tolerance can be countertherapeutic* (Ogden, 2010). Therapists and clients alike are shaped by the reinforcing comfort of the middle of the zone, but that will never expand the window. It may even narrow across time. Instead, we want to work collaboratively at the edges so that capacities are actively building. We teach the client to provide arousal ratings related to their window of tolerance so that they can provide important feedback to the therapist during the sessions themselves, as well as self-assess outside of sessions. See chapter 4 for information on expanding the window of tolerance.

Connecting Case Conceptualization to Treatment

Based on the case conceptualization, we consider whether mindfulness would be a part of the treatment plan (see chapter 3). Once we determine that integrating mindfulness into treatment is appropriate, we engage the client in a discussion of treatment planning, including conveying the why and how of mindfulness as relevant to the client's case conceptualization. An essential aspect of these discussions is allowing space for dialogue with the client to share their beliefs about, and experiences with, mindfulness. Within a trauma-informed framework, collaboration is a central tenet of our treatment planning.

We empower the client to share their preferences and concerns, prioritizing client choice, which enhances the client's sense of control (Clark et al., 2015). This means that we should not use a mindfulness approach if the client objects to the rationale for why we want to integrate mindfulness or to the strategies themselves. Some concerns may be resolved if a client's questions or beliefs are acknowledged and the why and how of mindfulness are adequately described. Providing examples of how mindfulness can facilitate client skill with attentional processes, including unhooking from rumination (or worry), as well as enhancing emotional acceptance and coping with painful emotions, such as sadness, shame, disgust, or anger, may increase client interest in or acceptance of using mindfulness in therapy.

In setting the stage for this work, it may be beneficial to describe mindfulness as a mindset the client can bring to trauma therapy. A mindful mindset involves an openness and nonjudgmental curiosity or willingness to explore trauma-related experiences and observe their symptoms and day-to-day experiences. Mindfulness helps the client sit with painful experiences without pushing them away, increasing both emotional acceptance and distress tolerance. As we move forward in treatment, we introduce, describe, and provide the rationale related to the why and how of each mindfulness exercise, empowering the client and enhancing their perceptions of control (see chapter 6 for specific information).

Our case conceptualization is scaffolding for the treatment plan. Once we have a strong understanding of the connections between trauma and mindfulness, that is, an idea why mindfulness may be useful to intervention with trauma survivors, the next step is to translate our case conceptualization into our treatment plan. In this step, we consider which mindfulness mechanisms are most salient to the presenting problem(s) within the traumagenic context, and then we identify mindfulness practices or strategies to target those mechanisms. Next, we will illustrate how we can connect the case conceptualization and treatment planning to integrate mindfulness into treatment.

For many trauma survivors, the dysregulation of a particular emotion(s) is central to the client's current impairment in functioning. These emotions typically include fear (anxiety, panic), shame, guilt, regret, sadness (disappointment, grief, loss, despair), anger (rage, irritability), and disgust. Many clinicians overlook that trauma sequelae may also include the dysregulation of positive emotions (for instance, anhedonia as dysregulation of pleasure or joy).

When focusing on building a client's capacities related to tolerating and regulating a particularly challenging emotion, we recommend a focus on two mindfulness mechanisms: emotion regulation (chapter 9) and change in perspective (chapter 10). For emotion regulation, practices such as mindfulness of emotion or working with difficulty are both helpful options for engaging exposure processes. For change in perspective, acceptance practices reduce rumination (which is typically nonacceptance thoughts) and self-compassion practices are helpful in developing kindness and gentleness toward painful emotions. Chapter 3 outlines our systematic approach to treatment planning. Additional examples of the translation of case conceptualization to treatment planning, which connects client problems, mindfulness mechanisms, and mindfulness intervention options similar to this, are located in "Appendix 1: Treatment Planning for Applying Mindfulness to Trauma Sequelae" (http://www.newharbinger.com/54650).

Considerations Moving Forward

Before engaging in trauma-focused therapy, the client learns self-regulation skills that allow them to observe, tolerate, and label physical reactions without overwhelm. Mindfulness skills facilitate this process of self-regulation. However, it is essential we privilege client safety when teaching mindfulness skills. Because mindfulness and meditation practice can increase the awareness of internal states, trauma survivors may experience an increase in the frequency and intensity of negative emotional states and traumatic memories when using these practices.

Emerging research suggests the presence of trauma symptoms, rather than a history of trauma, predicts distress during meditation (Zhu et al., 2019). It is important to be understanding of the impact of trauma and have knowledge and personal experience with mindfulness, to increase discernment in choosing or introducing practices to our clients. Client safety increases when we maintain our own personal mindfulness practice (Strand & Stige, 2021), which deepens our understanding of the potential challenges and benefits that arise from mindfulness. When we embody mindfulness and compassion in our work with trauma survivors, we serve as models for integrating these practices. See chapter 5 for an in-depth discussion of safety and mindfulness with trauma survivors.

Conclusion

A trauma-informed case conceptualization is fundamental to our work with survivors. Many presenting problems clinicians help to address are adaptations developed to cope in a traumagenic context. It is essential that we take a nonpathologizing stance regarding the trauma-related symptoms of our clients, considering what was "normal" or "adaptive" in that context. We can use mindfulness to enhance safety by maintaining the trauma survivor's physiological arousal within the window of tolerance. Mindfulness skills can broaden or widen this therapeutic window, which increases client coping capacity and decreases vulnerability to trauma-related cues. In addition, mindfulness may address trauma-related distress, such as reducing physiological arousal, increasing attentional control and capacity for self-regulation, and fostering acceptance of unwanted experiences.

CHAPTER 3

Treatment Planning Based on Client Needs, Preferences, and Readiness

Treatment planning includes complex decision-making about client presentation and needs, as well as client preferences and readiness. When you are considering whether mindfulness will be a part of the treatment plan for a trauma survivor, it is important to think through several considerations. In this chapter, we will discuss these in detail. First, we describe trauma-sensitive principles and their application. Second, we discuss the stage model for trauma treatment. Third, we address the choice between trauma-focused and trauma-informed treatment. Fourth, we discuss protocol-based approaches versus process-based approaches. Finally, we consider if mindfulness will be a part of treatment, and if so, whether it includes an intensive emphasis on meditation or mindfulness-informed psychotherapy.

Trauma-Sensitive Principles

Trauma-sensitive care considers the relevance of trauma history, trauma adaptations, traumagenic contextual factors (both present and past), and relational dynamics to case conceptualization and treatment planning. Our approach privileges collaboration with the trauma survivor and emphasizes the trauma-informed principles of safety, empowerment, respect, and positive regard. In addition, the therapeutic relationship and traumagenic relational dynamics, as well as other cultural and contextual factors, are important considerations for the integration of mindfulness in a trauma-sensitive manner (for further information, see Briere & Scott, 2015; Clark et al., 2015; Courtois & Ford, 2016; Treleaven, 2018).

Safety

Safety is the most central of the trauma-sensitive principles. We prioritize safety because during the traumatic experience, the trauma survivor lacked safety and control (Herman, 2015). The basis for safety is respect, positive regard, and the consistent therapeutic presence of the mindful trauma therapist. Our own mindfulness enhances attunement, which helps to ensure that the trauma survivor feels seen and heard and that their priorities, goals, and needs are considered. Safety is enhanced by our awareness (and ongoing assessment) of the trauma survivor's psychological adaptation patterns, self-safety (such as suicidality or self-harm) and external threats to safety (such as ongoing abuse in a romantic relationship or neighborhood violence). Client emotion regulation is an important aspect of psychological safety and, as such, a priority for our work because it contributes to the effective processing of information and memories (for further discussion, see chapter 4).

We enhance safety through stability, continuity, and predictability, which occurs when we establish clear, consistent, and appropriately flexible procedures and boundaries for the therapy process. Continuity in the scheduling of sessions (for instance, weekly at the same time and day of the week), meeting space (if multiple rooms or seating configurations are available), and organization of each session provides a sense of predictability, enhancing clients' perception of control. Feeling safe during the recall of traumatic memories is an essential part of successful trauma processing (Briere & Scott, 2015).

The pacing of treatment overall, as well as within each session, affects the client's perceptions of control and safety. We recommend conceptualizing each session as having three key components: guiding mindfulness practices (or facilitating trauma processing), intervening as needed on dysregulated physiological arousal to stay in or return to window of tolerance, and engaging in inquiry for consolidation (see chapter 6). Invitational (versus directive) language and trauma-sensitive modifications (for instance, the *choice* of mindfulness exercises with eyes open or closed) also enhance safety and a sense of control.

Empowerment

Empowerment involves enhancing the trauma survivor's sense of control and agency. It centers on choice and includes actively building the survivor's capacity to be engaged in the collaborative decision-making aspects of treatment. Empowerment begins with respect and positive regard (Briere & Scott, 2015). This attitude influences our responsiveness, the invitation of questions and feedback from the client, and the organization of sessions to flexibly address any client concerns. Empowerment involves holding space for the trauma survivor to express their understanding of their experiences and subsequent traumagenic responses, which destigmatizes the trauma adaptations the survivor developed to cope with their traumatic past. This includes normalizing and validating such responses by educating the client about the functional purpose of traumagenic psychological adaptations.

An essential component of empowerment involves informed consent (information about the treatment process) and psychoeducation. Clients need adequate information about the nature of the treatment to make an informed choice. Psychoeducation regarding the impact of trauma, trauma adaptations, and treatment options, including mindfulness interventions, are all part of the dynamic and ongoing nature of informed consent. By itself, psychoeducation is empowering because it increases the survivor's understanding of their difficulties while destigmatizing them (Herman, 2015). Seeking input from the trauma survivor relates to decisions throughout the course of therapy; thus, informed consent is not static. It is important to consider that traumagenic relational dynamics, such as submissiveness, may negatively affect the client's initial ability to engage in decision-making, in which case scaffolding may be helpful as autonomy, self-trust, and assertiveness develop.

Therapeutic Relationship & Traumagenic Relational Dynamics

The quality of the therapeutic relationship is essential to trauma-sensitive psychotherapy. In addition to respect and positive regard, we model attitudes of compassion, acceptance, and nonjudgment. We begin our work with clients by acknowledging the challenges (such as psychological pain) that the trauma survivor is choosing to face by engaging in psychotherapy. In this context, we express appreciation for the trauma survivor's courage and strength. Although we do not make promises to the client about outcomes, we should instill hope by avoiding reinforcing the survivor's hopelessness, helplessness, or demoralization (Briere & Scott, 2015) and instead discussing recovery processes.

It is likely that traumagenic relational dynamics, including transference and countertransference, will be present. Traumatic transference can be especially powerful, placing the therapist into the roles of rescuer, bystander, or perpetrator (Herman, 2015). This may manifest as client feelings of mistrust, sensitivity to power dynamics and rejection, or patterns of excessive dominance or submissiveness. The traumagenic origin of these dynamics is important to recognize (for further information on traumagenic relational dynamics, see Courtois & Ford, 2016; Herman, 2015)

Contextual Factors

Trauma-sensitive mindfulness considers individual, contextual, and cultural factors in treatment with trauma survivors. Many of these contextual factors connect to the emphasis on safety and can include access to and stability of resources, such as housing, food, health insurance, and employment. Early assessment of the extent and quality of social support can inform treatment planning as well as case conceptualization, especially when interpersonal trauma is familial or intergenerational.

We must consider cultural variation in the presentation of trauma adaptation, including differences that emerge related to gender role expectations, ethnic or racial differences, and exposure to trauma. Individuals who identify as part of a minoritized group (such as racial, ethnic, or sexual minorities) experience additional unique and hostile stressors that form a context in which they experience chronic traumatic events. Oppression and racism as a trauma are distressing in their own right but also can exacerbate responses to other traumatic events, such as a natural disaster or interpersonal violence (Williams, 2018). We also attend to intersectionality, the interlocking oppression that individuals experience from having multiple oppressed identities (Gómez, 2023). Trauma-sensitive mindfulness must integrate an understanding of these powerful forces.

David Treleaven (2018) shared a poignant clinical example of how a mindfulness breathing exercise could be invalidating (and potentially harmful) when the therapist rushes to reduce physiological reactivity without first acknowledging the significance and enormity of that client's recent experience of racial aggression. Even in the absence of an acute incident of discrimination or identity-based violence, we must be sure to acknowledge systemic traumas, such as the historical traumas of colonialism and enslavement, and cultural traumas, such as the forcible separation and assimilation and education of Indigenous children in US boarding schools.

Central Considerations in Treatment Planning

In keeping with the principles of trauma-informed care of empowerment and collaboration, our approach engages in collaborative treatment planning and invites the client to provide input about their preferences. At the same time, we are active guides in this process, offering the various options that are appropriate and specifying the benefits and challenges of each option. We stipulate what is known about the therapy based on its evidence base and provide our recommendations based on the clinically relevant recommendations. If certain treatment options are not available due to current clinical issues (for instance, treatment delivery would go against best practice guidance), the therapist also provides this information, including a discussion of contingencies related to the treatment options. The client is then empowered to make a treatment choice based on their preferences, capacities, and appropriate options.

There are many important considerations relevant to treatment planning. We will walk you through some of the major elements to consider in this phase.

The Stage Model for Working with Trauma Survivors

Best practice guidelines for psychotherapy with trauma survivors adhere to using a stage model that facilitates optimizing patient outcomes and quality of care without compromising safety (Forbes et al., 2020). The stage model includes the following three stages: 1) stabilization and safety, 2) processing trauma, and 3) reappraisal of traumatic memories into more adaptive views of the self, others, and the world (Cloitre et al., 2012; Courtois & Ford, 2016; Herman, 2015). Note that mindfulness practices can be therapeutic for trauma survivors at each one of these stages.

For clients who are not yet stable enough to safely engage with trauma processing, initial treatment goals include developing skills for tolerating painful emotions, interacting with distressing memories, and managing day-to-day stressors without turning to seriously destabilizing strategies (such as self-harm, suicidal behavior, and substance abuse). The stage model guides our thinking in working with trauma survivors. Client safety is promoted by thinking through stage model considerations. At the same time, we must also be careful not to slow client progress by using overly rigid interpretations of the stage model.

It is important to note that the stage model has had some controversy surrounding it. Central concerns expressed by those who disagree with the stage model include that this approach may potentially and unnecessarily delay symptom relief from trauma processing, may reinforce avoidance, and could communicate to clients the belief that they are unable to handle trauma processing (De Jongh et al., 2016; Resick et al., 2012). Our position is that these perspectives can be synthesized by having a stabilization phase *when needed for safety* prior to providing trauma-focused treatment for individuals with severe post-traumatic stress disorder (PTSD) or complex PTSD (CPTSD). Mindfulness functions as a highly effective intervention for building safety, as it allows for collaborative tracking, therapist support, and interventions as needed to build capacities in the service of widening the window of tolerance.

> We encourage you to engage trauma processing as soon as the client is open and able to (i.e., can engage with trauma memories without compromising safety).

Research demonstrates that most individuals do not experience exacerbation of symptoms during trauma-focused therapy; furthermore, among those that do, many still rapidly benefit from treatment, showing significantly reduced symptoms shortly thereafter (Harned et al., 2012; Larsen et al., 2016). Therefore, we encourage clinicians to engage in trauma processing as early in treatment as the client is open to it (willingness, preference) and is able to do so (able to engage with trauma memories without compromising safety). In this vein, we adhere to the stage model, which means we address safety and stabilization prior to engaging in trauma-focused therapy that involves intensive contact with avoided trauma content that the client perceives as overwhelming.

We agree that therapists can be overly inclusive about which threats to safety and stability would prevent a client from trauma-focused therapy. To illustrate, for many years it was widely accepted that substance use disorders (SUDs) had to be treated prior to treating PTSD. When studies began allowing individuals with SUDs to participate in trauma processing, positive outcomes in both PTSD and substance use were demonstrated, establishing that PTSD treatment also can improve SUDs, prompting a burgeoning set of concurrent treatment models. Consistent with this, we encourage trauma processing as early in treatment as is feasible.

We offer some heuristics related to managing safety. First, at a most basic level, we do not do trauma processing when there are current severe life-threatening behaviors (such as suicidal behaviors and self-harm), which often function to facilitate coping with overwhelming trauma memories and trauma-related emotions. Instead, we work very actively on building the capacity to tolerate the emotions related to trauma memories and trauma history.

Second, we need to prevent the client from experiencing such intense distress that learning fails to occur. When a client is extremely dysregulated, emotional processing and cognitive restructuring are not available, and effective consolidation cannot occur even if insights could be attained. We draw upon the evidence-based dialectical behavior therapy (DBT) prolonged exposure (DBT-PE) protocol (see Harned, 2022) to guide our heuristics regarding safety. We have a high threshold for the threats to safety that are required to be under full control before engaging in trauma processing. Specifically, we would *not* exclude clients with milder potential threats to safety (such as passive suicidal ideation), eating disorder symptoms that are not medically destabilizing, or SUDs, provided clients have sufficient control to abstain from substance use before and during the actual trauma interventions and home practice. Rather, we anticipate that some of those symptoms may in fact improve via treating trauma, particularly as they often function to reduce the experiencing of distressing trauma symptoms.

In summary, we want to ensure that the treatment plan allows for safe engagement in trauma processing, implemented in the manner preferable for the particular client, when they can cope more constructively and adaptively, or at least inhibit extremely unsafe problem behaviors.

In this book, we advocate for a *process-based approach* that includes a principle-based integration of mindfulness into trauma intervention. It makes sense that therapists should exercise great care and forethought in deciding when to implement trauma processing with a trauma-focused protocol (for instance, prolonged exposure [PE] or cognitive processing therapy [CPT]). However, a process-based approach allows for principle-based implementation of therapeutic interventions, such that brief trauma processing may occur through narrative exposure and emotional processing during a single session or a few sessions without immersion in a trauma-focused protocol (see chapter 5, "Pivot to Trauma Processing"). The client and therapist may choose to move into narrative exposure and emotional processing somewhat spontaneously in response to naturally arising trauma memories or trauma-related information. Thus, we can be dialectical in our approach to stage work and dabble in trauma processing as needed, which can help us assess the client's window of tolerance and capacities for doing this work.

Trauma-Informed and Trauma-Focused Therapies

Interventions for trauma survivors may be generic, trauma-informed, or trauma-focused. A generic treatment is not trauma-informed at all; that is, the intervention is not attentive to trauma or to working with trauma survivors. Many trauma survivors report receiving generic treatments in prior therapy.

Trauma-informed therapy attends to the relevance of trauma and conceptualizes symptoms as psychological adaptation to trauma.

Trauma-focused therapy is centered on trauma processing, which typically includes exposure to traumatic memories.

In contrast, *trauma-informed therapy* is attentive to links to trauma history and conceptualizes symptoms using the trauma-adaptation model. This type of therapy applies trauma-informed principles (safety, trustworthiness, empowerment, collaboration, and attention to culture and identity influences) and integrates the five themes of trauma (safety, trust, power and control, esteem, and intimacy).

Finally, *trauma-focused therapy* is centered on trauma processing, typically including exposure to trauma memory, exploring cognitions and beliefs about the trauma, and engaging in cognitive restructuring of inaccurate, distorted, problematic, or unhelpful beliefs. In trauma-focused therapy, the focus of each session is on the traumatic event(s) and sequelae as directly linked to the traumatic event, primarily through emotional and cognitive processing.

Best practice guidelines for treatment of trauma survivors specify that acutely suicidal individuals necessitate stabilization prior to engaging in trauma-focused treatment (Forbes et al., 2020). In such situations, we do not proceed with trauma-focused therapy, but rather focus on providing trauma-informed care. At the same time, we work toward trauma processing because it is so therapeutically potent.

Protocol-Based and Process-Based Approaches

In a *protocol-based approach*, the clinician has a manual that tells them how to approach the treatment step by step, typically including instructions for each session in a particular order that the clinician follows, attending to adherence while tailoring for the individual. Strengths of these types of approaches include increased consistency facilitating clinical trials, being able to tell the client how long the treatment will likely take, and perhaps some benefits to clinician confidence in delivery.

In contrast, in a *process-based approach*, the therapist is guided by principles governing processes of change (for instance, exposure, appraisal, cognitive defusion, and self-compassion), applied as relevant to case conceptualization, treatment plan, and context. Thus, when using trauma-focused protocols, there is ongoing trauma-focused work in each session. However, when using process-based approaches, there may be movement in and out of trauma processing in such a manner that the therapy is consistently trauma-informed as well as trauma-focused *during particular sessions or chapters of work*.

> In a process-based approach, the therapist is guided by principles governing processes of change, applied as relevant to case conceptualization, treatment plan, and context.

The approach we describe is a process-based, trauma-informed approach. It is also trauma-focused when relevant, if clients have the capacity to stay in their window of tolerance and feel willing to do that work. This does not mean avoiding distress or intense emotion; those are part of trauma recovery due to the nature of trauma itself. Rather, it means we avoid dysregulation and flooding, and we do not proceed without affirmative consent. If beneficial, we can also be dialectical here—a process-based therapy overall might include a protocol (such as PE or CPT) as these trauma-focused protocol therapies are the gold standard of treatment for PTSD and have the protocol-associated benefits noted above.

Alternatively, we often remain process-based in the trauma-focused work, applying principles of emotional processing or cognitive processing to a client's narrative exposure (telling the story of a particular traumatic event). The process-based approach allows us to be extremely flexible, modulating the amount of trauma processing as needed for the client to stay physiologically regulated while discussing the memory, in the process building capacities through resourcing strategies to facilitate expanding the window of tolerance.

The integration of formal mindfulness practices into psychotherapy allows for a targeted development of therapeutic processes that promote trauma recovery and decrease trauma symptoms. Furthermore, our approach emphasizes psychological safety (see chapter 5), and the integration of mindfulness gives us an opportunity to teach and guide various safety-enhancing strategies that help the client self-regulate and expand their window of tolerance. Thus, mindfulness becomes a training ground for the client to practice implementing safety-enhancing strategies that allow them deliberate control over dysregulation of the autonomic nervous system (ANS).

> Integrating mindfulness allows the client to practice implementing self-regulating strategies that intervene on physiological and neurobiological trauma adaptations.

While most therapies for trauma address cognitive, emotional, and behavioral elements, they often overlook the physiological elements that are extremely influential in trauma-related dysregulation (somatic therapies as a notable exception). Sensory-based, safety-enhancing strategies, such as grounding techniques and developing dual awareness (simultaneous awareness of the present moment and trauma memory), are of particular capacity-building importance, as they equip the client with key skills relevant to trauma processing.

Mindfulness-Based Interventions

Mindfulness may address mechanisms underlying trauma-related distress, such as reducing physiological arousal, increasing attentional control and the capacity for self-regulation, and fostering acceptance of unwanted experiences. Mindfulness-based interventions (MBIs) for trauma survivors can reduce symptoms of PTSD, depression, and anxiety (Goldsmith et al., 2014; Gallagos et al., 2015; Kelly & Garland, 2016; Jasbi et al., 2018), and increase resilience (Reyes et al., 2020). MBIs seem to be particularly useful in reducing avoidance and numbing symptoms of PTSD (Banks et al., 2015).

In addition, MBIs may shift trauma-based appraisals, such as decreasing shame, increasing acceptance, and decreasing attachment anxiety in survivors of interpersonal violence (Goldsmith et al., 2014; Kelly & Garland, 2016). Research examining MBIs for traumatized populations is still emerging. Empirical evidence is limited almost exclusively to controlled studies of MBIs, such as mindfulness-based stress reduction (MBSR) or mindfulness-based cognitive therapy (MBCT).

Distinguishing Between Types of Mindfulness-Based Therapies. Mindfulness-based psychotherapies encompass many different types. They are primarily cognitive behavioral therapies (CBTs). There is also literature about psychodynamic approaches, although less rigorously studied. Mindfulness-based psychotherapies include experiential practice and both Socratic teaching and direct teaching of mindfulness concepts. The mindfulness practice component may be applied in brief practice (for instance, five to ten minutes) or in longer duration practices (for instance, thirty to forty-five minutes), and may occur in every session or occasionally.

All of these therapies are typically referred to as mindfulness-based psychotherapies or MBIs. For clarity and distinction in this section, we will refer to those that emphasize longer-duration mindfulness practice in each session and are centered on mindfulness practice as *meditation-based therapies*. These therapies, including MBSR (Kabat-Zinn, 1990) and MBCT (Segal et al., 2013), are typically provided in group context allowing for longer duration sessions (typically two to two and a half hours) and therefore allow for longer meditation practices. The experience of longer practice offers a distinct meditation experience.

On occasion, these therapies are also implemented individually (such as individual MBCT; Paterniti et al., 2022) or intended for individual therapy (such as acceptance-based behavioral therapy [ABBT]; Roemer & Orsillo, 2020). At those times, typical modifications include reducing the duration of practices to a more feasible duration for individual therapy.

Other MBIs (that are not meditation-based) incorporate mindfulness practices and exercises at varying degrees of regularity and length. For example, in DBT (Linehan, 1993; Linehan, 2014), there is a brief mindfulness practice in each skills training session and in each DBT consultation team meeting. Alternatively, in acceptance and commitment therapy (ACT; Hayes et al., 1999), mindfulness practices are viewed as one of a variety of experiential exercises that can teach concepts like cognitive defusion and experiential acceptance, so a mindfulness practice may be used once every few sessions, while concepts relevant to mindfulness are discussed weekly.

> Ethical therapists do not use mindfulness interventions they are not qualified to provide.

In treatment planning discussions, we clearly distinguish between meditation-based therapy and mindfulness-based therapy. We are careful not to describe outcomes associated with meditation-based therapies as the likely outcome of other mindfulness-based therapies. Importantly, ethical therapists do not provide mindfulness-related interventions they are not qualified to offer; for instance, integrating twenty-five minute meditations when the therapist themselves has direct experience with only five minutes of practice. Instead, you can provide five-minute mindfulness interventions and offer additional resources, such as information on meditation centers in the community.

Some clients may choose to engage in mindfulness-based therapy and to enroll in a local or online meditation-based group. In collaboration, the therapist and the client decide together—with the client holding ultimate informed consent and decisional power—which therapeutic approaches will be implemented.

Integrating Mindfulness into the Treatment Plan

Mindfulness processes are uniquely well suited to help trauma survivors manage their distressing symptoms, build capacities that traumagenic contexts may have inhibited—or perhaps even actively suppressed or prohibited—and recover from episodic or chronic traumatic stress responses. There are four processes (mechanisms of mindfulness) cultivated through mindfulness practice: attention regulation, body awareness, emotion regulation (appraisal and exposure), and changes in perspective. Each of these processes influences the client's relationship to their difficulties and painful experiences (historical and current) in distinct ways, elaborated on in chapters 7–10.

> **Processes Cultivated via Mindfulness**
> - Attention regulation
> - Body awareness
> - Emotion regulation
> - Changes in perspective

Our approach emphasizes an intentional, thoughtful approach to the selection of mindful practices. We believe this is far more therapeutic and appropriate to psychotherapy than clinicians choosing a mindfulness practice to introduce based on whatever practice happens to occur to them in the moment. We encourage a model in which mindfulness and its clinically relevant mechanisms of change are integrated into treatment planning. In this model, we design a treatment plan that is directly relevant to elements of the case conceptualization. Our treatment plans designate clinically relevant processes that we intend to cultivate using mindfulness. Then we implement practices targeting the relevant processes.

In chapter 1, we discussed trauma sequelae in detail, conceptualizing them using the psychological adaptation to trauma model. This framework helps clients view trauma symptoms as historically adaptive but currently maladaptive or less adaptive than presently available alternatives. In the table "Domains of Trauma Adaptation" in chapter 1, we identify common trauma sequelae and symptoms in each domain of psychological adaptation.

As you look at this table, you can identify which adaptations are present for a particular client and consider which of the mindfulness processes are relevant to the client's presenting problems contributing to dysregulated distress or disruptions in functioning. We typically approach the cultivation of the four mindfulness processes in the order that we have listed them here, as each process integrates skills built in the prior process. That said, they can also be integrated independently if that is more suitable; if the client struggles with entering directly into emotion regulation or change in perspective practices, scaffold by circling back to attention training or body awareness.

For an exploration of each domain and the various trauma adaptations that have outlived their usefulness, are overgeneralized, or are harmful to the client and therefore need to be replaced, as well as guidance on relevant mindfulness processes to consider in treatment planning, please see Appendix 1 (http://www.newharbinger.com/54650). Regardless of the treatment plan details, if mindfulness is integrated, we must also attend to considerations regarding psychological safety and effective learning.

Psychological Safety

One of the strengths of our approach is intentional, systematic attention to building increased psychological safety (elaborated in chapter 5). This applies to meditation and managing trauma-related content for clients who are overwhelmed or dysregulated by that content. We are attentive to enhancing safety through three modalities.

First, we have a preparatory session teaching the client about the window of tolerance and physiological arousal ratings, options for independent modification during practice (such as opening the eyes or changing posture), and a few strategies for responding to difficulties during meditation (such as anchors, grounding techniques, or downregulating hyperarousal). Second, we emphasize therapist implementation of modifications and strategies to promote safe experiences of meditation as needed. Third, if the client has an extremely distressing or challenging experience during mindfulness practice in session, the therapist implements various interventions to help them return to *physiological equilibrium*, providing the client with skills for managing trauma-related intrusions and other overwhelming or adverse experiences.

Effective Learning

Another consideration that we are very attentive to is effective learning processes. For clients whose trauma adaptations include severe emotion dysregulation, we want to be mindful of how this problem can get in the way of effective learning. Learning requires *acquisition* (developing new understandings), *consolidation* (unifying information into a stable and lasting memory), and *generalization* (applying learning more widely than the context in which it was learned).

> Severe emotion dysregulation can disrupt learning by interfering with:
> - acquisition (of new information)
> - consolidation (unifying information, storing into memory)
> - generalization (applying knowledge in other contexts).

Experiencing severe emotion dysregulation can disrupt learning through problems in acquisition and consolidation, and generalization is not possible without those. As we will discuss in chapter 4, when clients are emotionally dysregulated, they are also physiologically dysregulated in ways that interfere with effective learning (for instance, intense hypoarousal disables cognition). A strategy we often use to mitigate this problem is to revisit or review key content (insights about patterns or strategies used for intervention) in the following session when the client is regulated and able to process information.

We can also structurally enhance consolidation and generalization by ending sessions with reflection and a summary or beginning sessions by reviewing key elements of the prior session. For many clients, one or both strategies are helpful as a standing tradition structured into each session. We also use inquiry to facilitate acquisition, consolidation, and generalization. In addition, we attend to reviewing home practices and discussing reflections to promote consolidation from that sphere, emphasizing the generalization function of home practice.

Contraindications: Attending to Context and When Not to Use Mindfulness

Mindfulness is not always appropriate or helpful. There are some presentations (such as psychosis) for which we might be more cautious to introduce mindfulness. There may also be individuals with presentations for which mindfulness is appropriate and part of their treatment plan, and still there are some sessions in which the context is not appropriate for initiating a formal mindfulness practice; these occur when there is a safety issue present or an important, time-sensitive situation that requires more active attention. We will review relevant considerations.

Individuals experiencing psychosis. When a client presents with psychosis, mindfulness needs to be approached with great caution, and you should proceed only if you have knowledge of managing psychosis. Otherwise, approach it as a contraindication (okay to integrate informal mindfulness; avoid formal mindfulness practice) or refer to a specialist.

If you have the appropriate expertise to proceed with caution, Shonin and colleagues (2014) provide recommendations for using mindfulness with individuals experiencing psychosis. They suggest the following adaptations: 1) mindfulness practices of a shorter duration (fifteen minutes or less), 2) long periods of silence should be avoided, 3) additional instruction of anchoring or grounding techniques (they suggest the body scan and counting the breath), 4) individualized attention, 5) insight-based meditation should be avoided, 6) the clinician should have at least three years of supervised mindfulness practice and experience providing instruction to others, 7) longer duration of treatment may be needed.

When integrating mindfulness abiding by these recommendations, it is also important to be knowledgeable about enhancing safety in meditation (see chapter 5).

Acute safety risk. In the context of an acute safety issue, mindfulness is *not* an appropriate intervention; instead, we pivot away from our treatment plan and triage risk assessment and safety planning to the top of therapeutic priorities. If risk assessment indicates that the client is an imminent risk to themselves or someone else, safety planning must be the central priority of the session until adequately addressed.

It can be hard to estimate the amount of time needed for safety planning or means restriction, therefore we must triage by allotting as much time as needed to managing safety concerns. Risk assessment and safety planning are reviewed in detail in "Appendix 2: Risk Assessment and Safety Planning" (http://www.newharbinger.com/54650). If someone is making suicide communications, engaging in suicide preparations or planning, a desire to die, or a plan with access to means or method, the focus must immediately turn to safety planning and means restriction. Safety planning is well established as a central intervention to mitigate suicide risk (Stanley & Brown, 2012; Stanley et al., 2018). Means restriction is one of the most important parts of safety planning as it appears to dramatically reduce suicide risk for at risk individuals (Barber and Miller, 2014).

Time-sensitive clinical opportunities. Another situational context in which we pivot away from mindfulness is when there is an important, time-sensitive situation that requires more active attention. For example, a client who typically experiences emotions in a more blunted manner and is now feeling emotions, and those emotions carry important information that benefits from verbal processing and therapeutic discussion, particularly as related to rarely available change contemplation. Other examples include a client in an intimate partner violence context feeling fear in the acute aftermath of an abuse episode or a client alarmed by a health event (such as a seizure) related to substance abuse.

If the client typically uses mindfulness for cognitive defusion and other decentering and has remained more detached in emotional processes, we pivot away from mindfulness. Instead, we focus on leveraging emotional information for activation of protective and safety-oriented, health-oriented, or recovery-oriented behaviors. This is particularly important in the context of intimate partner violence, as processing reactions to abuse episodes are time sensitive. Once the client moves into the contrition phase of the cycle of violence, which typically follows abuse episodes, the abusive partner leverages attachment-oriented strategies and expresses sorrow, promises of improvement, and expressions of deep devotion (Walker, 1979). These intermittent reinforcement processes alternating with intense aversive arousal produce traumatic bonding (Dutton & Painter, 1993). Therefore, as trauma therapists who understand the cycle of violence, if there is opportunity to catch someone in the natural emotions following an abuse event, we prioritize gathering clinically important elements immediately, knowing it may not be available by the next time we see this client.

Acute overwhelm and physiological dysregulation. Mindfulness is not therapeutic when the client is outside of their window of tolerance experiencing hyperarousal or hypoarousal (see chapter 4). This is often associated with trauma-related intrusions. In the context of intense physiological dysregulation, cognition may be impaired or disabled, impeding therapeutic learning. If we are already in a practice, we begin by offering practice modifications. However, if dysregulation maintains, continued efforts at mindfulness may exacerbate distress. Instead, at such times, we focus on implementing safety-enhancing strategies to return to physiological equilibrium and stabilize psychologically (chapter 5).

Balance deficits; avoid increasing excesses. Interventions ideally facilitate skill acquisition to balance deficits and shift maladaptive strategies to adaptive strategies to promote enhanced well-being and reduced symptoms. Britton (2019) highlights that using mindfulness practices without careful consideration of case conceptualization can lead to increasing excesses and may exacerbate symptoms. We believe that our approach of careful consideration of which mindfulness mechanisms to cultivate and, based on that, which practices to implement helps to avoid this pitfall. We encourage you to think about behaviors (cognitive and physical) and categorize deficits and excesses so you can consider which mindfulness processes to emphasize and deemphasize for your client.

As you can see, the issue of integrating mindfulness into therapy with traumatized clients is, for the most part, not one of contraindication, but more of thoughtful consideration and awareness of competence. There may be additional times when turning to a mindfulness practice seems dismissive of a client concern or avoidant of more extensive processing. We recommend seeking feedback from clients about when and how mindfulness practices are useful, as well as when and how they feel unhelpful or get in the way of other things that the client would like to attend to in therapy. This is an important discussion to have periodically in a collaborative, exploratory manner.

Conclusion

Our approach is a process-based therapy that is trauma-informed across the course of therapy and trauma-focused in certain sessions. We approach treatment planning collaboratively, first providing thorough information about treatment options and clinically relevant considerations and then empowering the client to choose their preferred treatment plan. Integrating mindfulness practices paired with inquiry can help the client build capacities relevant to trauma recovery. Integration of safety-enhancing strategies helps trauma survivors safely engage in mindfulness while providing opportunities to practice skills essential to tolerate trauma processing.

In circumstances when physical safety is at risk, mindfulness is secondary to addressing safety needs as comprehensively as possible. Therefore, risk assessment must occur immediately and, if needed, must be followed by safety planning, managing risk factors with an emphasis on means restriction. A mindfulness practice is not the appropriate clinical priority during a session when there is imminent risk. When psychological safety is at risk, we engage in safety-enhancing strategies.

Part 2

Integrating Mindfulness into Treatment for Trauma Survivors

CHAPTER 4

Expanding the Window of Tolerance

In this chapter, we introduce strategies we can use to help the trauma survivor expand the window of tolerance, as introduced in chapter 2. The window of tolerance is a guiding framework and useful illustration when working with trauma survivors. First, we will revisit some key features of the concept of the window of tolerance and its relevance to psychotherapy with trauma survivors. Next, we will discuss some considerations for the mindful trauma therapist as they engage with the trauma survivor, helping to titrate arousal and avoid overwhelm

Following the traumatic experience, many survivors continue to suffer from unconscious, automatic sensitivity to trauma reminders (triggers). This automatic process is carried out by the autonomic nervous system (ANS). The psychological adaptations that follow often include fear, shame, and rage, numbing, and negative beliefs about the self, which intensify the distress of trauma survivors. This dysregulated system makes it difficult for the trauma survivor to modulate extreme emotional states, which can involve heightened activation (hyperarousal) or states of deactivation (hypoarousal), often associated with overwhelm.

It is important to note that the arousal states occur in response not only to threatening experiences, but also to the *anticipation* of such events (Corrigan et al., 2011). This means that prolonged anticipatory states, as in ongoing childhood abuse or domestic violence, also lead to overactivation of the sympathetic (in states of fear or anger) or parasympathetic (in states of depression or despair) nervous systems. The freeze or immobilization response may occur because of the coactivation of the sympathetic and parasympathetic branches of the ANS, much like simultaneously stepping on the brake and the gas pedal of an automobile (Treleaven, 2018).

> A hallmark of trauma is the biphasic rollercoaster, the rapid shifting between states of hyper- and hypoarousal, with little time in the optimal zone of arousal.

A hallmark of trauma is the rapid shifting or alternating between hyper- and hypoaroused states, with little time in the optimal zone of arousal, called the biphasic rollercoaster (Corrigan et al., 2011). In this rollercoaster, trauma cues, reactive behaviors, and emotional states affect one another and shift the trauma survivor in and out of the extreme zones of arousal.

Imagine the following scenario: an intrusive memory elicits hyperarousal and subsequent emotional binge eating (a self-soothing strategy), which then triggers the negative thought, *I'm a disgusting person with no self-control*. This shifts the trauma survivor into a state of hypoarousal, increasing isolation and a focus on traumatic memories (maintaining hypoarousal). Then, the traumatic memories trigger a flashback of rage (hyperarousal), then shame (hypoarousal), then self-directed rage (hyperarousal), then substance intoxication (hypoarousal), and then withdrawal nightmares (hyperarousal). In this way, the trauma survivor pings back and forth between the extreme states of hyper- and hypoarousal, rarely remaining in the optimal arousal zone (Corrigan et al., 2011). Educating the trauma survivor about the biphasic rollercoaster and how to cope effectively is an important part of trauma therapy. Mindfulness skills will help to reduce the reactivity that elicits extreme and rapid shifts in arousal.

The window of tolerance is the optimal zone of arousal in which emotions are tolerable and experience can be integrated (Siegel, 1999). When inside this optimal zone, we feel grounded, open, curious, and present; we can effectively regulate our emotions, tolerate life stress, and engage in flexible strategies for coping and self-regulation. For our purposes, the window of tolerance encapsulates the optimal level of regulated arousal, within which the trauma survivor can process their experience cognitively (thinking and talking about it) and remain connected to their body (Clark et al., 2015).

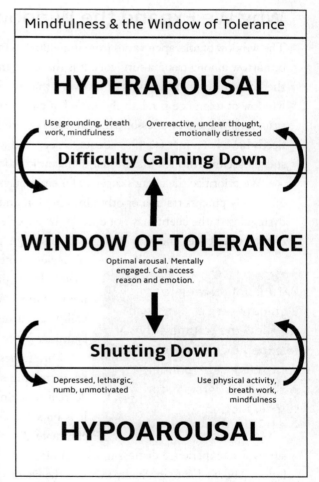

Adjacent to the window of tolerance are two zones of dysregulation: hyperarousal and hypoarousal. Individuals can become triggered by internal or external cues, shifting into a dysregulated state and subsequent hyper- or hypoarousal. When in either of the two states, the trauma survivor cannot process or integrate information in an adaptive way to promote growth and recovery. The mindful therapist helps the survivor to use attention regulation and body awareness to identify somatic cues indicative of physiological arousal and to identify its potential trigger(s). By explaining the psychophysiology of trauma and the window of tolerance, the therapist teaches the client to notice the cues that they are shifting into either zone of dysregulation.

Client overwhelm can occur at either end of the window of tolerance by activation of the fight-flight system. When the sympathetic nervous system becomes triggered and activated in session, trauma survivors may describe feeling distress, hyperarousal, feeling overly reactive, having racing thoughts, or having difficulty processing information. In contrast, hypoarousal involves a state of nearly shutting down. This state involves a deactivation of the system in which the trauma survivor may look spaced out or dissociated, drowsy, or unengaged (such as failing to initiate dialogue or not responding to therapist comments). Clients may report feeling numb, lethargic, or unmotivated. At extreme levels, the hypoarousal can manifest as a state of freeze where the client is immobilized. See chapter 5 for stabilizing interventions to implement.

Why We Expand the Window of Tolerance

The window of tolerance varies from individual to individual but is typically more compromised or narrow among trauma survivors. It is the space in which trauma processing occurs, so it is to the advantage of the survivor's recovery that we broaden their capacity for this work. The window of tolerance is relatively stable but can vary for each individual related to time of day, situational factors or stressors, the presence of trauma-related triggers, and whether biological needs have been met (such as adequate sleep and nutrition). Furthermore, we can expand the stable baseline through intentional therapeutic processes.

We prioritize the client's capacity for emotion regulation because it is necessary for them to effectively process trauma or other information and integrate the new meaning that occurs. If dysregulated, the client may not encode the experience fully, may not consolidate the meaning of the experience, and may struggle to generalize new learning. Clients can use mindfulness strategies to broaden the window of tolerance and reduce their vulnerability to trauma triggers. Our process of engaging in inquiry (detailed in chapter 6) scaffolds the client's ability to investigate, consolidate, and generalize new learning.

> We are not striving to eliminate distress. Instead, we allow the trauma survivor to experience distress in a controlled, safe manner, within their capacity for self-regulation.

Mindfulness skills can widen the window of tolerance by increasing the client's distress tolerance while also decreasing vulnerability to trauma-related cues or triggers. It is important to understand that we are not striving to eliminate distress. Instead, we want to allow the trauma survivor to experience distress in a controlled, safe manner, within their capacity for self-regulation. The goal is to gradually increase the client's capacity and gently expand the window of tolerance. In fact, staying in the middle of the window of tolerance can be countertherapeutic (Ogden, 2010). We teach the client about the window of tolerance so that the client can provide important feedback to the therapist during the sessions and self-assess outside of sessions.

We can target the window of tolerance as we guide the session, observing client response to know when to shift the focus as needed. In other words, we organize the session to titrate client arousal. We support the client so they remain within the window of tolerance while engaging with difficult stimuli, providing feedback to help modulate emotional and physiological responses. Strategies to help the trauma survivor anchor to the present moment and return to the window of tolerance if needed include a variety of grounding techniques (discussed in chapter 5).

Before helping our clients to expand their window of tolerance, we help build a foundation of self-regulation. This foundation involves resourcing the trauma survivor. Resourcing involves the client taking in information, experiences, and support. In this case, the therapist helps resource the client by helping them prioritize overall wellness through healthy engagement in self-care, including nourishment and hydration, sleep, social connections, physical activity, and meaningful experiences with nature and spirituality. Once the client learns how to modulate arousal, we can teach the client to expand the window of tolerance (Ogden, 2010). To expand the window of tolerance, the client must be willing to maintain contact with high (yet tolerable) levels of distress (for instance, related to disturbing trauma-related material) during the therapy session. We aim to work near the farthest edges, or margins, *within* the window of tolerance.

How to Expand the Window of Tolerance

We empower the trauma survivor with transparency and psychoeducation of concepts related to our work together—a fundamental component of resourcing the client. A key feature of this work is explaining the psychobiology of the trauma response, including how it relates to emotion regulation. The concept of the window of tolerance is an essential part of this psychoeducation in helping trauma survivors understand the nature of their distress. As trauma, other adverse childhood experiences, and a genetic predisposition narrow the window of tolerance, most trauma survivors will enter therapy with a need to expand it. This happens by boosting the general capacity for emotion regulation and working specifically in the margins by helping the trauma survivor modulate distress that occurs at the edge of the window as they near dysregulation.

We invite the client to engage in mindfulness skills, such as observing and describing to discern whether physiological arousal or emotional experiences are within the window of tolerance. Mindfulness facilitates detachment from experience so that the trauma survivor can observe their emotional state or arousal more objectively with nonjudgment and curiosity. This state of being, called *the observer self*, can help trauma survivors adopt a more open, accepting, and mindful stance on their experience that maintains arousal within the window of tolerance by reducing reactivity (for more on the observer self, see chapter 10). Focusing attention on the body and using the mindfulness skills of observing and describing, the trauma survivor will observe signs of physiological arousal, including subtle changes that occur as the arousal builds or dissipates. They then can observe the intensity of emotional experiences to allow arousal to extend to the margins, but not exceed the window of tolerance.

Safety and the Therapeutic Relationship

The window of tolerance expands as the trauma survivor gains additional capacity to self-regulate. Trauma survivors benefit when the therapist is supportive, connected, and attuned. Fostering safety within the therapeutic relationship is a fundamental element of building the client's self-regulatory capacities. We foster safety through emphasizing choice, collaboration, and empowerment, as well as attunement. Resourcing the trauma survivor through psychoeducation about trauma and mindfulness enhances a sense of client predictability, control, and safety. We model safety by engaging in compassion, acceptance, and nonjudgment. Notice that our own mindfulness practice will help us cultivate these therapeutic qualities.

Emotion Education

While explaining the window of tolerance, it is useful to set a foundation of general understanding of emotions. A trauma-informed, didactic, educational approach can facilitate the development of emotion regulation skills for trauma survivors in therapy. Teaching about the nature and function of emotion can increase the client's motivation for working with difficulty and distress. When we educate the client about emotion, our goal is to ascertain our client's level of knowledge about their emotional experiences—exploring and perhaps gently correcting (mis)conceptions about emotions—using mindfulness.

Education about emotion is important for all clients, but especially important for trauma survivors. This is because traumatic experiences, especially during childhood, impede or interfere with experiences of learning about healthy models of emotion and emotion regulation (for more discussion, see chapter 9). In the process of emotion education, we are inquiring into understandings held about emotions, their expression, and the level of acceptance or avoidance connected to specific emotional states (or facets of expression). Cultural mores and gendered expectations affect the experience and expression of emotional states as well. For instance, many cultures expect men to be stoic and not show emotional vulnerability, so when vulnerability is present, it is expressed as anger or irritability as this is more acceptable than sadness. Similarly, generalized anxiety is more likely to be expressed as worry in Western cultures, whereas in non-Western cultures, we are more likely to see anxiety expressed as somatic concerns.

We should assess each client's knowledge of emotion and the source of such understanding. Survivors' experiences with trauma likely affect their understanding of emotion and capacity for emotion regulation, resulting in the overuse of suppression or avoidance, which leads to less understanding of the emotional experience overall. We tend to see less elaborate emotional vocabularies and difficulty sensing, identifying, or naming emotional states (alexithymia) among trauma survivors. Providing information about the purpose or function of emotion (for instance, to communicate pain or other states to the self or to communicate with others) helps to set the foundation for why emotional experience is important for trauma recovery, motivating the trauma survivor to engage in informal exposure (see below), and to learn to tolerate and explore painful emotional experiences.

It may be powerful, in discussions of the sources of emotional understandings, to discuss perpetrator strategies. For example, if anger was forbidden and punished, the effect is typically submission or acquiescence (such as decreasing self-protective options in childhood sexual abuse or intimate partner violence). Similarly, perpetrator messages that the client is dramatic and overemotional may have taught emotional suppression and self-invalidation, and the effect is typically an increasing likelihood of a victim staying silent about abuse.

The trauma survivor may benefit from ancillary materials or handouts that provide basic emotion information, including lists of emotion words and an emotion wheel that explains the connection between different emotions, the blending of emotions, and the increasing complexity of emotion. The client can learn the unique signature of emotion in their body, such as feeling hot, chest tightness, and a sense of a physical agitation in the case of anger (the fight response).

One of the first skills the trauma survivor will learn is awareness of the signs of overwhelm, or that their experience is outside the window of tolerance. See chapter 8 on body awareness for more information. Emotion education should be rooted in the context of the psychobiology of trauma (fight, flight, freeze, and fawn responses) and discussion of the extreme vacillation between hyper- and hypoarousal states among trauma survivors. Throughout the process of emotion education, we help the client to engage in self-compassion, given that trauma survivors can feel a sense of shame or inadequacy related to their impoverished emotional understandings.

Containment Skill

The hallmark feature of many cognitive behavioral therapy (CBT) approaches for trauma survivors is to curb avoidance, which includes denial, minimization, and suppression. Containment is an intentional intervention used to reduce physiological overwhelm that can, on the surface, look like avoidance. Yet, its function is much different. It is critical for the mindful trauma therapist to recognize the *purpose or function* of avoidance among trauma survivors, which is the hallmark of being trauma-informed.

> When avoidance is present, this is a sign the trauma survivor does not yet have the self-soothing skills to tolerate negative affect in that specific context.

The purpose of avoidance typically is to titrate or reduce overwhelm that comes from facing traumatic memories, emotional flashbacks, or trauma-related sensations. To operate in a safe and trauma-informed manner, trauma survivors need options (skills) to manage emotional overwhelm and reduce the physiological dysregulation that leads to avoidant behavior. Meaning, we seek to contain the level of physiological arousal so that the trauma survivor can learn and engage in therapy effectively.

We assess the survivor's capacity for experiencing trauma-related experiences and the capacity for self-soothing or emotion regulation. When avoidance is present, this is a sign that the trauma survivor does not yet have the self-soothing skills to tolerate the negative affect in that specific context. Avoidance is ubiquitous among trauma survivors (with the exception of post-traumatic embitterment disorder). Thus, the mindful trauma therapist should enter every new therapeutic encounter with assessment of the need to teach strategies to tolerate emotional states and widen the window of tolerance. Next, these needs are incorporated into the treatment plan. In chapter 3, we discussed the need to begin with a focus on safety and stabilization before moving into trauma processing (formal exposure).

> Containment involves temporary avoidance to enhance emotional control and safety when overwhelmed or under-resourced with an intentional commitment to returning at a later time.

Containment involves teaching the trauma survivor how to intentionally decenter or distance themselves from memories or feelings until emotional tolerance has increased to face the traumatic stimuli without overwhelm. This can mean that within a session, we "step in" to shift attention, thereby titrating emotional overwhelm in the moment, modeling skills or strategies the trauma survivor can use in the future. To be clear, overwhelm is not equivalent to distress. The client is learning distress tolerance through informal exposure. However, when distress becomes too severe, the trauma survivor is outside their window of tolerance (overwhelm occurs), and therefore, learning is impaired. Containment strategies are implemented temporarily until the client can remain engaged with trauma content and stay within the window of tolerance, bringing with it the added benefit of maintaining a sense of safety and control. They allow the client to set aside overwhelming trauma-related content. While some might refer to this as avoidance, it is *intentionally* moving away from the stimuli in a way to *enhance* emotional control and safety, paired with the commitment to return with greater capacities.

Thus, a simple shorthand to distinguish avoidance and containment is actually about purpose and intentionality, as well as whether it is temporary. Teaching the trauma survivor to notice and observe signs of emotional overwhelm, temporarily disengage from trauma-related stimuli, and implement strategies to shift their physiology back into the window of tolerance enhances self-efficacy and a sense of control. It ultimately widens the window of tolerance, lessening the perceived need to engage in avoidance behaviors and allowing for trauma processing.

Informal Exposure

When integrating mindfulness into therapy with trauma survivors, we distinguish between informal and formal exposure. With *informal exposure*, we identify opportunities in the therapy session to replace avoidance with approach behavior. This might include inviting the trauma survivor to turn toward, rather than avoid, experienced emotion such as shame or sadness.

Informal exposure occurs with naturally arising experience in session (versus a formally planned trauma-focused exposure) and is a practice of tolerating aversive and painful emotions.

Informal exposure is an essential practice to widen the window of tolerance. We help the trauma survivor to titrate the emotional experience to avoid overwhelm while working at the edges of the window of tolerance, building increased capacity to tolerate the experience. Strategies for titration might include pausing to implement shifting attention, grounding exercises, or decentering strategies that can facilitate a less embodied state of distress. In this context, we focus on gently guiding or instructing the trauma survivor to help them cultivate curiosity, tenderness, and self-compassion as they explore the painful experience (this could be an emotional state, a distress-provoking topic, or a memory).

Informal exposure is a practice in allowing, tolerating, and being curious about challenging emotions and provides the opportunity for a change in perspective as the trauma survivor can begin to consider the painful emotions as tolerable and manageable. The process of informal exposure is a means of applying numerous mindfulness concepts, including observing and describing, nonreactivity, nonjudgment, and acceptance in everyday life, providing opportunities to practice mindfully approaching challenging experiences or painful states.

In chapter 9, we discuss several practices that are relevant to the process of informal exposure, including mindfulness of emotion and working with difficulty. If these practices are overwhelming, we can titrate by engaging in deliberate, volitional detachment to reduce intensity of the exposure, with an aim to reduce the likelihood of dissociative detachment. Although informal exposure differs from an exposure protocol (formal exposure) associated with trauma-focused therapies, such as prolonged exposure (PE) and cognitive processing therapy (CPT), there are elements of overlap in how exposure can be titrated with mindfulness approaches. We turn to a discussion of formal exposure next.

Memory Processing and Formal Exposure

Trauma processing is a priority for trauma recovery due to its therapeutic potency. Therefore, we should introduce emotional processing of traumatic experience as soon as the client has the capacity to do so. Memory processing, or what we refer to here as formal exposure, is a common component of CBT approaches to trauma treatment. With memory processing we adhere to the tenets of trauma-sensitive care (see chapter 3), by maintaining a collaborative therapeutic alliance that emphasizes empowerment of the trauma survivor, making them the primary determiner who has control of whether to engage in memory processing (formal exposure).

When engaging in trauma processing, it is important to continue to do so in the context of mindfulness attitudes, such as nonjudgment, acceptance, and self-compassion. We modulate the client's psychophysiological arousal through guidance that will enhance safety, helping the trauma survivor remain within the window of tolerance. These strategies include titrating exposure to decrease intensity, downregulating arousal, grounding techniques, and responding to painful emotions. For a thorough review of trauma processing, we refer readers to other sources (Courtois and Ford, 2016; Steele et al., 2017).

Titration of trauma processing can include pacing the trauma narrative (Rothschild, 2000) into three stages: 1) naming the trauma (in one sentence, not detailed, just "the headline"), 2) outlining the trauma with a label of the main incidents (one sentence per incident), and 3) filling in the details of each incident, elaborating the description of events. Throughout each of these steps, we are actively observing for signs of hyperarousal or hypoarousal, checking in with the client, and using strategies to maintain the window of tolerance, if needed.

If the client is flooded (is outside the window of tolerance), we do not proceed into the second stage. Instead, we encourage strategies to shift arousal, including diaphragmatic breathing, labeling emotional experiences, entering observer mode, or engaging in physical activity (such as standing or pushing against a wall). If the client can maintain or return with relative ease to their window of tolerance, we proceed with additional steps, continuing to monitor arousal.

Metaphor

We may find that using metaphor or analogy can be a useful way to explain mindfulness concepts and avoid unnecessary jargon. The weather is a common mindfulness metaphor that can help illustrate the transiency of emotion or thought (such as clouds drifting). In mindfulness-based interventions (MBIs), a metaphor conveys information often within a story, poem, or kōan. They can make difficult concepts less abstract, allowing a bit of distance from the experience because they usually involve a third person perspective.

The distance between the client's experience and the metaphor creates safety to experience difficult emotions, helping to expand the window of tolerance. For example, to help reduce a sense of shame or unworthiness a trauma survivor might have following an automatic response such as fawning, we might compare the trauma survivor's automatic response to a trauma cue as akin to the physical reflex of pulling our hand away after accidentally touching a hot stove (Doyle, 2022). This would help the trauma survivor see that fawning is not an intentional, purposeful response, without addressing it directly.

The detachment involved in the use of an analogy or metaphor creates space for the trauma survivor to generate their own conclusions or meaning, applying the concept to their own lived experience. In many cases, the metaphor involves an abrupt shift in meaning-making that helps the trauma survivor grasp the concept and its relevance, which facilitates learning and remembering the concept.

Conclusions

Widening the window of tolerance is a fundamental aspect of psychotherapy with trauma survivors. We accomplish this by working "in the margins," such that the trauma survivor is encouraged to engage in emotional processing at the highest level of distress tolerable without crossing outside the window of tolerance into hyperarousal or hypoarousal. An important element of successful trauma processing is the capacity of the trauma survivor to widen or expand their window of tolerance. This enhances their capacity to process increasingly challenging emotions and distress in the service of processing trauma.

Working within the window of tolerance facilitates safety and the efficacy of trauma processing, as well as a greater self-understanding for the trauma survivor. This is the basis for their growth in emotion regulation and sets the stage for new understandings of their traumatic experiences and their aftermath. In this chapter, we focused on strategies to teach the trauma survivor how they can widen the window of tolerance to increase their capacity for trauma processing and general functioning in everyday life.

CHAPTER 5

Safety-Enhancing Strategies for Mindfulness and Trauma-Related Overwhelm

One of the fundamental elements of our approach is promoting the practice of safety-enhancing strategies. These strategies help trauma survivors develop conscious, intentional control over two essential processes: physiological dysregulation and difficulties staying in the present-moment experience (for instance, flashbacks). The client's use of these strategies helps them expand their window of tolerance to include trauma-related cues (internal and external) and reduces the intensity of responses to trauma-related intrusions (such as intrusive memories). In addition, sometimes clients may have intensely adverse experiences in meditation (for instance, intrusions or dissociation) and these same strategies, along with some practice modifications, can be helpful to clients in staying in or returning to the window of tolerance. Note that in this chapter, we will refer to formal mindfulness practice consistently as meditation to distinguish between formal mindfulness practice and informal mindfulness (application of techniques and attitudes in daily life, which is not associated with any adverse effects).

For some clients, physiological dysregulation occurs on a regular basis. In such cases, we teach strategies focused on tolerating trauma-related cues (internal and external) embedded in their daily lives. If we begin to integrate meditation, we may be more likely to include the "Learning the Landscape Phase" (see below). For other clients, physiological dysregulation may occur only infrequently, although they may still be quite intense. In such circumstances, we include just one preparatory session to discuss safety-enhancing strategies as applied to meditation and intrusive experiences, overwhelm, and physiological dysregulation when those occur in daily life.

Given our book's emphasis on meditation (formal mindfulness practice), we will discuss these skills as related to challenges that may arise in meditation, although we emphasize the importance of generalizing application of these skills if clinically relevant. For some clients, the use of these strategies both in their daily lives and in mindfulness will be a central aspect of treatment, while for others it will be in the background and relevant only as needed.

Certain elements of the recommendations in this chapter are specific to meditation, such as offering practice modifications, guiding instruction of safety-enhancing strategies, and how to gently transition out of meditation when needed. In addition, we will discuss other safety-enhancing strategies that are generalizable outside of meditation if trauma-related intrusions or dysregulation occur. All the practices are listed, classified by category, in the handouts named "Safety-Enhancing Strategies" (http://www.newharbinger.com/54650). The handouts include distinct therapist and client versions, particularly for Modifications to Mindfulness Practice and Trauma Processing.

Distinguishing Typical Challenges from Adverse Experiences

We must be able to distinguish *typical challenges* during meditation from those that are adverse experiences. Typical challenges include discomfort, distress, and intense emotion and *are not to be treated as adverse events*, even if clients experience them as unpleasant. We do not want to overreact to emotions arising during practice, as that would implicitly negate messages inviting clients to allow emotional experiencing. If clients have historically overrelied on emotional inhibition or overcontrol strategies, allowing emotional experiencing may come routinely with initial discomfort and difficulty. If clients have been suppressing or avoiding trauma-related memories or emotions, decreasing avoidance may temporarily increase intrusions; however, this will typically subside with interventions of process-based emotional or cognitive processing. Therefore, we pivot to trauma processing as relevant.

In addition, increasing awareness may bring distressing realizations. Clients may become more aware of painful emotions, problematic patterns, or notice ways that are behaving outside of their values. They may recognize that they are in an abusive relationship, their manager's behavior is belittling and mocking, or that they acquiesce instead of assertively setting boundaries when their kids misbehave.

Furthermore, if clients increase awareness without developing the attitudes and emergent processes of mindfulness, awareness is likely even more painful. While becoming aware may be difficult, the context of meditation brings an opportunity for new responses, which we explore through practice and consolidate via inquiry. These typical challenges are discussed throughout the book. In this chapter, we concentrate specifically on adverse meditation-related experiences.

Meditation-Related Adverse Experiences

At times, trauma survivors report challenging or intensely distressing experiences that arise during meditation. These occur when clients experience flashbacks, intrusive memories, reactions of panic, hallucinations, depersonalization, or suicidal ideation, and they require our immediate clinical attention. We use the language of adverse experiences here to be consistent with the literature and to differentiate these from typical meditation challenges. However, *with our clients* we label these as distressing, challenging, difficult, or overwhelming experiences that occur during or following meditation so as not to add appraisal-influencing language. We also use the client's language to demonstrate our recognition of how they are experiencing it.

It is well established that trauma survivors have an increased risk of experiencing meditation-related adverse experiences (Goldberg et al., 2022). The therapist's ability to skillfully manage these through trauma-sensitive mindfulness modifications and interventions is essential for facilitating stabilization and reducing the likelihood of enduring symptoms and impairment (Magyari, 2016; Treleaven, 2018). Effective therapeutic responses involve validation, assessment, intervention as needed, and subsequent monitoring. We may also seek consultation from knowledgeable sources in our local community or resources discussed later in the chapter.

> **Therapeutic Response to Adverse Experiences**
> 1. Validation
> 2. Assessment
> 3. Intervention when needed
> 4. Subsequent monitoring
> 5. Seeking consultation as needed

Meditation-related adverse experiences occur to both novice and expert practitioners across traditions, and length of practice does not appear to be a reliable predictor. Lindahl and colleagues (2017) investigated the types of practices being engaged at onset of adverse effects, and practitioners reported a broad variety of types of meditation practices, including concentration (such as mindfulness of breath), insight (such as noting or open monitoring), body scan, kōan, loving-kindness, tonglen, and visualization practices. Given that adverse experiences can occur across a broad range of mediation practices, we need to be prepared that adverse effects may occur, and if they do, we need to facilitate stabilization using the safety-enhancing strategies discussed in this chapter.

Conceptualizing Meditation-Related Adverse Experiences

As therapists, we value both content competence and cultural competence. Therefore, our conceptualization of these experiences is situated within the relevant knowledge available through spiritual and religious teachings (for instance, historical texts and meditation teachers). In this context, these experiences occurring during meditation are recognized as known effects labeled *nonordinary states of consciousness* (NSC).

VanderKooi (1997) summarized that in her interviews with Buddhist teachers from three traditions, they all "understand NSC as phenomena that often emerge as practice progresses" (p. 40). Accordingly, in a culturally informed perspective, these experiences may be viewed as naturally occurring sequelae of meditation rather than indicators of psychopathology. Scientific insights suggest that a neurobiological model would account for some of these experiences and might even be a positive indicator of a period of increased neuroplasticity that can be leveraged for new learning in psychotherapy (Lindahl et al., 2014).

We believe that both the clinical and spiritual, religious, or cultural perspectives are true and valid and provide important insight regarding adverse experiences. Rather than seeing these perspectives though an either/or lens, we hold them together in dialectical synthesis, such that we do not neglect clinical responsibilities and, at the same time, do not overreact and infer psychopathology. Thus, we do not assume psychosis when someone reports a hallucination during meditation, any more than we would if someone hallucinated in a sensory deprivation tank.

Regardless of conceptualization, if a problem is causing great distress or promoting functional impairment, it is critical to support and intervene. In a culturally responsive framework, the central question is not whether these experiences are rooted in psychopathology or spirituality, but rather whether they require our support and intervention (Lindahl et al., 2019).

Nonetheless, the conceptualization still needs to be approached thoughtfully, as the therapeutic alliance may suffer if the therapist and client don't have a shared conceptualization of the problem. The therapist's ability to understand the client's worldview and belief system is central to the client's appraisal of therapy following meditation-related adverse experiences (Lindahl et al., 2019). Thus, if the client believes their experience is a normative process that occurs in meditation, we adopt that as a primary conceptualization for the current difficulties. Lindahl and colleagues (2019, p. 19) summarize: "Recognizing the forms of culturally valid and nonpathological experiences is basic to spiritual and religious competence for clinicians."

Resources on Meditation-Related Adverse Experiences

Mindful trauma therapists must prepare to respond to meditation-related adverse experiences by intentionally learning and practicing the safety-enhancing strategies in this chapter. To learn more about meditation-related adverse experiences, we recommend the *Meditation Safety Toolbox*, a robust resource toolkit developed by neuroscientist and clinical psychologist Willoughby Britton (http://sites.brown.edu/britton/resources/meditation-safety-toolbox; Clinical and Affective Neuroscience Laboratory, n.d.), which includes meditation safety resources from various mindfulness centers and programs as well as an extensive scientific review of meditation-related adverse experiences.

In addition, Britton, Lindahl, and colleagues have developed online training courses available through the nonprofit organization Cheetah House to provide information about meditation-related adverse experiences (http://courses.cheetahhouse.org). To read more about prevention and intervention, we recommend books by Rothschild (2000; *The Body Remembers*) and Treleaven (2018; *Trauma-Sensitive Mindfulness*), and Magyari's chapter (2016; "Teaching Individuals with Traumatic Stress").

Informed Consent

Trauma-informed and ethical practice includes informed consent and preventive interventions whenever possible. Therefore, once we determine that the treatment plan may be enhanced by integrating meditation, our next step involves a collaborative discussion with the client involving informed consent about the treatment plan. Informed consent includes discussion of potential benefits of mindfulness (mediation) relevant to your specific client, as well as acknowledgment of potential negative effects. This is a basic ethical expectation when we are doing clinical work and make changes in the treatment plan.

However, we do not want informed consent to unhelpfully alarm the client or make them hypervigilant, given that could itself exacerbate difficulty. In addition, some clients may not have any meditation-related adverse experiences. Britton (2016) emphasizes that, most vitally, we should never offer inaccurate or misleading assurances that meditation is totally safe or has no side effects. We tailor our discussion of benefits and risks to the client's specific presentation. For example, we would tell a client who reports frequent flashbacks that it is possible they could have an intrusive memory during meditation and that we will prepare in advance so they have safety-enhancing strategies to implement if that were to occur. For many clients, we provide less specificity because there are no clear, specific, and likely risks to prepare for.

Britton (2016) notes that typically mindfulness teachers provide this information at a very general level, offering an example from mindfulness-based cognitive therapy (MBCT) participant handouts: "You might find that taking the MBCT course is challenging for a number of different reasons" (Segal et al., 2013, handout 6.2, p. 3). This type of general statement is helpful for reducing the likelihood of client hypervigilance and overmonitoring for potential symptoms, which can itself exacerbate meditation difficulties.

These strategies may not prevent an intrusion from occurring, but they will help clients return to physiological equilibrium and can also be used when intrusions arise in their everyday lives. You and the client may both find it comforting to know that in one study, most people who endorsed experiencing meditation-related adverse effects were still equally as glad to have practiced meditation as those who did not have adverse effects (Goldberg et al., 2022).

Preparation Session(s) to Enhance Safety in Meditation

We frame the preparation session as a resourcing session, offering various ways to help make practice more comfortable for the client, as well as introducing various strategies that they may use if they are experiencing difficulty. This is typically one session but may be more depending on client needs and clinical process factors; the emphasis is skills training in safety-enhancing strategies.

Some clients will say they don't need that because they are already meditating independently. In such cases, we explain that because challenging experiences during meditation can occur to both novice and expert practitioners—including meditation teachers—we would still want to have one preparatory session if they are open to it, given our commitment to promoting safety in meditation. That said, we would not insist on it. During the preparatory session, the strategies are taught and practiced; they are discussed in application to meditation and other contexts in which such strategies might be helpful to the client.

Practice Modifications to Enhance Safety

We begin with practice modifications that can be implemented during meditation when challenges arise. Sometimes, this might allow someone who is approaching the edge of their window of tolerance to continue practicing with an enhanced sense of safety. The client can implement the client practice modifications independently, and we integrate the therapist practice modifications by adding them within the standard meditation instructions (for instance, "Pausing momentarily to turn our attention to external awareness, listening attentively for sounds").

Client's practice modifications. We provide these recommended practice modifications to the client in advance and encourage them to implement these during meditation if they are having difficulty. One of the most helpful modifications is keeping the eyes open or opening the eyes when beneficial (for instance, when feeling disoriented), as this provides **sensory grounding** in present-day surroundings. Another sensory grounding strategy emphasizing taste is *keeping a candy or lozenge in the mouth* during the practice (Treleaven, 2018). The client may also invite any **shifting of the body** that feels helpful. Talk the client through it, suggesting different options: *shifting posture* (shifting how you are holding your abdominal muscles and spine, elongating and engaging core, then releasing slightly so that posture has ease rather than effort), *position* (changing how your legs or body are positioned, standing up), or *support* (adding a pillow or bolster to support you, removing something that now feels uncomfortable). We encourage clients to make relevant modifications whenever it feels beneficial or necessary during practice.

We encourage clients to experiment with brief practices to learn more about what works and feels safe. Our message to clients is that longer is not better, more challenging is not excelling, and more striving is not more mindful. Rather, what we consider effective is 1) working on skills for staying in the window of tolerance, 2) maintaining psychological safety, and 3) identifying mindfulness practices that feel safe and helpful to practice, and then expand further. We also remind clients to let us know if they need us to pause or stop during a practice; it is important to state this explicitly, as most clients assume they must stay silent during meditation.

> Our message is that longer is not better, more challenging is not excelling, and more striving is not more mindful.

Therapist's practice modifications. One of the most powerful practice modifications is to **include therapist and client dialogue** during the meditation (Frewen & Lanius, 2015). This allows us to integrate into the practice the questions of inquiry ("What do you observe as we notice sounds?" "How does that feel when you are reminded to take a soft tone mentally?") as well as discussions of additional safety-enhancing strategies ("If you are feeling overwhelmed, perhaps we can do some elongated exhalations now, together"). This moment-to-moment tracking allows the therapist to provide guidance and modifications as relevant and augments the practice with increased relational resourcing.

You might consider a **trauma-sensitive starting sequence** for meditations, like the one Magyari (2016) developed, for example. First, she guides brief mindful movement (stand, stretch) prior to sitting in stillness or silence. Second, she orients to time and place and offers a reminder of options to practice with eyes open or closed. Third, she guides sensory grounding in the support of the chair or cushion and floor, particularly emphasizing the soles of the feet. Fourth, she instructs deep diaphragmatic breathing with long audible exhalations for down-regulating arousal. Finally, she provides reminders to bring calming internal resources, especially self-compassion, into the practice when inner struggle arises.

If needed due to client's frequency of intrusions or intensity of dysregulation, we can broaden the window of tolerance safely by using **titration**, starting with smaller components and adding more when appropriate. One titration strategy is engaging in *shorter practice periods*, extending duration once skills are developed for staying in the window of tolerance. Another is *taking small pauses to integrate movement* (such as stretching arms up, then slowly moving them out and down). We encourage the client to engage in spontaneous movement interventions that are guided by bottom-up somatic urges (for instance, leaning off the side of the chair or stretching in a twist that feels desired), highlighting such instances as examples of body awareness and responsiveness.

Another way to titrate is *taking structured breaks for resourcing* to build capacities and reduce dysregulation (Treleaven, 2018). One way to do this is *pendulation*, moving attention between safe or calming stimuli and distressing stimuli to provide resourcing and build capacities to stay present with challenging stimuli (Steele et al., 2017). All of these practice modifications can be incorporated into meditation guidance, facilitating the safe expansion of the window of tolerance.

Skills Acquisition in Preparatory Session(s)

This is a great time to teach the client about the window of tolerance or refer back to the concept if discussed prior (see chapter 4). Treleaven (2018) recommends having the client begin to practice rating their arousal on a rating scale (0 = *hypoarousal*; 5 = *optimal zone of arousal*; 10 = *hyperarousal*), encouraging them to regularly practice rating arousal (typically leveraging body awareness) in various situations. We let the client know that they will be using this scale to notice and rate arousal before and after mindfulness practices, as well as if there is distress or difficulty during a practice. Many sexual trauma survivors express distress toward the term "arousal," describing it as a trauma cue. We have found that modifying to "physiological arousal" neutralizes the term, allowing new associations to be formed with the word.

It is important to socialize clients to not persist in meditation practice when they are already outside of the window of tolerance (Treleaven, 2018). We emphasize that we feel very strongly about them *not pushing through* in ways that might make it more likely to exacerbate adverse experiences. We highlight that no learning occurs outside the window of tolerance due to cognitive difficulties in both hyperarousal (such as disorganized or racing thoughts) and hypoarousal (such as slowed or inhibited cognitive processing).

As the client considers their rating system, we clarify together which numbers mark the edges of the window of tolerance for them and how they will let us know during meditation if they are outside of their window of tolerance. It is very important that we know the number on each side that transitions into dysregulation, as this indicates when to intervene.

> We intervene as the client *approaches* dysregulated arousal, *before* they move into that level of arousal.

In preparatory session(s), we review various strategies with the client, providing instructions for implementation during meditation. We review the handouts "Safety-Enhancing Strategies," selecting a variety of skills to point out with brief explanations and some to discuss in more depth, integrating practice where relevant. While some strategies are specific to meditation (such as opening the eyes), most of these skills are also applicable to other situations when intrusive memories arise, emotional experiences feel overwhelming, or dissociative experiences occur. As we teach strategies, we discuss other applications for these skills. Clients are welcome to identify an external grounding object that may be useful to them during practice (for example, a rock or picture on the wall). It is also helpful for the object to be replaceable (not a particular rock but any rock).

We often teach **anchoring** in the preparatory session, a helpful technique for both staying present and maintaining intentional awareness. As we guide, the emphasis is on experiencing and noticing anchor sensations. An anchor is a place to focus our awareness that helps us orient to the present-moment sensory experience. Identifying an anchor that feels safe and accessible will be resourcing if difficulties arise during practice (Treleaven, 2018).

Anderson and Farb (2018) observed that mindfulness-based interventions (MBIs) primarily use somatosensory anchors of attention (such as breath-focused awareness), although anchors can rely on various sensory modalities (somatosensory, auditory, and visual). Their study showed that meditation-naïve individuals do have a preference for particular anchors, and interestingly, their preferences often change following practice. This research suggests that different people find different anchors helpful, and they don't always anticipate correctly what their most helpful anchor will be. Thus, we recommend experimenting with each client to identify their preferred anchor, upholding the trauma-informed principles of empowerment, choice, and collaboration.

We provide instructions for *somatosensory anchors*, guiding with anchor options one at a time (feet, hands, breath in belly, breath in chest), *auditory anchors* (attending to sound), and *visual anchors* (imagery, visual object of attention). Anchor options are especially important with trauma survivors, given that an external focus of attention is typically less prone to difficulty than an internal focus of attention (Treleaven, 2018); note that somatosensory anchors are internally focused, while auditory and visual anchors are externally focused.

For many clients, the preparatory skills review is sufficient to proceed into the work laid out in other chapters as relevant to case conceptualization and the treatment plan. However, for some clients—those with frequent flashbacks or intrusions, panic, or severe emotion dysregulation—we may choose to engage in what we affectionately call the *learning about the landscape phase*: an assessment-rich, slow start-up phase promoting safety in meditation.

Learning about the Landscape (Slow Start-Up) Phase

There are some clients for whom we have concern about a higher likelihood of adverse reactions (clients reporting frequent panic attacks, flashbacks, transient stress-related psychotic symptoms, or struggle with dysregulation). For these clients, we add a preliminary learning about the landscape phase (typically two to three sessions) in which we implement brief meditations (approximately five minutes) and work on building skills in tracking arousal and staying in the window of tolerance. This slow start-up phase offers ample opportunities to practice arousal ratings, provide interventions when arousal is moving toward the edges of the window of tolerance, and gain information about client preferences for particular strategies.

We observe the client during the brief practices, monitoring for signs of approaching hyperarousal (muscle tone rigid, hyperventilation, exaggerated startle response, or excessive sweating) or hypoarousal (muscle tone slack, collapsed, or rigid, flat affect or dysregulated intense affect, observable dissociation, or pale skin tone; Treleaven, 2018). When we observe these signs, we offer instructions encouraging the client to engage their preferred anchor and return attention there any time it is resourcing to them; we also integrate the preferred anchor into instructions during practice. We suggest options for modification. We will continue to use arousal scale check-ins during the practice to bolster client skills in noticing and rating arousal and for momentary assessment, given that hyperarousal and hypoarousal may not be observable during meditation.

We try brief versions of a few different types of practices consistent with targeted mindfulness processes (such as attention and body awareness) to learn more about client arousal responses. Ideally, clients identify some meditations that have safety signals from the arousal system, initially practicing those while building strategies to stay in the window of tolerance. We do not need to disrupt meditation to avoid discomfort or mild distress—those that arise and can be dealt with during practice—however, if needed to prevent emotional flooding, we offer practice modifications and begin to integrate safety-enhancing strategies into the guidance.

> As the client builds capacities, the window of tolerance expands through repeated psychologically safe experiences.

The most important outcome needed in this phase is that we ensure the client can use strategies to stay in or return to their window of tolerance, at least with therapist guidance and instruction. Otherwise, we are cautious to proceed from this phase into meditation until we have done more work with self-regulation and the client can use those strategies effectively. If the client is repeatedly experiencing overwhelm during brief practices and is unable to implement strategies effectively with guidance in session, we do not implement home practice of meditation nor do we implement longer practices. Instead, we continue to scaffold and work with the client to intervene to balance physiological arousal.

As the client can engage in certain practices without dysregulation, we use those to develop further skills. We remind them throughout that as they build capacities, the window of tolerance expands, which will occur only through repeated, psychologically safe experiences. When we begin to extend the duration of the brief practices, we return to the safest practices and lengthen them before introducing other or more challenging practices. At the stage of extending duration, we may try variations of the practice or other practices sharing relevant safe characteristics.

During this phase, our emphasis in home practice is on generalization of insights from the practice through informal mindfulness practice (mindful awareness in everyday life), not on meditation. For example, if during the brief practice the client notices having a high volume of harsh self-criticism and associated feelings of sadness and shame, then home practice might be: notice the self-criticism, notice emotions, and consider what responses might come next. The client might spontaneously generate helpful alternative responses or might increase commitment to learning to modify judgments or develop self-compassion.

Therapeutic Management of Meditation-Related Adverse Experiences

After the preparation session (and, if needed, the learning about the landscape phase), we begin integrating meditation into therapy. We offer modification strategies during practice by providing choices for modifications within the instructions, instructing on how to work with challenges that arise and pausing to check in for arousal ratings if we are concerned about the client. Aside from doing our best with preparation and monitoring the client's arousal during practice to modify instructions as needed, our emphasis is on effective responses if meditation-related challenges, distress, or adverse experiences arise.

There are four central types of meditation-related challenges or adverse experiences that we will discuss (for discussion of additional factors, see Lindahl et al., 2017). These include trauma-related intrusions (such as flashbacks or intrusive memories, emotions, or thoughts), overwhelm (such as panic or emotional flooding), perceptual disturbances (such as dissociation or hallucinations), and suicidal ideation. We discuss each separately, although these experiences may cascade and co-occur (flashback → overwhelm).

Meditation-Related Adverse Experiences

- Trauma-related intrusions
- Feeling overwhelmed
- Perceptual disturbances
- Suicidal ideation

There may be times when meditation needs to be paused or discontinued. Most of the time, we are pausing just for today while pivoting to safety-enhancing techniques. Sometimes we recommend discontinuing for a few weeks or more, until the client has more skills for staying in and returning to the window of tolerance outside of meditation, then returning to the learning the landscape phase. Rarely, reactions may be so concerning that therapist and client decide together that meditation is too risky to continue. In such circumstances, the client can still safely apply informal mindfulness in daily life, but we would caution against continued meditation practice.

Trauma-Related Intrusions During Meditation

Trauma-related intrusions are one of the most frequently reported meditation-related adverse experiences, with 25.8 percent of meditators reporting meditation-related traumatic reexperiencing in one study (Goldberg et al., 2022). Intrusions include flashbacks and intrusive memories, emotions, thoughts, or images. Flashbacks are different from other intrusive memories; flashbacks feel *here and now* (reexperiencing) and include sensory elements (visual, auditory, olfactory, tactile, or gustatory (taste), whereas intrusive memories feel *there and then*, meaning they are remembered (not reexperienced) and are typically strictly visual memories.

Trauma-related intrusions occur in response to trauma cues and in the context of reduced busyness or avoidance. In meditation, physical and mental busyness is quieted, and we are welcoming and attending to emotions and body sensations, both of which may include trauma-related cues. This is not a problem to avoid; trauma survivors live their lives with these emotions and body sensations, and learning to tolerate them and decouple them from trauma associations is an essential aspect of trauma recovery. Thus, our emphasis is on skillfully managing intrusions and returning to physiological equilibrium and, in the context of a flashback, maintaining a present-moment awareness.

> Learning to tolerate trauma-related cues and decouple them from trauma associations is an essential aspect of trauma recovery.

Trauma adaptations may include hypersensitivity to threat cues (including internal ones like intrusions), so when trauma survivors increase awareness of internal experiences—especially if their arousal system is outside of their window of tolerance—their attention is likely to go to internal threat cues, causing overattending to trauma-related stimuli (Forner, 2017; Treleaven, 2018). Continued internal attention can make it difficult for the client to disengage from trauma-related memories, emotions, or thoughts; it can be particularly helpful to shift the focus to external stimuli (such as auditory or visual sensory grounding).

In our guidance and interventions, we emphasize how the client is responding to the intrusion and questions, rather than the intrusion itself or its content. When we address intrusion experiences with support, guidance, and interventions as needed, clients gain the skills for taking care of themselves when intrusions occur, which can be generalized to other contexts. Trish Magyari (2016) describes well this central benefit of mindfulness for trauma survivors: "The combination of learning to be present in this moment of one's life, along with very specific and concrete instructions on how to 'be with' one's own experience in a way that is healing rather than retraumatizing, triggering, or otherwise self-injuring" (p. 340).

What to Do When Trauma-Related Intrusions Occur During Meditation

When a trauma-related intrusion occurs during meditation, we may or may not be aware of it, as the client is often silent and relatively still. If a client is sad or tearful during practice, this is *not* a signal that we need to stop the practice; rather, as noted prior, we want to cultivate allowing emotional experiencing and to convey that this is not problematic, offering guidance in compassionate response. However, if we become aware that a client is dysregulated (for instance, sobbing intensely), we pause and invite them to check in, reiterating our wish for clients to let us know if they are having a flashback or feel overwhelmed by intrusions. Typically, we do this during the practice by including additional instructions to clarify if a pivot is needed, such as, "Emotions are welcome and greeted as kindly as possible during mindfulness. And at the same time, if you are feeling overwhelmed or having a memory that makes it hard to participate in the practice, letting me know by speaking up, raising your arm, or lifting your foot so that I can support you in the experience." Note that we provide the nonverbal notification options because sometimes clients may have difficulty forming verbal communication in intensely dysregulated states, such as extreme hypoarousal.

If a client lets us know they are experiencing a trauma-related intrusion during meditation, we narrate a pivot and engage strategies. The first step is to pause or discontinue the practice; we insert a mindful ending narrating our pivot: "Given that you are having an intense experience that we want to attend to, we are going to pause the practice at this time. We honor this shifting of our attention as a skillful practice in fostering responsiveness."

It is important to convey care in a calm manner, attentive to not add therapist anxiety to the client's experience. We then begin guiding safety-enhancing strategies (see http://www.newharbinger.com/54650). We encourage trying a variety of strategies, one at a time, paced so that the client can follow the guidance and see how that strategy feels before you introduce additional instruction. We express nonjudgment, acceptance, and compassion as we respond to the experience (Magyari, 2016).

We check in with the client, asking them to rate physiological arousal using the arousal rating scale discussed in preparatory sessions, clarifying whether they are inside or outside of the window of tolerance. If it was a manageable intrusion and the client's arousal rating conveys that they are inside the window of tolerance, we continue with the meditation, integrating minor modifications (for instance, adding attention to the preferred anchor).

Treleaven (2018) highlights that trauma survivors "will tend to reflexively orient toward trauma-relevant stimuli" (p. 116), making it difficult to stay in the window of tolerance; therefore, he encourages shifting attention toward external stimuli. One practice modification described above that addresses this effectively is pendulation (moving attention between distressing stimuli and safe or calming stimuli). This technique provides resourcing, builds capacities to stay present with challenging stimuli, and titrates the process to reduce intensity.

If the client is outside of the window of tolerance, we do not reengage the meditation; instead, we shift to intervention techniques. First, we invite the client to **describe emotions**.

Labeling emotions, denoted by the neuroscience slogan "name it to tame it" (Siegel & Bryson, 2011), involves naming emotions without explaining or justifying the feeling or going back into the narrative of what caused the emotion, with notable influence on subjective experiencing. Our colleague Erin Walsh, clinical psychologist with a neuroscience emphasis, offered this client-friendly explanation of the neuroscience behind this skill: "During labeling of emotion (verbal processing), the prefrontal cortex is often activated, while subcortical brain structures, such as the amygdala, often show reduced activation. Because the prefrontal cortex is central to emotion processing and regulation, and the amygdala is frequently activated during experience of negative emotions (such as fear, threat, danger), it is hypothesized that this 'top-down' control of subcortical brain regions decreases both neural and subjective hyperarousal (chronic fight/flight activation)" (E. C. Walsh, personal communication, July 17, 2024). When the client provides emotion descriptions, we validate the emotions described and reinforce labeling emotions as a foundational emotion regulation skill.

Second, we assess whether the client has **dual awareness** of the intrusive memory, emotion, or sensation; that is, the ability to keep their sense of the present moment while they are aware of remembering the past (Rothschild, 2000). If the client is experiencing a flashback and is unable to separate past and present, it is not safe or effective to continue meditation nor to do any work with trauma-related material, as it is much more likely to cause destabilization than benefit. In these states of flashback or when the client is outside of their window of tolerance, we focus on guiding them in containment (see below), followed by shifting awareness to external cues and other safety-enhancing strategies.

STRATEGIES FOR REDUCING EMOTIONAL INTENSITY

We facilitate stabilization using safety-enhancing strategies. During or after an intrusion, we typically begin with **containment**, a technique in which the client compartmentalizes overwhelming content (trauma memories and unbearable emotions) when they do not have adequate space or resources for managing it, with a commitment to returning to the content at a time when capacities are more available (ability to use skills to stay in or return to the window of tolerance). We can differentiate containment from avoidance through the intentional return to the content once capacities and context can be leveraged to facilitate effective processing and integration of new learning (see the "Pivot to Trauma Processing" section below).

To guide containment, we invite the client to identify their preferred container (for example, chest, bank vault, jars, or box; Steele et al., 2017). Once the client selects the type of container, we guide visualization of the container (the color, shape, texture, and size), and then the client placing the overwhelming memory or emotion into the container and closing it. Some clients prefer to have a lock on their container, in which case we add locking the container at the end of the sequence. The final step is making the commitment to return to it when greater capacities and resources are available (for instance, during the next session, after a few sessions emphasizing safety-enhancing strategies, or in a few months).

If the client is distressed and struggling to implement containment strategies, we typically shift to **anchoring the end**, a technique for helping the client orient to the trauma being in the past—developing **dual awareness** during a flashback or time disruption experience. We anchor the end, adapting from Steele and colleagues (2017): "You are here, in this room, with me now. Even as this painful memory is present, you know in some part of your mind that if you are here with me, it is over. Perhaps there is a memory of a moment in when there was a sense of knowing that it was over. Holding onto the moment, the one that anchors the end. And here we are now; this is now after the end."

For clients who experienced chronic trauma, and thus the end of one event was not the end of trauma, Steele and colleagues (2017, p. 448) offer, "…as you know for certain that event ended, you are also aware of here and now with me, after all the times you were hurt have ended. This is the end after the last end, where you are no longer hurt. This is here and now, where it is safe… Let your entire mind, your entire body, all parts of you feel and sense and know for certain that the past, all the past, is over, and you are in the present."

We also use **dual awareness slogans**, such as: "You have already survived," "The danger is not happening now," and "Something old is getting cued." Clients may have slogans noted in phones or in their wallet, a reminder for times when the past feels here-and-now. We also integrate "Past-Present Discernment" (see chapter 8; client worksheet: http://www.newharbinger.com/54650), a skill leveraging body awareness to facilitate dual awareness, which can be integrated as a safety-enhancing strategy. For an array of more cognitive strategies for separating past from present, we recommend the *Finding Solid Ground* program materials (Schielke et al., 2022).

> Dual awareness offers high magnitude reductions in distress by intervening on the inaccurate here-and-now quality of flashbacks.

GROUNDING TECHNIQUES

Grounding techniques orient the client to the present moment and thereby reduce the overwhelmed feeling. They are helpful in many situations and essential when the client is having a flashback or time disruption, as present-moment awareness enhances the capacity for dual awareness. This is powerfully regulating and offers high magnitude reductions in distress by intervening on the inaccurate here-and-now quality of flashbacks, likely linked to sensory reexperiencing of the memory. Grounding techniques have either cognitive or sensory emphasis. When clients experience hypoarousal or extreme hyperarousal, cognitive processing is impaired and sensory grounding—which is unaffected—should be emphasized.

Cognitive grounding techniques. Cognitive grounding techniques use mental processing to orient to the present-moment experience. Functionally, we are facilitating dual awareness and activating the prefrontal cortex, which, as described in greater nuance above, subdues the fight-or-flight activation. One technique is **orienting to the surrounding environment and to context**, asking orienting questions (for instance, the weekday, month, season, or location).

Another cognitive grounding technique that is particularly useful in the context of trauma processing is **organizing** by summarizing and reviewing information, categorizing, identifying key themes or elements at a high level. For example, after trauma processing, we might summarize: "You were so courageous today and with strategies you were able to stay present through the session—lovely! You labeled some very important elements of the event, like the relationship between their accusations and your self-blame, their laughter and your shame, and you noted that you have a new certainty that you did in fact tell them to stop and you were crying, so there shouldn't have been any miscommunications. Let's give that a chance to settle with you over the next few days."

Organizing reduces cognitive load, making challenging information feel less overwhelming. If there are relevant gaps in information or aspects that are confusing or unclear (for instance, regarding trauma memory), we acknowledge them, recommending letting uncertainty be (acceptance) and allowing things to unfold.

Sensory grounding techniques. Sensory grounding techniques focus on body sensations and leverage the fact that the sensory system typically remains available even when the cognitive system is not (such as the case in extreme hypoarousal). Sensory grounding emphasizes noticing the present-moment sensory experience, supporting the development of dual awareness. We typically choose one particular sensory system and guide noticing that sense. Note that although in mindfulness practice we typically emphasize experiencing sensation over thinking about sensation, in contrast in grounding practices we are interested in bringing cognitive processes online in relation to the present-moment sensory experience, facilitating dual awareness.

We focus on *vision*, instructing in opening the eyes, observing visual input. We can guide noticing a picture on the wall (colors, textures, and describing components), looking at the therapist (notice my compassionate expression, notice the bright teal of my shirt), looking at an object, or identifying colors in the room. Frewen and Lanius (2015) suggest: "Look at my ugly coffee mug," noting that the use of humor can facilitate a return to the window of tolerance.

We use *sound*, offering guidance in bringing awareness to sounds of heating or air-conditioning, traffic, birds chirping, and the sound of your voice. We attend to *tactile (touch)* sensory input by guiding the client in any of these options: feeling the feet on the ground, feeling the fingers resting on the thighs or the arm of the chair, feeling the back against the chair, bringing awareness to sensations of fabric against the skin, or holding and feeling an object.

We engage *smell* by guiding the client in bringing awareness to a natural scent (such as an essential oil) or spice (such as cinnamon or cardamom). We can use *taste* by guiding attention to the taste of a mint, sipping a drink, or chewing gum. When intervening with intense arousal, we recommend using a cinnamon fireball or intensely sour candies. Finally, we use *multisensory grounding techniques*, guiding the client in clapping the hands (touch and sound), stamping the feet (touch and sound), and feeling and looking at an object (touch and vision).

TECHNIQUES FOR DOWNREGULATING HYPERAROUSAL

When a client is experiencing hyperarousal, we use techniques to downregulate arousal back into the window of tolerance by activating the parasympathetic nervous system. The client's attention is likely fixated on the distressing experience; our instructions emphasize redirection of attention, reminding gently and firmly that we do not attend to old trauma-related content when we are outside of the window of tolerance, encouraging containment, and providing verbal guidance in downregulating strategies.

Our go-to strategy for downregulating hyperarousal is **elongated exhalations**, leveraging the exhalation's activation of the parasympathetic nervous system. This is not a mindfulness of breath practice; do *not* provide guidance in noticing sensations of the breath as this increases attention to internal sensations, which may be disruptive to downregulation if they include trauma-related cues. We typically provide instruction in counting silently—out-breath twice as long as in-breath (four in, eight out), or adjusted for client preference while maintaining a nonequal ratio (out-breath and parasympathetic > in-breath and sympathetic), continued for a few minutes. We highlight breathing without strain or striving, allowing adjustments to rhythm as beneficial. Another version of elongated exhalations is long, audible sighs (Magyari, 2016).

Crying arises as a naturally occurring biological emotion regulation process. It activates the parasympathetic nervous system and releases feel-good hormones—oxytocin and endogenous opioids (endorphins)—that reduce physical and emotional pain. When a client cries during practice, we guide: "Letting your body provide you with soothing hormones as you cry… Letting this pass through by not adding to the pain. No need to review the events that caused the distress in this moment… Inviting kindness toward this pain that is here."

In the online therapist materials (http://www.newharbinger.com/54650), we suggest numerous skills for downregulation of hyperarousal, including "Progressive Muscle Release." Additional strategies include using **ice** or an ice pack, a **self-regulating touch** through touching the lips or procerus muscle, **vagus nerve activation** (by listening to calming music, for instance), **gentle stretching**, using a **weighted blanket**, and **visual imagery** of a calming or peaceful place.

TECHNIQUES FOR UPREGULATING HYPERAROUSAL

When a client is experiencing hypoarousal, we engage techniques that upregulate arousal back into the window of tolerance by activating the sympathetic nervous system. We often begin by working with the breath. One strategy is **elongated inhalations**, which activates the sympathetic nervous system. We follow the same instructions as above for elongated exhalations but switch the ratio so that sympathetic in-breath is longer than parasympathetic out-breath. The second strategy is **quickened breathing**, inviting a *slightly* quickened pace of breathing, without rushing or straining (avoiding hyperventilation), activating the sympathetic nervous system.

Another technique for upregulating arousal is **activating muscles**, which activates the sympathetic nervous system. We guide the client in multipart activation: sitting forward in a chair, engaging thigh muscles, placing hands on thighs, engaging arm muscles by pressing into the legs, elongating posture, pushing feet into the ground, and activating legs. Alternatively, guiding the lifting and lowering of arms, leaning, wiggling, and scooching. We can also use *challenging balance*, guiding options such as standing on one foot (if balance is challenging, lifting the heel of one foot and steadying with toes on the ground), switching legs as needed.

We also activate muscles through *movement*, stimulating the sympathetic nervous system. We invite swiveling, swaying, standing up, moving arms, and squatting slightly (activates the strongest muscle groups). Once increased movement is available, we might guide getting the blood pumping, inviting waving arms, marching, or dancing; willingness can often be enhanced by adding music. If movement is particularly helpful or the client tends toward hypoarousal, we may integrate more movement-based meditation (for instance, walking mindfulness).

If the client experiences such severe hypoarousal that they are immobilized, we use the **starting small technique**, inviting small movements and then getting bigger (Steele, 2018). We guide slight movements of the fingers or toes. When those movements are available, we invite the movement of the hands or feet, then arms or legs, and finally inhabiting an active (not collapsed) posture.

RESPONSIVENESS TO PAINFUL EMOTIONS

When clients experience trauma-related intrusions during meditation, they may experience many painful emotions, such as shame, sadness, despair, disgust, fear, and horror. Therefore, it is helpful to use techniques that teach the client how to be responsive to painful emotions so they can practice a new alternative to habitual self-judgment and self-loathing. Note that this is informal mindfulness practice (off the cushion), applying the ideas of mindfulness in daily life and in session.

One way of being responsive to painful emotions is through **resourcing**, which involves the client taking in information, experiences, and support. One important method of resourcing is *providing psychoeducation*, in which we offer some information about what they experienced ("Experiences like this happen with meditation sometimes; they are related to the increased awareness and attention of mindfulness") and suggest responsible websites, such as Cheetah House (http://www.cheetahhouse.org) and Meditating in Safety (http://meditatinginsafety.org.uk), and books, such as Treleaven (2018; *Trauma-Sensitive Mindfulness*). We also encourage resourcing through social support and by being around loved ones (pets, partner, friend, or neighbor). We emphasize their *receiving* and taking in the support and care that is offered, not pushing it away out of habit.

We also attend to **restorative activities**, which help to reestablish balance. This may be simple, such as hydrating and nourishing (even if appetite is poor). At home, clients can engage in meaningful or restorative activities that capture their attention, such as gardening, time in nature, physical activity, or artistic creativity. Clients can also practice allowing themselves to rest when rest is needed.

Self-soothing reduces the intensity of painful emotions, quieting the agitation of the autonomic nervous system (ANS). The client may drink something soothing or smell an essential oil. We guide the client in practices such as placing the hand on the chest or holding themselves in a hug for as long as that feels soothing or pleasant.

Finally, a powerful response to painful emotions is **self-compassion** (see chapter 10 for self-compassion practices). For many clients, this is a departure from typical responses of self-judgment, self-berating, self-shaming, self-mocking, and contempt. If self-compassion is challenging, we start with *tenderness*, fostering the client's tender and caring stance toward themselves. Remember that tender is both the painful quality of the wound (it still feels tender) and the gentle stance toward it (approaching it tenderly).

KEEP GENERALIZATION IN MIND

It is important to remember that although the experience may disrupt the mindfulness practice, it is also a therapeutic opportunity. If the client experiences intrusions at other times, even infrequently, or fears having intrusions and not being able to handle them, we highlight that what we did in session to return to the window of tolerance can be generalized to other times when intrusions are experienced. Toward the session end, we may assist the client in making some notes on their client handouts (see "Safety-Enhancing Strategies"), marking the strategies they applied and how they were helpful.

Over time, as you implement safety-enhancing strategies, you will have an increasing sense of when to use which strategies. It is very important to practice these; they will make you a more skilled, responsible, and trustworthy mindful trauma therapist. Remember to guide only to the level of what you know (Pollak, 2013), meaning that if you practice for ten minutes in your own meditation practice, then you guide ten-minute practices, and so on. If you never use choiceless awareness, then you do not guide choiceless awareness.

Experiential knowledge leads to personal reference points on the practices you are leading and the experience of sitting still with yourself for that amount of time. For example, most people who have never meditated for thirty minutes may not realize how hard that is, how much restlessness or agitation or boredom can arise, the physical discomfort issues typical during practice, or how it feels to sit with painful emotions and try to find self-compassion. We encourage you to build your own skill set as an important part of enhancing safety in meditation for the clients whom you guide in practice.

Pivot to Trauma Processing When Readiness Arises

The most potent way to reduce intrusions and expand the client's window of tolerance is trauma processing. Thus, we invite clients to let us know at any point when they feel ready to talk more about specific traumatic events. In our process-based approach, we have a great deal of flexibility to pivot to trauma processing when readiness arises. Sometimes flashbacks or intrusive memories will motivate a client to express that they want to discuss that memory further. A common catalyst for this motivation is our letting clients know that trauma processing is the most effective way to reduce intrusions. However, there is a very important caveat: to effectively and therapeutically process trauma, they must have either dual awareness abilities (maintaining present-day awareness while remembering the trauma) or very strong skills in safety-enhancing strategies to facilitate staying in the window of tolerance while remembering the trauma. In the latter case, we promote dual awareness through integrating awareness of present-day stimuli and context while discussing the trauma memory and its impact on the client.

> **Prerequisite for Trauma Processing**
>
> Either:
>
> 1. Dual awareness (maintaining present-day awareness while remembering the trauma).
>
> 2. Ability to use safety-enhancing strategies to facilitate staying in the window of tolerance while remembering the trauma.

Intrusions have a strong relationship to avoidance (including nondeliberate forms like dissociation). This assertion is not meant to be blaming; we validate that avoidance provides relief in the short term, and we also recognize that long term, research shows that avoidance behaviors in response to intrusions are associated with increased likelihood of intrusions (Steil & Ehlers, 2000). Therefore, if the client expresses readiness to engage in trauma processing, long term this will be optimally effective for reducing trauma symptoms. If the client does not yet meet the requirements noted above, then we continue to build capacities using safety-enhancing strategies, *emphasizing present-moment awareness as scaffolding for dual awareness.*

Trauma processing is not to be done through meditation, and it is a priority in trauma treatment due to its therapeutic potency. Therefore, if the client has the capacities to engage in emotional processing of the traumatic experience, we pivot to trauma processing, mindfully and explicitly pausing the focus on mindfulness for any number of sessions. Importantly, as we shift into trauma processing, we bring with us the attitudes of mindfulness, practicing nonjudgment, acceptance, and compassion in the processing of trauma memories.

We also bring our safety-enhancing strategies, as many of these strategies (decreasing emotional intensity, grounding techniques, and responding to painful emotions) are helpful during the processing of trauma memories. In particular, integrate strategies for modifications of trauma processing (see handout) as needed. For a thorough review of trauma processing, we refer readers to other sources (Courtois & Ford, 2016; Steele et al., 2017). We will touch briefly on a few titration strategies, which we encourage you to integrate with other safety strategies described above, in particular emphasizing dual awareness and grounding strategies.

TITRATION TECHNIQUES

Consistent with the concept of titration (doing small pieces of work with an emphasis on staying regulated, building further as capacities are available; Steele et al., 2017), when the client experiences extensive emotional flooding, we encourage doing small pieces of work that build onto one another to build capacities at the edges of the window of tolerance. As always, therapeutic processing of trauma memories cannot occur when the client is outside of the window of tolerance. If the client moves outside of their window of tolerance while telling their narrative of the trauma, pivot briefly to implementation of safety-enhancing strategies, including grounding techniques, dual awareness practices, and downregulating arousal.

One very helpful example of titration is Babette Rothschild's (2000) *pacing the trauma narrative* by dividing it into three stages (see also chapter 4, "Memory Processing and Formal Exposure"). The first stage is naming the trauma at a one sentence level. We offer, "Just the headline, not the whole story." The second stage is outlining the trauma by labeling the main incidents. Each label is one short sentence without details. The third stage is filling in the details; the client elaborates on the events. Throughout each of these steps, we are actively engaged in observing the client for signs of hyperarousal or hypoarousal, checking in with them and getting physiological arousal ratings, and using strategies as needed to facilitate staying in the window of tolerance. If the client is flooded by naming the trauma and has difficulty returning to their window of tolerance, we do not proceed to the second stage; instead, we return to building awareness of the ANS and practicing strategies to return to physiological equilibrium. If the client can stay regulated or effectively apply strategies to return to their window of tolerance, we proceed with additional steps with continued monitoring of arousal.

A titration strategy that we use to reduce client dysregulation at the thought of talking about their trauma is to *begin by talking about what happened after the trauma* (Rothschild, 2000). The aftermath of trauma can be complex and retraumatizing in various ways. When a client thinks telling the story is too distressing, starting with what happened after the trauma reduces the load when they get to sharing the trauma event, thus functioning as preliminary titration. Furthermore, when they get to telling the worst part of the trauma event, they are very aware of the part that comes after and that they have survived (Rothschild, 2000).

If the client is struggling with maintaining present-moment awareness, we often use a technique of creating a present-moment sensation to promote dual awareness. We guide the client in *creating a present-moment sensation* that they can be aware of (for example, finger moving up and down the arm or standing up and moving) while talking about the trauma (Rothschild, 2000). We instruct maintaining awareness of the present-moment sensation that they are creating.

Overwhelm and Dysregulation During Meditation

Trauma survivors may experience a state of overwhelm during meditation and in their daily lives. This accompanies reactions of anxiety or panic, emotional flooding or numbing, intense distress, dissociation, or immobilization—emotions and states that mark experiences that are unbearable to the client or beyond current capacities or resources. These intense reactions are accompanied by dysregulation of the ANS (hyperarousal or hypoarousal). We conceptualize this category as overwhelm, marking that we are outside of the client's window of tolerance.

Clients may experience overwhelm in the context of trauma-related intrusions as well as a variety of other experiences that can occur during meditation, including perceptual disturbances (see below), challenging emotional experiences, and somatic distress (Lindahl et al., 2017). Anxiety is one of the most frequently reported meditation-related adverse effects, with 27 percent of participants reporting it in one study (Goldberg et al., 2022).

What to Do When Dysregulation Occurs During Meditation

When dysregulation occurs during meditation in session, we respond by engaging safety-enhancing strategies without conveying therapist anxiety or emotional reactivity. How clients react to distressing experiences during meditation can have an immense influence on whether they move through the experience gently or escalate in reactivity. As you know, once they are outside of their window of tolerance, no learning will occur. Therefore, as the overwhelmed feeling rises, our emphasis shifts to safety-enhancing strategies, using pivots like those described for intrusions, beginning with those that can be integrated smoothly into the practice (such as opening the eyes, shifting posture, and elongated exhalations).

Here is the best part—you already learned all the relevant strategies in the intrusions section. You can review the online therapist materials (http://www.newharbinger.com/54650) and integrate techniques from categories of Reducing Emotional Intensity, Grounding, either Downregulating Hyperarousal or Upregulating Hypoarousal (depending on the client's physiological arousal ratings), and Responding to Painful Emotions. You'll decide based on contextual factors what category of intervention would be most useful and implement techniques from that section of the handout. At the end of the session, we ask for arousal ratings and summarize the strategies we used, discussing the client's experience as they make notes for themselves on their client handouts ("Safety-Enhancing Strategies") about what was helpful and in what way.

We highlight that although the experience was distressing and we wish it hadn't occurred, the silver lining is that the client has learned some techniques for coming back into the window of tolerance, providing an opportunity for skills acquisition or generalization. Typically, the client will be back in the window of tolerance by the end of the session. If not, we encourage connecting with their support system or engaging in a restorative activity after the session (refer client to handout, "Responsiveness to Painful Emotions," see restorative activities category).

At times, it may be necessary to go beyond safety-enhancing strategies. One important resource is social support, and we encourage clients to connect with others who are regulating and resourcing to them. They can also access social support through Cheetah House support groups, or a local meditation center may offer spaces for discussing meditation challenges. At times, clients may benefit from medication, so you may refer them to consult with a psychiatric prescriber. In the varieties of contemplative experiences (VCE) study, practitioners reported that medications were helpful to them in facilitating stabilization and reducing distress and functional impairments (Lindahl et al., 2019).

We notice closely what practice elements seem to be associated with dysregulated arousal, seeking out practices in which the client feels safe. For example, interoceptive awareness may be very difficult for a survivor of childhood sexual abuse due to somatic reminders of trauma; once we know that, we can shift to practices emphasizing externally focused awareness. Many mindfulness practices emphasize noticing internal thoughts, emotions, and sensations, which may be exceedingly painful for trauma survivors who experience self-loathing, shame, and self-disgust (Forner, 2017).

In our experience, finding meditation-related challenges to be overwhelming or unmanageable within the practice is more likely for clients whose adaptations involve severe or pervasive emotion dysregulation, difficulty with distress tolerance, or trauma-related intrusions (for instance, occurring in patients with post-traumatic stress disorder [PTSD], dissociative disorders, and BPD). For these clients, it is often effective to begin with externally focused attention practices (see chapter 7; add modification of attention regulation practices for auditory or visual anchoring rather than somatosensory).

Perceptual Disturbances During Meditation

Clients may report experiencing perceptual disturbances during meditation, such as hallucinations (perceptual experience in the absence of external stimuli), illusions (distortions of actual external stimuli), depersonalization (estrangement from one's body or out-of-body experiences), derealization (estrangement from others or surroundings or things seeming dreamlike, unreal, or foggy), and distortions in time or space (Lindahl et al., 2017). Clients have a broad range of reactions to these experiences—they may seem unfazed and discuss the event disinterestedly, they may see it as a positive or complex spiritual experience, or they may view it as emerging psychopathology. First, understand how your client conceptualizes the experience.

Most perceptual disturbances are likely related to neurobiological phenomena. For example, Lindahl and colleagues (2014) provide neurobiological explanations for light-related hallucinations during meditation, drawing on well-established empirical knowledge of sensory deprivation (minimal sensory input) and perceptual isolation (uniform, consistent, or unstructured stimuli) contexts, which they demonstrate are analogous to meditation. In addition, they highlight neurobiological findings that suggest visual hallucination experiences may indicate that the brain is in a state of enhanced neuroplasticity, allowing for increased capacity for new learning and growth, consistent with the conceptualization throughout Buddhist literature (Lindahl et al., 2014). Thus, these experiences may be less of an indicator of emerging psychopathology and more of an indicator of a period in which enhanced learning can occur.

There are a few questions to consider in conceptualizing the perceptual disturbance. If a client reports a hallucination, the first question is whether this is part of a trauma memory—if it is, we conceptualize it as an intrusion rather than a perceptual disturbance. Similarly, if a hallucination happened when falling asleep (hypnagogic hallucination) or upon waking (hypnopompic hallucination), it could be sleep-related rather than meditation-related (Waters et al.,

2024). Beyond clarifying these aspects that are relevant to assessment, we mainly focus on attending to the client's emotional reactions to the experience.

What to Do When Perceptual Disturbances Occur During Meditation

When a client has an experience like this, they will typically let you know during inquiry, or if it was during home practice, in the next session. We always start with assessment, leading with curiosity and characterizing the experience—what occurred, the duration, and how they felt during the experience. We are also interested in the client's reality testing (for instance, "I knew it wasn't really there"); in our experience, clients have always retained reality testing capability. Further, we invite the client to rate physiological arousal. If they are not overwhelmed, we engage in resourcing by providing psychoeducation, letting them know that these things happen sometimes during meditation, that they appear to be related to neurobiological phenomena that occur during meditation, and often resolve without intervention. We let them know that we would like them to follow up with us if they continue experiencing such phenomena.

If a client has reported depersonalization or derealization, it might be helpful to engage in some grounding techniques. Downregulating hyperarousal or upregulating hypoarousal are also helpful; as dissociative experiences can occur in both hyperarousal (such as in a panic attack) and hypoarousal (such as in shutdown collapse states), you will need to reference the client's physiological arousal rating to determine which to use.

If the client is overwhelmed or highly distressed by a perceptual disturbance experience, we guide them in safety-enhancing techniques from the "Safety-Enhancing Strategies" handouts, specifically "Reducing Emotional Overwhelm" and either "Downregulating Hyperarousal" or "Upregulating Hypoarousal" (depending on the client's physiological arousal ratings). We ask about what they are doing after the session and consider safety (for example, if they are driving), inviting them to walk around for a while outside before driving away if needed. To reduce stress in controllable ways, we encourage the client to emphasize stabilization after the session—biologically by focusing on hydration, balanced eating, balanced sleep, and avoiding alcohol or substances, and psychologically by being gentle and compassionate with themselves.

If the client is highly destabilized by the experience, we recommend *briefly discontinuing meditation*, and when ready to return, going back to the learning the landscape (slow start-up) phase to titrate meditation and promote safety. Destabilization following perceptual disturbances is often associated with two factors: 1) duration (disturbances enduring after discontinuing meditation) and 2) the psychological response to the experience (anxiety; catastrophic appraisal).

If the central problem is the duration (or both), we discuss with the client whether they might benefit from a consultation with a psychiatric prescriber (preferably one who understands meditation-related phenomena). This kind of adjunctive intervention is recommended if the experience worsens or intensifies over time, or proliferates into new symptoms (Lindahl et al.,

2020). If the central problem is the psychological response, we work with this psychologically by trying to reduce hypervigilance, anxiety, and catastrophic interpretations.

When considering the client's emotional response to the experience, be aware that intense anxiety or distress often have an exacerbating effect on the trajectory. A hallucination may not be so distressing if the client views it as a passing event, relating to it nonjudgmentally and as a transient present-moment experience, or sees it as a culturally contextualized experience. However, if the client responds to the experience with intense anxiety, they may often make catastrophic future predictions (such as, *Now I am psychotic; This will happen all the time now*); we have seen this progress into destabilization and deterioration. To mitigate this, you can guide the client in responding to thoughts about the experience with *nonreactivity* (letting things be as they are, observing them without reacting) and grounding in the present moment (focus on cognitive grounding or externally focused sensory grounding with visual or auditory anchors).

If the client is not destabilized by the experience, you definitely do not need to be either; if they are, then they need you to stay steady. Remind yourself of why such phenomena occur (likely neurobiological changes during meditation) and that these experiences are often not indicators of emerging psychopathology. That said, we are attentive to subsequent monitoring for symptoms given that such symptoms can endure (Goldberg et al., 2022).

Suicide Ideation During Meditation

Clients may report suicide ideation (SI) during meditation. They will typically tell us about it during inquiry after the practice, and they may describe thoughts or images. Sometimes, these are downstream effects of emotions about other difficult experiences (such as shame associated with trauma-related intrusions). Other times, clients will report a purely emotion-driven process (likely elicited by habitual emotion–thought associations) such as feeling deep sadness and experiencing SI.

For many trauma survivors, during periods of chronic trauma, SI may have brought the comfort of an escape from ongoing abuse and extensive sequelae; therefore, trauma-related stimuli (internal and external) may become habitually associated with SI and reinforced by subsequent relief or comfort. For some of our clients, there is greater specificity in the habitual association, such as *shame* → SI or *feeling trapped* → SI.

What to Do When Suicide Ideation Occurs During Meditation

When a client reports SI, we assess further. We briefly gather information about the cues or prompting events that led up to this to better understand the SI context. For some trauma survivors, SI was a psychological adaptation to trauma, providing the comfort of escape as a (maladaptive) emotion regulation strategy. Thus, it can arise in response to painful trauma-related memories or emotions, reoccurring due to well-worn associative networks. We validate suffering or sadness, the discomfort of the intensity of shame, and distress at surprising intrusive suicidal thought as fits circumstances. However, we must move rapidly into risk assessment. The client should not leave our office after reporting SI without conducting a risk assessment and, if necessary, engaging in safety planning. This can be very brief if SI is passive but will be more extensive if SI is active and involves a plan or intent. See Appendix 2 (http://www.newharbinger.com/54650) for detailed information about risk assessment and safety planning.

Conclusion

Meditation (formal mindfulness practice) comes with typical challenges and risks of more serious meditation-related adverse experiences. Trauma survivors are particularly vulnerable to experiencing meditation-related adverse experiences, so it is very important for the mindful trauma therapist to review this chapter thoroughly to understand the relevant risks and how to work with them to ensure client safety.

For flashbacks, dual awareness is an essential process to emphasize and develop. We conceptualize meditation-related perceptual disturbances as occurring due to neurobiological processes producing reactions (such as hallucinations) that are well-established phenomena arising during or following meditation (Lindahl et al., 2014).

We have offered you a structure for a preparatory session that helps to resource the client with strategies, skills, and techniques that we have offered in this chapter and the accompanying online therapist materials (http://www.newharbinger.com/54650). Learning the various categories of safety-enhancing strategies will help you know how to quickly select relevant strategies in session.

CHAPTER 6

How to Use Mindfulness in Session

When implementing mindfulness practices in the context of therapy sessions, the therapist has many considerations to bear in mind. In this chapter, we will discuss therapist skills for integrating mindfulness into session, including how to introduce mindfulness practices, choices in language and instruction during mindfulness practices, ending the practice, embodying qualities of mindfulness, and general recommendations.

> The mindful trauma therapist affirms the client's first-person knowledge and fosters their self-awareness and self-trust.

The most important therapeutic tasks follow the mindfulness practice: the culling of knowledge gleaned from experience, the consolidation of this learning, and the generalization of this learning. Therefore, in addition to effectively leading a mindfulness practice, we attend to therapeutic processes. In a mindfulness-based approach, we include both experiential and instructional learning; however, we emphasize and privilege experiential learning.

The mindful trauma therapist uses an approach that affirms the client's first-person knowledge and fosters their self-awareness and self-trust. We will discuss the use of inquiry to facilitate consolidation and generalization. Furthermore, we will discuss how therapists can be thoughtful and methodical in the selection of mindfulness practices. Finally, we will review when it might be unhelpful to include a mindfulness practice in session.

Guidance for Integrating Mindfulness into Session

The therapist embodies qualities of mindfulness, bringing them to life in practice instruction and inquiry. The therapist's presence and approach to instruction and dialogue provide experiential learning of processes relevant to mindfulness; therefore, this is an approach that emphasizes the *therapist's use of self*. The client experiences the therapist's embodiment of qualities and attitudes, including a welcoming, nonjudgmental stance, curiosity, acceptance, compassion, and equanimity, as they interact with awareness of pain, aversion, discomfort, joy, calm, wonder, or whatever arises; this facilitates the client's own cultivation of these qualities. Our

> Our therapeutic embodiment of qualities and attitudes of mindfulness is developed through our personal mindfulness practice.

embodiment of qualities and attitudes of mindfulness is developed through our personal mindfulness practice, and therefore they are authentic and values consistent as well as being recommendations from a theoretical paradigm. If you are struggling to access these qualities, see chapter 11.

The mindful trauma therapist brings an experiential and exploratory approach to psychotherapy, helping trauma survivors attend to and relate to their experiences in new ways. For therapists who were trained to take a more directive or instructive style, this will mean attending to style (explore rather than explain), leaning more heavily on skills such as Socratic dialogue paired with a stance of truly not knowing. The therapist embodies this in asking their questions, and at times, when the client asks questions seeking a correct answer.

Client: I tried not to cough, but it hurt. What should I do when I think I may need to cough during a practice?

Therapist: What a beautiful yearning to learn more. I'm eager to hear more from you about what you notice around this now that you are curious. You'll have to let me know. What happens when you observe the urge and try to suppress the cough? Sounds like it hurts. What happens when you let yourself cough? Can you do both strategies with kindness? We have so much to learn about how to relate to the urge to cough during practice. There is certainly no rule that you may not cough during practice. And yet, you may notice that you had one in your mind and that it got privileged over your physical needs.

Common Humanity

Mindful trauma therapists often use the language of *we* when describing relatively universal experiences to invite awareness of common humanity. Common humanity reminds us that suffering is a part of life and places our experiences as part of the larger human experience (Germer & Neff, 2015). This can help shift experiences that might feel separating and isolating into feeling like part of the human experience. As trauma survivors may feel very alone and separate due to their trauma experiences and often from secrecy and shame following the trauma, this is a crucial concept during therapy.

Because the *we* is also a form of self-disclosure, note that all considerations related to judicious self-disclosure apply here. It is therefore applied thoughtfully, with consideration of personal factors with regard to client benefit and therapist limits (for instance, therapist says "we" referring to trauma survivors). With intentionality, the mindful therapist integrates the language of *we* frequently when discussing themes and patterns that are common to most people (for instance, wandering minds, judgmental minds, and noticing worries).

Therapist: "When we notice our minds wandering, this is a real opportunity to notice how we interact with ourselves around challenges. We can be curious about how we approach that, and about how it feels to experience that approach."

Disruptions During Practice

It is best to minimize disruptions during a mindfulness practice, so we recommend silencing phones, tablets, and computers. However, it is not imperative to have a quiet environment that includes no disruptions. Although clients may prefer that, if we believe that we must have a pristine, silent, uninterrupted space in order to practice mindfulness, it becomes far less accessible than if we learn to practice *with* distractions. If individuals comment on their reactions to distractions during the inquiry process, that too becomes fodder for inquiry.

Client: I heard the toilet flush and felt so annoyed. It basically ruined my practice.

Therapist: Beautiful. You observed the sound of the toilet flushing, and you noticed feeling annoyed. And then this thought about 'ruined my practice'—what does that mean?

Client: It interrupted the practice, and then I couldn't get back into the same mindset.

Therapist: What if the toilet flushing is actually part of the practice, just as any sound you hear might become an object of attention or distraction during practice?

Client: It was just so frustrating that it was hard to let go of.

Therapist: I get that. Then what happened?

Client: Eventually I just forgot about it… I guess I went back to listening to your words.

Therapist: And the annoyance—what happened to that?

Client: It just passed.

Therapist: Oh, it passed! I am curious about how, at first, it was hard to let go of the annoyance. And yet, although you didn't do anything to fix it, after some time it still shifted. And those shifts affected the process! I'll be eager to hear more about how you work with sounds or disruptions in your mindfulness home practice this week.

Providing Instruction in Mindfulness

Providing instruction in mindfulness practice involves a thoughtful approach to each element of the practice. We will discuss components, including introduction of a mindfulness practice, instruction and language choices during a practice, and ending the practice. That experience is then followed by an inquiry process, which we will discuss in the next section of this chapter. Across

> There is a developmental arc to instruction. Early on, we use more words to help harness and focus attention; later, more silence is useful in providing space for relevant reflection.

sessions for each individual client, there is a developmental arc to instruction. Early in the client's use of mindfulness, we may use more words to encourage the client to harness and focus their attention; later, more silence is useful in providing space for relevant reflection. Even early in instruction, leave enough silence in between guidance to enable the practitioner to experience what happens to attention.

Introducing Mindfulness Practices

When introducing the practice, we typically describe a very brief general overview of the practice (for instance, "We will attend to the breath." "I will read a poem." "We will do a gratitude practice together."). It is helpful to orient to the practice duration (for instance, "This practice will be about ten minutes"). For certain practices, additional instruction may be helpful (such as identifying target individuals for loving-kindness meditation). However, most of the time, the majority of instructions can be provided within the mindfulness practice in ways that provide guidance, direct the client's attention, and offer new ways of relating to their experience. Instructions are typically rather brief given the emphasis on experience.

> Trauma survivors have adapted to ignore and suppress their needs and to mistrust or block somatically based information, which we counter by teaching responsiveness as a meaningful self-care option.

Working with discomfort. If it will be a longer sitting practice, it is helpful to discuss discomfort (such as legs falling asleep or back pain) and options for responding. We often encourage individuals to use such experiences as a choice point—an opportunity to choose between alternatives. One option is to sit with the discomfort, to observe the experience and use it as part of the practice. The other option is to consider what can be shifted and, if one chooses to, mindfully shift and observe the experience following the shift, using it as part of the practice. The sitting through and observing is often what therapists and clients think one "should" do; the alternative option often surprises therapists and clients alike.

We emphasize that through noticing the choice point, making mindful decisions, and then collecting information with curiosity following those decisions, our wisdom about how to take care of ourselves effectively deepens. Although many traditions emphasize the first option in the service of nonreactivity, we believe that the second option offering responsiveness is of *equal importance* to the recovery process of trauma survivors. This is particularly true because so often trauma survivors have learned through their traumatic experiences and traumagenic contexts to ignore and suppress their needs and to mistrust or block somatically based information, which we counter by teaching responsiveness as a meaningful option for self-care.

There is not a preferred or optimal choice; however, we are curious if someone habitually declines the other choice. Then we want to be curious about how it might be to practice the alternative choice. This is especially true if the client articulates a desire or need for the other experience (for instance, "I wished I could just move my leg. I kept feeling these urges to move my leg").

Curiosity about responsiveness example:

Client: I had lots of thoughts about my leg cramping and the uncomfortable feelings.

Therapist: So you observed a lot of attention to physical discomfort sensations. What did you notice about the uncomfortable feelings?

Client: It was mostly pain, and I felt really agitated. I kept getting distracted by the sensations in my leg.

Therapist: So important. There was this agitation rooted in discomfort. How did you respond to that?

Client: I was frustrated with myself. I hate that it's so hard for me to do this right; I know that I'm supposed to be still and quiet.

Therapist: What if we consider that at times you might choose to shift something slightly—perhaps moving or shifting in such a way that alleviates some of those sensations of discomfort? What would happen if you did stretch your leg out in that moment when you feel it cramping? And maybe then settle back into stillness?

Client: I didn't even know that was an okay option.

Curiosity about nonreactivity example:

Client: I felt some embarrassment about all my fidgeting. I think I had a harder time settling because I was fidgeting so much.

Therapist: So you noticed some distraction or even disruption from all of the movement. What are you taking from this?

Client: I guess I would like to be more still. I just fidget out of habit.

Therapist: You might see if you can hold that as an invitation, to ride the urges sometimes and to find out more about what happens when you are more still.

Therapist (holds dialectics and instructs active responsiveness to potential for harm or injury):
And we know that right beside that, you have the other choice. If something hurts, then responsiveness is strongly, perhaps unequivocally, preferred.

Posture. We provide guidance on how to sit so the body is supported by the bones and muscles. We encourage a posture that is elongated without being rigidly held or requiring great effort.

The typical instructions we use are: "Inviting the posture to take on a sense of dignity, we mark the experience of shifting out of automatic pilot and into mindful awareness."

Our typical context in session is the client sitting on a chair or a couch; in that case, we provide instructions to place the feet flat on the floor, making contact with the ground. If the feet don't reach the ground, consider offering a small block or bolster to put under the feet; this again teaches responsiveness and care, permitting and encouraging receiving support and finding more ease and less effort. This will also take the pressure off the lower back. If meditation cushions are used—which for us is more typical in a group context—we provide instructions to center the shoulders over the hips, and we often offer small bolsters under the knees; this helps individuals sit cross-legged with more support and reduces discomfort.

Gaze. It is helpful to discuss that the eyes may be open or closed per client preference. This is an important trauma-sensitive adaptation, and some meditative traditions are more prescriptive about form. If the client leaves their eyes open, they can look slightly downward, keeping their gaze relaxed with a soft focus. Some trauma survivors may prefer open eyes because the eyes being closed is distressing or may elicit feelings of vulnerability and worries about safety. Furthermore, keeping the eyes open can help with awareness of present-moment stimuli and facilitate the distinction between past and present if flashbacks occur during mindfulness practice. In addition, eyes open helps address problems with sleepiness. Finally, in some traditions (such as Zen and Tibetan Buddhism), eyes open are encouraged to facilitate generalization to everyday life.

Conversely, some clients may find that closing the eyes facilitates turning inward or makes it easier to disregard distractions around them. Therefore, we encourage offering the choice and encouraging clients to find what works best (the method that is most facilitative of meditation) for them. Again, we activate trauma-informed principles of choice and empowerment, opportunities for self-awareness, self-trust, and self-responsiveness.

Mindfulness practice introduction includes:

- brief overview of current practice
- orientation to duration of current practice
- if long, brief discussion of response options for discomfort
- brief instruction regarding posture and gaze.

Instruction and Guidance During the Practice

We start the practice by marking our shift out of automatic pilot and into mindful awareness. This is most typically a bell, but this is not a requirement for mindfulness. You could use other markers to signify this switch (for instance, the postural instructions offered above). Once the practice begins, there are many things that the mindful trauma therapist tries to keep in mind in providing instruction and guidance.

Providing choices. First and foremost, we provide choices embedded throughout the practice. We instruct the core practice as recommended while seeking out the myriad of opportunities for individualization that do not disrupt the essence of the practice. Offering a range of alternatives embedded in instruction invites the client to notice how their experience fits into an array of options rather than a single instruction. This fosters the development of more nuanced self-awareness and noticing of preferences or inclinations, which may have been historically suppressed, inhibited, or judged and rejected. Finally, for trauma survivors, having opportunities for agency through choice can be a crucial part of healing.

Example: "Letting our awareness follow the sensations of the breath. Perhaps noticing some sensations of the breath at the nostrils or on the lips… Perhaps observing the sensations of the rise and fall of the chest with each breath, the expansion and contraction of the ribs, or the swell and ebb of the belly with each breath. Choosing one area, follow the sensations of each breath with fresh curiosity."

Offering invitational language. We guide mindfulness practices using invitational language, offering opportunities rather than providing commands. Therefore, we avoid language of imperatives (should, must, ought). Invitational language includes starting with: "Inviting awareness to focus in on the left foot…" "Taking a few moments to settle in…" "Allowing the breath to move in and out as it does…"

Using the present participle. Instructions are structured using the present participle (-ing verbs) and offer guidance that facilitates the client's sense of experiential immersion. Using the present participle allows instruction to parallel the observing or participating in experience as it unfolds from moment to moment. Examples of using present participles in instruction: "Bringing attention to the sensations of sound…" "Resting awareness on the shoulders…" "Shifting your attention from the wrist to the forearm…"

Offering encouragement paired with a nonstriving and accepting attitude. We suggest and invite while demonstrating acceptance and gentle awareness through instruction. For example, we might offer instructions framed by: "As best you can, let the body soften here for a moment." "Without striving, perhaps letting something release with the exhalation." "With a light touch…"

Our enthusiasm for the client's mindful awareness of experiences is nonpreferential. Whether the client describes an experience that was calm and peaceful, sad and painful, or agitated and irritable, we welcome the description and eagerly pursue detailed information about the experience with great curiosity. It is particularly important to be welcoming and affirming of experiences of pain, discomfort, and aversion.

Offering guidance for mind wandering. We offer guidance for mind wandering and a nonjudgmental stance toward this happening. In most cases, the instructions will emphasize refocusing attention on the chosen object of awareness.

Therapist: "Taking a moment to observe where attention is focused, perhaps noticing that the mind has wandered away from the breath. Celebrating the moment of noticing, which is followed by the opportunity to shepherd our awareness back to the breath. Noticing the temperature change with the inhalation. Following the sensations that present themselves into our awareness."

There is one notable exception around the instruction to provide guidance for mind wandering: choiceless awareness (open monitoring) practices. In these practices, attention is placed on whatever enters awareness, with an emphasis on nonreactivity to content. In such practices, the therapist does *not* provide instruction on mind wandering, as this reflects a fundamental misunderstanding of the practice. Here, we are interested in how the client relates to the thought process of mind wandering or the content it has wandered to, looking for a deeply textured description of what they may notice as we would any other object of awareness (such as sound, emotion, or muscle sensation).

An example instruction during a choiceless awareness practice, spoken across a practice with silences for contemplation: "Noticing what awareness is focused on. Perhaps observing that the mind has been generating judgments. Hmmm. If we notice judgments, we might begin with noting whether we feel caught up in them or are simply noticing them. Are the judgments you notice directed at you or at others, or both? Are the judgments critical or preferential, or are both present? What about the tone—is the tone light, harsh, or even scathing? You may notice that a feeling accompanies these judgments. Perhaps you may name that emotion, nonjudgmentally acknowledging it, without trying to fix it or having to do something about it."

Pacing. It is helpful to have a time-keeping device as we want to track time during the mindfulness practice (which can be challenging when you provide an embodied mindfulness presence), ensuring completion of practice with time to engage in a full inquiry about the experience. In longer or more complex practices, it is particularly important to attend to pacing. It is the therapist's responsibility to observe time and ensure space is available for deep inquiry.

Ending the practice. A few minutes before completing the practice, it is helpful to orient to the upcoming end of the practice (for instance, "As we approach the end of our practice…" "In our last few minutes of practice now…"). This prevents the end from being jarring and offers an opportunity to facilitate transition. At the end of the practice, the therapist should avoid instructions like, *Return to the room* or *Come back to this session,* as these signify that the practice has been something different from that, when mindfulness is about being in the present moment. Even if we are using imagery or an intentional practice, we are experiencing ourselves in the present moment as we visit with the imagery or the intention.

Our typical instructions for ending include inviting awareness and beginning to engage metacognition about the practice: "As we prepare for the end of our practice, noticing our current experience—observing the emotional state, the mental pace of activity or content of thought, sensations. Perhaps a moment of remembering the experience at the start of the practice, perhaps noticing ways that your current experience may feel different… In the last few minutes of our practice, identifying if there is anything that you would like to take with you from this practice. Perhaps the way you are deeply noticing, or particular ways you are relating to your experiences, or qualities you have cultivated in your practice that you would like to take with you from this practice into the rest of this hour, this day, this week."

By providing orientation to the upcoming transition of the practice ending, we provide the client with the opportunity to engage with the transition in a way that is perhaps less jarring or abrupt. Trauma survivors are often sensitized to discomfort with unpredictability because traumatic experiences are typically marked by a lack of predictability or control. Predictability allows clients to prepare themselves for what is ahead, providing an opportunity to have more control over our experience. Note that at the end of the excerpt, we have provided a generalization prompt.

Inquiry: A Facilitator of Therapeutic Integration and Consolidation

The inquiry process is a key element of enhancing the therapeutic benefit of mindfulness practice. After completing an in-session mindfulness practice, we use the inquiry process to facilitate the client's building awareness, consolidation, and generalization. We engage the client in a contemplative dialogue, embodying qualities of mindfulness to facilitate experiential learning.

The inquiry process we use is drawn from mindfulness-based cognitive therapy (MBCT; Segal et al., 2013); the process has been elaborated as a core therapeutic process of MBCT (Woods et al., 2019). In our work providing MBCT, we have often had clients come to the process who, despite having experience in mindfulness, are uncertain about how it can be leveraged to enhance mental health, highlighting the gap in typical or standard teaching of mindfulness. Further, although many therapists do incorporate mindfulness into therapy sessions, they are often uncertain about how to effectively and therapeutically follow up on a mindfulness practice. The inquiry process is specifically tailored to facilitate therapeutic processing.

The inquiry process consists of inquiring about experience across three layers. The first layer is *building awareness*, in which we encourage the noticing of direct sensory experience. Second, *tracking and contextualizing*. Here, we put observations into context and explore how this experience is different or similar to their everyday lives, facilitating consolidation of the experience. The third layer is *insight and generalization*, in which we explore how this is relevant for taking care of themselves and identifying application opportunities.

> **The Three Layers of Inquiry**
> 1. Building awareness.
> 2. Tracking and contextualizing.
> 3. Insight and generalization.

The three layers are to be approached as a dialogue in which the therapist and client collaboratively explore the client's experience and observations. We ask open-ended questions, rooted in curiosity, and paired with tenderness, compassion, and an inclination toward the befriending of experiences that may typically be judged or perceived as negative. The dialogue emphasizes observations, musings, and marvels about the client's experience and how they related to that experience. The inquiry process has been detailed in the MBCT literature, first described by Crane (2009) and elaborated further in the MBCT manual (Segal et al., 2013) and other guides (Woods et al., 2019).

Inquiry is an experiential process that unfolds rather than a rote set of questions and the receipt of their answers. That is, it feels more like a heart-to-heart discussion than an interview. Across sessions of participating in inquiry, clients begin to demonstrate an enhanced ability to notice and describe sensory and body-based information as they develop an interest in these aspects of their experience. They shift from forming interpretations of experiences and narratives about experience to inhabiting and describing direct experience.

In addition, they demonstrate an enhanced awareness of how they are relating to their experiences and how they treat themselves in the context of those experiences. Clients often develop an awareness of habitual patterns with contextual elements, which turns into opportunities for autopilot reactions to become considered responses. They may begin to notice more about the fluctuations in experience and the shifts in relating to the experience. They develop skills in leveraging the duality of being both a participant in their experiences and the observer of their experiences (metacognitive awareness). The client may benefit from engaging self-inquiry facilitated by prompts, as on the "Home Practice with Self-Inquiry" form (client worksheet: http://www.newharbinger.com/54650).

Layer One: Building Awareness

In this layer, we ask: "What did you notice during that practice?" We investigate the noticing and describing of the direct sensory experience. We seek out rich, textured descriptions of body sensations, feelings, and thoughts. When the mind habitually wanders, we explore to where (for instance, to pain sensations, planning thoughts, or self-judging thoughts). We ask

---

Therapist questions for layer one: building awareness

- *What did you notice during that practice?*
    - *Sensations in the body?*
    - *Sounds?*
    - *Emotions? Sensations associated with the emotions?*
    - *Thoughts? About the present moment, the past, or the future? (Perhaps categorizing input as memories, rumination, planning, worries, or self-judgment.)*
- *What was your reaction, if you had one, to these experiences? How did you relate to them?*

questions that invite information about what the client was aware of during the practice in various aspects of the experience while practicing the parsing or categorizing of experience. When continuing a line of inquiry further, we may also ask for permission.

Layer Two: Tracking and Contextualizing

In this layer, we ask: "How is this way of attending or responding different from the everyday way of responding? And then what happened? How did you feel about that or respond to that?" We explore the unfolding process of the experience, tracking across time how it shifts or fluctuates, highlighting impermanence and change.

Further, we consolidate a contextualized understanding of habitual patterns or contrasts to these patterns. This facilitates the client cultivating a meta-perspective on habitual ways of thinking or behaving and the opportunity to clarify contingencies (when…, then…) around the habitual behavior (Woods et al., 2019). For example, clients may notice that when they are harsh and punitive with themselves about mind wandering, they feel guilty and shameful,

---

Therapist questions for layer two: tracking and contextualizing

- *How might this way of attending or responding be different from the everyday way of responding?*
- *And then what happened? And then what?*
- *Did it stay that way the whole time, or did it shift or fluctuate?*
- *How did you feel about that or respond to that?*
- *When you noticed your mind wandering / your back hurting / your worries about your boss…*
    - *How did you feel?*
    - *What did you do? Did you let it wander? Did you start planning or getting involved with the thoughts? Did you bring your attention back?*
    - *What was the tone or style of that? Was it gentle, harsh, patient, annoyed, judging, amused? And what feelings or sensations did you notice in response to the gentle / harsh / annoyed redirection?*
- *How does bringing awareness to the gentleness / harshness / annoyance affect the experience of it?*
- *Is this a familiar pattern? What do you recognize in it as familiar?*
- *Do you think of this habitual pattern as helpful, neutral, or harmful and problematic?*

whereas when they are gentle and firm with themselves, they can redirect attention more effectively in the absence of the aversive emotions that arise from scathing self-judgment. The therapist helps the client to consolidate new learning.

Layer Three: Insight and Generalization

In this layer, we ask: "How might this relate to taking care of yourself in the context of trauma symptoms? How is this relevant to your healing and recovery process?" We investigate the application of reflections and new understandings to facilitate generalization. Here, we try to apply the new insights by forming ideas for supporting oneself during difficult times or the regular ups and downs of everyday life.

> Therapist questions for layer three: insight and generalization
> - *How might this relate to taking care of yourself in the context of trauma symptoms?*
> - *How is this relevant to your healing and recovery process?*
> - *How would you like to take this with you?*
> - *What an opportunity this is. What is the invitation here?*
> - Consolidating with an open-ended question:
>
> Example: "So you noticed that when I'm guiding with gentle statements acknowledging fallibility, you give yourself a lot of grace; that feels more pleasant and helps you remain more aware of all the times you're effectively staying mindful. And my instructions about celebrating noticing mind wandering helped you focus on building a sense of mastery around the ability to practice. What are you taking with you from this?"

Choosing Strategies and Techniques

We have noted the importance of therapists approaching the selection of mindfulness practices thoughtfully and methodically. Although many therapists may have historically been somewhat arbitrary or indiscriminate, selecting whatever mindfulness practice came to mind, we strongly encourage therapists to select an appropriate mindfulness practice based on case conceptualization and systematic understanding of the intervention plan as relevant to the practices.

Mindfulness practices improve well-being and mental health through one of several processes. Hölzel and colleagues (2011) have offered a model delineating the four overarching processes underlying the effectiveness of mindfulness meditation: 1) attention regulation, 2) body awareness, 3) emotion regulation, involving appraisal and exposure, and 4) change in perspective. These four processes can guide therapist selection of mindfulness practices.

In part 3 of this book, "Implementing Mindfulness Using a Process-Based Approach," we provide extensive scaffolding for the therapist's selection of mindfulness practices targeted toward the relevant therapeutic intervention processes. Each chapter represents one of the four processes targeting various problems or symptoms. The approach uses a skill-building framework, viewing clients (and therapists) as being able to build and strengthen skills through practice.

Using the heuristics that we provide, the therapist selects practices based on the process that is currently being cultivated and strengthened. For example, we focus on enhancing attention regulation; cultivating this process involves learning to notice and direct attention, practicing skills in harnessing and shifting attention, and collecting information and making deliberate choices about where to foster attention and where to redirect attention. We choose a practice that facilitates these attentional components, such as a focal attention (concentration) practice or a body scan.

In another example, the therapy may focus on cultivating a change in perspective; fostering this process involves cognitive defusion, acceptance, compassion, and other processes. The therapist will choose a practice that fosters the relevant qualities, such as a kōan, loving-kindness, or a self-compassion practice.

Conclusion

In this chapter, we have emphasized the therapist's embodiment of qualities and attitudes of mindfulness that are developed through our own mindfulness practice. Through experiencing these qualities in the therapist's instructions and inquiry, the client learns to inhabit qualities including curiosity, gentle and welcoming awareness, nonjudgment, acceptance, and compassion.

We view responsiveness as no less important—perhaps more important—than nonreactivity or discipline. The inquiry process is a key element of enhancing the therapeutic benefit of mindfulness practice. This includes three layers: 1) building awareness, 2) tracking and contextualizing, and 3) insight and generalization. We privilege experiential learning through mindfulness practice and inquiry-based consolidation. We choose mindfulness strategies with intention drawn from clarity about function.

Part 3

Techniques for Implementing Mindfulness Using a Process-Based Approach

CHAPTER 7

Mindfulness, Attention Regulation, and Trauma

In this section, we organize approaches to mindfulness-related intervention into four overarching mechanisms: attention regulation, body awareness, emotion regulation, and changes in perspective. These interact with one another to enhance self-regulation (Hölzel et al., 2011). Some mindfulness practices will emphasize or enhance specific domains, but not all mindfulness practices will address these four different processes to the same extent. Notably, when there are difficulties in these domains of mindfulness, psychopathological states can emerge. As we approach integrating mindfulness into psychotherapy with trauma survivors, we consider these mechanisms in relation to the model of psychological adaptation. We will dedicate a chapter to each of the four processes cultivated by mindfulness. Please refer to Chapter 3 and Appendix 1 if you want to reflect on the model of psychological adaptation and the treatment planning guidance that we offered.

The current chapter will focus on attention regulation in relation to integrating mindfulness into intervention for trauma. It is divided into two parts. The first part, "Background," will go into detail about how attention regulation relates to mindfulness and its relevance to traumagenic contexts and trauma sequelae. In the second part, "Clinical Applications," we will discuss how the mindful therapist can utilize mindfulness practices to enhance the development of attention regulation and how these practices may be relevant for specific types of trauma-related adaptations in clients.

Background: Attention Regulation in Mindfulness and Trauma

Attention is an essential part of mindfulness. Along with intention and attitude, it is one of three key components thought to embody mindfulness (Shapiro et al., 2006). Kabat-Zinn (2003) defines mindfulness as the awareness that develops through the process of intentionally paying attention, focusing on the present moment with a nonjudgmental attitude.

> Attention, as well as intention and attitude, are essential components of mindfulness.

In this context, the qualities of attention relate to our intention (the purpose with which we engage in mindful attention) and our attitude with which we engage in attention, such as an attitude of curiosity, acceptance, and nonjudgment. This kind of attention can enhance self-awareness and well-being. Further, mindful attention by the therapist also enhances the impact of psychotherapy. Fritz Perls, founder of Gestalt therapy, claims that the therapist's "attention in and of itself is curative" (Shapiro & Carlson, 2009, p. 18). Indeed, our capacity to be in attunement with our clients, facilitated by mindful attention, enhances our effectiveness as therapists (Shapiro et al., 2006).

For the client, attention regulation is relevant in numerous approaches to psychotherapy. For example, cognitive behavioral therapy (CBT) focuses on teaching clients to monitor behavior and observe automatic thoughts, including internal experiences such as imagery or feeling states, bringing attention to patterns of experience.

When engaging in mindfulness with an emphasis on attention, the goal is to sustain attention to current experiences, either internal or external. In a mindful approach, not only do we aim to sustain attention, we do so with nonjudgment and acceptance, as well as curiosity and openness. In mindfulness practice, attention is relevant to several skills, such as observing or noticing internal and external stimuli. This includes observing sensations, feelings, and thoughts, as well as external, surrounding stimuli. Attention training teaches intentional direction of awareness, which scaffolds the capacity to describe one's experiences (or what is observed) though mental labeling or noting, which is a foundational skill relevant to the emotion regulation process (see chapter 9). Importantly, attention regulation shifts us out of automatic behavior toward attending to our current behaviors and engaging intentionally.

Attention regulation can involve the ability to engage in the intentional shifting of awareness or switching—harnessing attention and moving from one object, stimulus, or mental task to another. Attention regulation is also relevant to the capacity for cognitive inhibition (of feelings and sensations or among competing stimuli).

> Attention regulation shifts us out of automatic behavior or autopilot.

There is preliminary evidence that targeting attention regulation with mindfulness in treatment may help to improve executive functioning and address problems related to attention regulation, such as found among individuals with attention-deficit/hyperactivity disorder (ADHD) and bipolar disorder (Hölzel et al., 2011). Shifting attention is also relevant for trauma survivors who struggle with rumination or worry, which are repetitive thought processes that are typically unproductive and distressing. Through mindfulness practices, we teach the client *experientially* how to intentionally unhook from sticky thoughts and shift attention to an alternative focus.

Meditation and Attention Regulation

Attention regulation can be enhanced through the practice of mindfulness meditation, which focuses attention on the experience of thoughts, feelings, and body sensations. Two types of mindfulness meditation, focused attention and choiceless awareness (also called open monitoring), are typically part of mindfulness-based interventions (MBIs; Lutz et al., 2008). In focused attention meditation, we develop attention regulation skills through sustaining our focus on a chosen object of awareness, which may be a sensation (such as the breath or taste) or an item (such as a rock, pen, or raisin; for example, see therapist materials, "Mindfulness of a Raisin;" http://www.newharbinger.com/54650). We integrate instructions, noting that whenever we notice that we are distracted, for example by a memory or thought about future events, we return our attention to the object.

In contrast, in choiceless awareness, we observe our thoughts, feelings, or bodily sensations as they arise and as they dissipate. We invite the client to monitor their experience from moment to moment in a nonreactive manner to identify emotional and cognitive patterns.

Mindfulness meditation practice enhances attention regulation in several ways. When we learn to disregard distractions and return our focus, we are practicing conflict monitoring or executive attention. The latter, also executive control, involves the capacity for shifting (or switching) to bounce from one task to another. When shifting is impaired, there is difficulty disengaging from a stimulus, such as the case in ruminative thoughts or in the context of an intrusive memory (Miyake et al., 2000).

People who meditate have more skill in maintaining focus, handling distractions (inhibiting), and juggling objects or tasks competing for their attention (Sumantry & Stewart, 2021). Attention regulation arises from skills in conflict monitoring developed in focused attention meditation, which includes monitoring the focus of attention, detecting distraction, disengaging attention from the source of distraction, and redirecting and engaging attention toward the intended focus or object (Lutz et al., 2008). Instruction in mindfulness increases capacities for orienting, another form of executive attention, which involves directing and limiting attention (Posner & Petersen, 1990). Mindfulness-based stress reduction (MBSR) and choiceless awareness meditation are associated with improvement in a third aspect of executive attention, alerting, which involves a vigilant state of preparedness (Hölzel et al., 2011).

Mindfulness promotes skills in sustained attention, meta-awareness, and the capacity to be present. Numerous studies indicate mindfulness helps to improve one's ability to sustain attention as well as inhibit distractions (Sumantry & Stewart, 2021). There is evidence that both focused attention and choiceless awareness meditation approaches improve attentional capacity, although some research suggests the executive control of attention is developed almost entirely during the initial phases of training, in relation to the practice of focused attention meditation (relative to the more advanced skill of choiceless awareness). Further, the attention monitoring skills learned through the practice of focused attention meditation exercises improves inhibitory control, reducing the tendency to experience distractions (Lodha & Gupta, 2022).

> Mindfulness helps us shift out of autopilot, a state of mind in which we engage in behavior without conscious intention.

Mindfulness practices improve awareness of thinking patterns (metacognition), which helps clients to identify when they are engaging in rumination or worry. A key aspect of metacognition is the point of shifting out of autopilot. This refers to a state of mind in which we engage in behavior without conscious intention; we lack awareness of the present moment. During autopilot, our mind engages in cognitive processes such as judgment, monitoring, and problem solving outside our conscious awareness (Crane, 2009).

While autopilot can be helpful when we are performing routine tasks or solving problems, it can be problematic if it facilitates maladaptive cognitive patterns such as worry and rumination. Mindfulness practices, particularly concentration practices, promote the client's capacity to notice when they are operating on autopilot. Noticing autopilot is one of the first steps in the development of metacognition skills.

Metacognition involves examining the pattern and nature of thoughts, contextual patterns of thoughts, and the usefulness of thoughts—for example, whether concern over danger is warranted—and how to respond to the pattern of thinking (either by taking action to increase safety or by taking action to reduce distress in the absence of actual danger). Thus, mindfulness helps to shift attention to the present experience and awareness of thinking patterns when rumination occurs.

Mindfulness practices, such as focusing attention, commonly on the breath or on an external object, increases capacity to do so in other contexts (for instance, to disrupt the cycle of rumination or worry and shift attention to the present moment). Over time, practices of mindfulness increase the capacity of trauma survivors to shift their attention in ways that promote disengagement from maladaptive or problematic patterns of thinking.

> Mindfulness practices improve metacognitive awareness, which involves noticing one's thoughts.

Purpose or Intent of Mindfulness Practice

Why we practice mindfulness—its intent or purpose—appears to influence potential outcomes. As stated earlier in chapter 2, knowing the *why* of mindfulness can enhance our interventions. In the context of learning mindfulness, the client's intention, purpose, or reason for the practice relates to the outcome. For instance, Shapiro and colleagues (2006) described research that indicated the participant's intention predicted their outcomes; individuals who engaged in mindfulness for stress management and self-regulation attained higher levels of self-regulation, whereas those whose goal was self-exploration attained higher levels of self-exploration. Thus, it is important for us to explore *why* the client may want to incorporate mindfulness practices into therapy, and for the client to set an explicit intention at the outset.

Attitude Toward Mindfulness Practice

How we engage in attention regulation—our attitude toward the practice of mindfulness—is vital (Shapiro et al., 2006). Awareness, without compassion, can lead to judgment and have a cold, critical quality (Kabat-Zinn, 2003). Shapiro and colleagues (2006) discussed the concept of heart-mindfulness from the two interactive figures in Japanese characters, which include both mind and heart. Our embodiment of the attitudes of mindfulness (see chapter 6) *experientially* teaches the client to approach attention to internal and external experiences with attitudes of acceptance, gentleness, openness, and compassion. Likewise, our attitude of curiosity invites the client to take interest in their experience as it arises, reducing the tendency to engage in self-criticism or judgment.

Attention Regulation in Trauma

As part of the survival response, activation of the sympathetic nervous system enhances the ability to perceive threat and identify danger and increases chances of survival through the fight-or-flight response. As such, humans evolved with an attentional bias towards noticing, processing, and remembering threat-related information. When living in a traumagenic context, whether in the present or past, there is a tendency to overfocus on perceived threats, even when danger is absent.

Not surprisingly, post-traumatic stress disorder (PTSD) is associated with deficits in attention and an attentional bias, which may be primarily due to problems disengaging from threat stimuli. Other research suggests that PTSD symptoms of hypervigilance and concentration problems may actually be due to problems in the orienting attention networks. In addition, there is evidence attentional difficulties interact with reexperiencing symptoms to increase PTSD severity (Punski-Hoogervorst et al., 2023), making attention regulation an important target for therapy with trauma survivors.

Individuals develop strategies to adapt to living in a traumagenic context. Even if the trauma is over and danger is in the past, the mind and body of a trauma survivor are often still functioning within a sustained fight-or-flight response. Disruptions in the capacity for attention regulation may be particularly relevant to specific adaptations and patterns, such as the cognitive patterns of worry, rumination, or self-blame, as well as difficulties disengaging from these patterns.

Intrusive thoughts and the tendency to focus on the future through frequent worry or revisit past experiences through patterns of rumination all involve a focus outside the present-moment awareness. In this case, attention is on future threats or reexamining previous threats or traumas rather than the present. Attention regulation skills can help the trauma survivor direct attention away from these unwanted memories or worries, instead focusing on the present-moment experience by releasing and shifting the attentional focus.

Trauma survivors may find themselves in a state of hypoarousal, accompanied by dissociation, impaired cognition, or being on automatic pilot. As discussed in chapter 1, the nature, extent, complexity, and developmental context of traumatic experiences can influence patterns of hyperarousal and hypoarousal. The oscillation of the two is particularly prominent among individuals exposed to complex developmental trauma. In this context, incorporating mindfulness to address attention regulation can be a core skill that facilitates the client's capacity to observe their internal states and learn skills for effective self-regulation, including body awareness and emotion regulation.

Attention-Related Disturbances in Trauma Survivors

Disturbances in attention are common experiences among trauma survivors. Numerous problems associated with disturbances in attention can arise, including difficulties with concentration, intrusive thoughts, worry, obsessions, rumination, absorption, as well as emotional numbing and detachment. Trauma survivors may also develop maladaptive patterns of thinking that involve displaced attention. In this case, attention is not present focused, instead shifting to worry about future events or rumination about experiences in the past.

> Trauma survivors may develop maladaptive thinking patterns that involve excessive present-moment attention to the future or past.

Both worry and rumination involve a chain of thoughts associated with negative emotional states, either anticipating future threats (worry) or focusing on past events (rumination). In each case, attention shifts from the present moment. Difficulties directing or shifting attention may exacerbate certain symptoms or problems, such as sleep disorders or pain disorders. Mindfulness can be useful to trauma survivors as they learn to disengage or let go of problematic thinking patterns, such as worry or rumination, or develop the capacity to shift attention to disengage from a focus on pain or other problems.

Concentration. Trauma survivors often experience concentration problems, which may occur in relation to PTSD, dissociation, depression, anxiety, ADHD, or outside the context of a particular diagnosis. In the case of PTSD, hypervigilance negatively affects the capacity for sustained, directed attention unrelated to potential danger, leaving traumatized individuals with difficulty focusing attention on mundane tasks. Such disturbances may involve difficulties sustaining attention in a directed way, such as concentrating on a necessary task for work or remembering upcoming events for a busy family calendar.

Difficulties in focusing attention or concentration may lead to difficulty completing tasks in multiple contexts, such as work, school, parenting, or other aspects of homelife (such as personal hygiene or preparing meals). Practices such as focused attention meditation can strengthen skills in maintaining directed attention for concentration.

Worry. Tendencies for worry often are present among traumatized individuals. Worry relates to future concerns of safety, threat, or danger, whereas rumination relates to past events, often connected to feelings of loss, hopelessness, and failure. Worry coexists with anxiety, muscle tension, feelings of dread, and the inability to relax. Worry is present in many types of psychopathology but is most pronounced in the case of generalized anxiety disorder. Those exposed to trauma may develop schemas related to themes of danger, safety, or trust, making worry a prominent concern.

Like everyone else, trauma survivors worry about general topics, but they also worry about trauma per se; for example, worrying about whether a partner's hostile mood may lead to physical aggression. They may have realistic worries about risk or danger associated with ongoing traumatic experiences or may experience unwarranted worry based on prior traumatic experiences when currently in a safe environment.

At such times, it is critical for the mindful trauma therapist to assess and determine whether worries are indicated—that is, a true and actual alarm connected to current threat—or whether the worry pertains to past traumatic experiences in the context of relative safety. For false alarms, mindfulness can be useful to reduce worry by shifting attention away from such thoughts and back to the present moment; this facilitates skills in differentiating past from present.

Rumination. Efforts to understand traumatic experiences or to counter gaslighting may result in thinking patterns similar to rumination, whether or not in the context of depressed mood. Rumination involves a pattern of repetitive thinking focused on negative topics. It can relate to experiences or thoughts about the self, such as self-judgment, self-blame, or self-denigration. Negative feelings can elicit rumination, and rumination can elicit negative feelings, creating a vicious cycle, often occurring in relation to depression or low positive affect.

Individuals who experienced trauma may ruminate by replaying traumatic experiences in their mind, such as incidents of interpersonal violence, to increase understanding, identify precipitating factors, or consider how they might have responded differently or more effectively. Mindfulness can be useful to trauma survivors in learning to disengage or let go of rumination and similar problematic thinking patterns.

Dissociation. It is important that trauma survivors develop awareness of dissociation and learn to return to the present experience. Mindfulness can be useful in this regard as it can help them develop the ability to predict and notice dissociation and return to the present. Learning skills to intentionally harness attention, such as focused attention meditation or other mindfulness activities that build observing and noticing skills, can improve dissociative absorption in particular (Zerubavel & Messman-Moore, 2015).

Absorption is a form of dissociation characterized by total immersion of attention on something and is often associated with distorted perceptions of surroundings, the self, and time. Noticing attentional drift is a primary task for the treatment of absorption. Attentional skills are the foundation upon which trauma survivors learn to return to, or remain in, the present.

Mindfulness helps survivors learn to predict and control dissociative processes, which enables the development of more volitional control of dissociation, which in turn increases perceptions of safety among trauma survivors who dissociate. In the literature, mindfulness skills frequently are discussed as a means of grounding (for example, attention to sensory input, an image, or object) to prevent or interrupt dissociation. Although we contend that mindfulness is more than grounding, it can be useful for this purpose as well.

Clinical Applications: Cultivating Attention Regulation with Trauma Survivors

A central aspect of our approach is that mindful trauma therapists are thoughtful about the selection of mindful practices that promote the desired therapeutic process—in this case, attention regulation. The mindfulness practices that best cultivate attention regulation can be categorized into 1) sustained attention practices and 2) practices that involve focusing, releasing, and shifting attention. Both of these categories employ focal attention; the choiceless awareness practices that were discussed earlier emphasize a shift in perspective more than attentional processes, so that type of practice is not included here but instead included in chapter 10. The practices we recommend for cultivating attention regulation are listed in the box and correspond to mindfulness scripts that are included in your therapist materials ("Mindfulness of Breath," "Mindfulness of a Raisin," and "Mindfulness of a Rock," "Body Scan," and "Five-Minute Breathing Space;" http://www.newharbinger.com/54650).

> **Mindfulness Practices That Cultivate Attention Regulation**
>
> 1. Sustained attention mindfulness practices
>   - Mindfulness of breath
>   - Mindfulness of a raisin
>   - Mindfulness of a rock
> 2. Practices that involve focusing, releasing, and shifting attention
>   - Body scan
>   - Five-minute breathing space

Attention Practices

Sustained attention practices involve maintaining intentional focus on an object of awareness. The practices emphasize noticing distraction and mind wandering, and redirecting attention back to the object of awareness. We convey to the client that the practice of concentration includes the process of attentional drift due to the nature of the human mind. We emphasize that the goal is not to stop the mind from wandering. Rather, the goal is to notice when attention drifts and then to deliberately shift and redirect attention to the intended object of awareness.

We also let clients know that through practice, they will learn to inhibit responses to distractions so when a thought arises, it might interrupt for ten seconds rather than a few minutes. For practices with concentration on an object, the usual focus is on either the breath, a raisin, or a rock. As needed, alternate; other food items can be used in place of a raisin and other objects can be used in place of a rock. Substitutions are encouraged to support empowerment, choice, and affirmative consent (maintaining a trauma-informed and safety-enhancing approach).

Practices that involve focusing, releasing, and shifting attention also involve maintaining intentional focus on an object of awareness. However, they build on that skill by incorporating the switching of the attentional focal point. Like the sustained attention practices, these practices emphasize noticing distraction and the wandering mind, and the redirecting of attention back to the object of awareness. Some clients find they can maintain their attentional focus with less effort in these practices, due to the novelty offered by the shifts in attentional focus.

We may also borrow other practices from MBIs, such as mindfulness-based cognitive therapy (MBCT), including the **body scan** and the **five-minute breathing space**, which can be

---

Using Process-Oriented Mindfulness Instructions Helps Cultivate Attention Regulation

Sustained Attention

- Resting awareness on (the breath).
- Noticing when our attention wanders, and gently guiding attention back to (the breath).
- When the mind wanders, as minds inevitably do, noticing that attention has drifted. Noticing if this is accompanied by judging. Letting go of judgments while guiding attention back to (the breath).
- Staying with (the breath), inviting curiosity about moment to moment changing sensations of (the breath).

Shifting or Switching Attention

- Releasing the focus on (the breath) and shifting the spotlight of awareness to (different type of stimulus).
- Letting go of the focus on sensations of (the breath in the nostrils and around the lips), and moving the spotlight of awareness to the sensations of (the breath in the belly).

incorporated to practice releasing and shifting attention. In the body scan, attention is focused on one area of the body at a time, then released and shifted over to another area of the body. In the five-minute breathing space, the first step is building present-moment internal awareness, the second step is gathering attention and resting it on the breath, and the third step is creating a broader holistic awareness.

In our approach, we intentionally select a practice that cultivates attention regulation and then provide instruction, using language that invites and encourages the client's conscious awareness of relevant capacities. See the box for some examples. This language is integrated into the mindfulness scripts in your online therapist materials as well. We follow each mindfulness practice with inquiry (see chapter 6 for more on inquiry process).

Inquiry

The inquiry process experientially teaches the client to be curious about aspects of the experience alongside the therapist. During the inquiry, the therapist invites reflection and follows threads relevant to the intentional direction of awareness, the influence of the client's attitude on the experience of awareness, distractions that arise, how these distractions are responded to, and eventually the inhibiting or minimizing of disruptions to attention. Through inquiry, we also amplify aspects of the experience that the client may be overlooking (for example, the moments that they held deep attentional focus, even if fleeting).

The examples we provide in these chapters will focus on discussion that occurs during inquiry or home practice review. Detailed examples of how to provide instruction in the attention regulation practices (and later, body awareness, emotion regulation, and change in perspective practices) are provided as scripts in the online therapist materials (http://www.newharbinger.com/54650). These scripts will show you how to instruct mindfulness practices to guide the process to be cultivated. Therefore, our focus in these examples is on how you therapeutically process the experience of the mindfulness practice through inquiry and of efforts at generalization through review of home practice.

EXAMPLE: INQUIRY FOLLOWING MINDFULNESS OF A RAISIN

In our first example script, we offer an excerpt from inquiry following a **mindfulness of a raisin** practice. To provide context for the client's post-traumatic reactions and the rationale for integrating mindfulness, we will briefly describe her trauma exposure; we do not provide any gruesome details. This client experiences severe hyperarousal in the context of PTSD that affects her ability to focus and concentrate. This client grew up in a home in a very dangerous area with high violence and crime, where her family experienced repeated robberies. One time, a gunshot came through the wall into the client's home. She regularly describes how exhausting it is for her to monitor vigilantly for danger and how this makes it more challenging to engage fully in her life. In prior sessions, we began exploring what she would attend to if she were not monitoring for danger. Therefore, we chose to integrate mindfulness emphasizing attention training to help her practice choosing the object of her awareness. The raisin practice was selected to help her explore how her intentional awareness can change her experience of a relatively mundane, edible object.

Example Script: *Client Finds Interest in Deep Awareness*

Therapist: What did you notice during that practice? What types of sensations did you observe?

Client: I thought that was so weird at first. Like, what are we going to do with this squished up raisin? Then I forgot about all that and just got caught up in the things you were saying and noticed all these color and texture elements that I never noticed before. I think I never really saw a raisin before.

Therapist: Were there other sensory experiences of the raisin?

Client: The smell! The smell surprised me. It smelled sweet and delicious and my mouth watered.

Therapist: How was this similar to or different from how you typically interact with raisins?

Client: I guess I was genuinely interested—I don't think I've ever been interested in a raisin before. I usually eat them in large handfuls or mixed with nuts in trail mix, so I've never really paid attention to a single raisin before.

Therapist: What was that like to pay attention to a single raisin instead of eating a handful?

Client: I would call it 'deep awareness.' Now I know so much more about raisins.

Therapist: Beautiful. How do you think this might be relevant to living with your trauma symptoms?

Client: I never pay attention to things in my life because I'm so busy monitoring danger—looking at doors and windows and keeping track of people's emotional expressions. It's exhausting. It feels like I want to make room for raisin moments.

Therapist: How inspiring. I want that for you as well. Would you like that to be your home practice? Finding 'raisin moments' for deep awareness and noticing what those experiences are like? Seeing if you can shift out of monitoring for danger and instead be deeply present with your experiences?

Client: Yeah, I think that would be really helpful.

EXAMPLE: INQUIRY FOLLOWING MINDFULNESS OF BREATH

In our second example script, we offer an excerpt from inquiry following a **mindfulness of breath** practice. This client is a young adult, a trauma survivor who struggles with anxiety, and for whom a primary source of impairment is that worry and other preparation-oriented behavior distracts her and creates problems with sustained attention toward other stimuli. Mindfulness of breath was introduced to practice choosing where her attention is placed rather than deeply engaging all thoughts that show up. Following the practice, we engage in inquiry.

Example Script: *Client Notices Distraction from Worry and Planning*

Therapist: What did you observe during that practice? What did you notice about your experience?

Client: I had a hard time. I would do it for a bit, and it would feel good, but then I would go back to thinking about how tomorrow is the last day to finish up my work project, and there's still so much I have to do. And there's an email I was supposed to send today that I didn't get to and that was nagging at me. I had knots in my stomach.

Therapist: Lovely job being aware of your experience. What does it mean when you say, 'I would do it for a bit'? How would you describe that?

Client: There were times, especially right when you would say something and after that, that I really was just noticing my breath and staying really present. I knew what you meant by 'sensations of the breath,' but I couldn't stay with it.

Therapist: And what was your experience in those bits where you were just noticing your breath and staying really present, feeling sensations of the breath? What did you observe?

Client: I felt movement in my chest, and the rhythm felt nice. That felt nice; it was centering. I felt moments of calmness, and the chatter was quiet. But then it would turn back on.

Therapist: Great, so you were noticing the movement between focused attention on the breath, which felt centering, and then you also noticed distraction, chatter. And it sounded like you were describing that, specifically, the distraction was planning and worrying—is that right?

Client: Hmmm. Yeah, I guess it was… I'm working on tomorrow, and that makes it hard to stay present. Huh.

(Quiet pause for reflection and consolidation.)

Therapist: How do you think that your experience of attention and awareness in this practice is similar to or different from the experiences in your daily life?

Client: Everyone who loves me—my mom, my partner, my friends—tells me to stop worrying so much. And the planning. I'm just always planning and preparing. Maybe I never really noticed how much I'm missing out on in the meantime.

Therapist: And now this cost—that working on tomorrow makes it hard to stay present—becomes more clear.

Client: Yes. And the planning is just another version of it. It doesn't stress me out like the worrying does, but it also totally gets in the way of paying attention.

Therapist: What powerful observations. How do you think you might take this with you into your daily living?

Client: I guess I can practice not getting distracted by worries and planning and trying instead to stay present?

Therapist: How will you do that? What will the first step be?

Client: I'm not sure.

Therapist: How about starting with noticing? Trying to notice when your mind is caught up in planning or worrying?

Client: Yeah, that sounds good. And then maybe I'll try to notice what's happening in real time, and see what I'm missing out on!

Therapist: Fantastic. What a great next step. I'm so curious what you will learn. Would you be willing to do that for your home practice and make some notes throughout the week to share your observations with me next session?

Client: Definitely; that sounds good.

In the examples above, the sessions ended with a home practice assignment that naturally emerged as a generalization of the insights from the mindfulness practice. If the session ended with a home practice assignment, the next session's agenda would include reviewing it to reinforce the importance of home practice. Home practice may focus on formal mindfulness practices or may take the insights off the cushion to practice mindfulness informally in everyday life around central, clinically relevant, habitual patterns. We treat home practice review with the same curiosity and interest that we approach the mindfulness practices, and our review provides opportunities for consolidation of generalization practice.

EXAMPLE: HOME PRACTICE REVIEW

In our final example script, we offer an excerpt of home practice review, which includes a discussion of what the person noticed, how they made sense of what they noticed, and what they are taking from the data they have gathered. It can take the form of inquiry but does not have to. In this example, the client is an older man who has struggled with persistent depression since adolescence. His mother suffered from severe depression and addiction, and was emotionally abusive, often belittling and mocking him. We have conceptualized his day-to-day disruption and impairment as driven by rumination, self-berating, and hopelessness. His home practice was to notice rumination by catching repetitive thoughts and notice his response and what proceeds.

Example Script: *Client Struggling with Rumination*

Therapist: What did you observe during your home practice? What did you notice about your experiences with your attention and how you interacted with rumination?

Client: I noticed that I can't stop thinking about the promotion I didn't get, how I got passed over and someone else is going to get my promotion. Everyone will lose respect for me. Yet again, it ends with *I'm a failure*.

Therapist: This has been very distressing for you. I'm hearing some judgmental and evaluative words. Would you be willing to nonjudgmentally describe the situation?

Client: I find myself thinking about the promotion that I didn't get. I get really stuck on not understanding why I didn't get it. It's been bothering me for days.

Therapist: Thank you; that was a fantastic nonjudgmental description. Did that feel different to you?

Client: It makes me feel a bit less fed up with myself. But only a little bit.

Therapist: Wonderful. Let's keep that up as we talk about this. Now, you describe ruminating about not getting the promotion; so, first of all, great job noticing that you are ruminating. And I'm hearing you go straight to the *I'm a failure* schema. (Client nods.) What happens then? What follows when the *I'm a failure* thoughts start?

Client: I immediately feel hopelessness and despair. And shame… I feel worthless, and I am embarrassed to face my team because they knew I thought I was going to get it.

Therapist: Okay, so right here is a spot where you jump to self-judgment—I'm a failure—and global self-judgment about the essence of who you are; and, inadvertently, this increases your suffering. And along with that, shame and embarrassment show up.

	And you are noticing that… such an opportunity! How are you responding when you notice?
Client:	Sometimes I'm just stuck in the hamster wheel between reviewing all the events, wondering what more I could have done or what I did wrong, and the failure thoughts. I'll be so mad at myself for a few hours. Sometimes I try to shift out of it by taking a walk or watching a TV show or something.
Therapist:	Sounds like sometimes you intervene and opt out of rumination by shifting your attention and sometimes you stay in it, is that right? That reminds me very much of what you were noticing in the mindfulness practice last week. What are you learning from these different options?
Client:	I think when I stay in the rumination and keep rehashing it, I just get more and more upset. One of those times, I got into a fight with my partner in the middle of that. When I get my attention off of the rumination, I still feel really sad about the promotion, but it's interesting that I don't feel the hopelessness and despair.
Therapist:	That's really profound. Is that clarity helpful to you?
Client:	I can't stop the thoughts from showing up, but I don't have to stay in them. And I'm especially seeing that I don't need to make them worse. (Client smiles.)
Therapist:	What's the tone of that? Is that gentle teasing or is that more like mocking or judging?
Client:	Maybe a little bit of both. I hear you about the mocking.
Therapist:	And how will this be relevant for you in terms of taking care of yourself in the face of your depression?
Client:	I think I really need to work on interrupting the rumination more. Maybe I just don't have answers to the questions, but either way, thinking about it all the time isn't helping me come up with answers. I just have to keep practicing doing something else with my mind instead.

Clinical Application Summary

The mindfulness practices that best cultivate attention regulation include sustained attention practices and practices that involve focusing, releasing, and shifting attention. We include language that emphasizes the intentional direction of attention. We acknowledge the inclination of the mind to wander and encourage the noticing of mind wandering and gentle returning of awareness to the object of attention. To foster the client's skills in observing and noticing experiences in relationship to objects of attention within attitudes of curiosity, nonjudgment, and acceptance, we use instructional language and the process of inquiry. These skills (attentional and attitudinal) can be generalized within the client's daily life through home practice assignments that may include either or both formal mindfulness practices and off the cushion applications of mindfulness skills.

CHAPTER 8

Mindfulness, Body Awareness, and Trauma

Body awareness is an important component of mindfulness practice for trauma survivors. It interacts with the other overarching mechanisms—attention regulation, emotion regulation, and changes in perspective—in a way that contributes to self-regulation (Hölzel et al., 2011). Body awareness is enhanced by attention regulation, and likewise, body awareness will increase the capacity for emotion regulation and shifts in perspective. An important function of body awareness is in service of obtaining information because bodily sensations provide signals to the trauma survivor about feelings, safety, or connection, providing data that increases emotional awareness and the capacity for emotion regulation. In practice, body awareness and attention regulation frequently are integrated, for example, with breath awareness or body scan exercises. A focus on increasing body awareness is relevant to the treatment of numerous mental disorders, including borderline personality disorder (BPD), eating disorders, and substance use disorders (SUDs; Hölzel et al., 2011).

The current chapter will focus on body awareness in relation to integrating mindfulness into intervention for trauma. There are two parts in this chapter. In "Background," we will discuss how body awareness relates to mindfulness and the relevance of body awareness to traumagenic contexts and trauma sequelae. The second part, "Clinical Applications," will go into detail about how the mindful therapist can utilize mindfulness practices to enhance development of body awareness and how these practices may be relevant to address specific types of trauma-related adaptations in clients.

Background: Body Awareness in Mindfulness and Trauma

Body awareness relates to mindfulness in several ways. First, the conscious awareness of sensory stimuli is the primary means of connection to the present—the here and now (Rothschild, 2000). Focusing or concentrating on the body increases present-moment awareness because it shifts attention away from cognition or emotional stimuli connected to the past or future and interrupts a stream of thought related to worry or regret. Mindfulness practices that concentrate on the body can direct attention toward bodily sensations, shifting focus away from one's thoughts or worries. Related, body awareness can contribute to the decentering of experience. Attending to bodily sensations or experiences with openness and nonjudgment can help us to "reperceive" a situation, to "see it with clarity and objectivity" (Shapiro & Carlson, 2009, p. 558).

Second, body awareness is a critical component of mindfulness because it promotes interoception, meaning paying attention to and being aware of internal bodily sensations, both the conscious and unconscious processes (Pérez-Peña et al., 2022). Mindfulness practices can enhance aspects of interoception, which includes sensing, interpreting, and integrating internal bodily signals. Interoceptive awareness involves the ability to access, identify, understand, and respond to patterns of internal bodily signals, which enhances the capacity for emotion regulation (Craig, 2015).

> Body awareness can increase emotional awareness and subsequent emotion regulation skills.

Body awareness is a precursor to emotion regulation, including the capacity to understand bodily signals and tolerance of body-related distress. Bodily sensations are part of the context in which we experience emotional or affective responses. When practicing mindfulness, we can notice and label these sensations. Body awareness permits the identification of sensations that signal the presence of specific emotions, increasing emotional awareness. In this way, emotion regulation develops from the increased awareness of bodily responses to emotionally provocative events or situations. The more advanced skill of noticing internal sensations and emotions without reactivity or merging with those experiences develops first with the skill of body awareness or interoception. Body awareness can involve challenging sensations that might elicit the desire to shift sensations, leading to behaviors that modulate or suppress such experiences. When working on cultivating emotion regulation (see chapter 9), we leverage the accurate detection and evaluation of cues related to physiological states and add in strategies to modify the emotional response.

Body Awareness in Trauma

The stress response involves the interaction between interoception and experiences of stress. When activated, the stress response system mobilizes the body to maintain homeostasis and survival. Within this system, there is dynamic communication between different parts, including the central nervous system (CNS), peripheral nervous system (PNS), and metabolic and immunologic functioning (Price & Hooven, 2018). For trauma survivors, this stress response can easily become dysregulated. This typically leads to hyperresponsivity to stress, which wears down the physical, mental, and emotional response systems.

Paradoxically, when there is a sustained activation of the system, responses can be downregulated, making the body less responsive or sensitive to cues, which translates into numbness or decreased sensitivity for internal states. This results in both hypersensitivity (hypervigilance) and hyposensitivity (underactivity) of the stress response system. The former leads to overly reactive responses that involve negative, potentially inaccurate interpretations or appraisals, whereas hyposensitivity involves a buffered responsivity of decreased responding. Exposure to sustained stress can thus lead to decreased interoceptive ability, including difficulties detecting, tolerating, and interpreting interoceptive cues (Price & Hooven, 2018). When traumatized individuals experience hyposensitivity, they also experience a diminished capacity to maintain body awareness, to notice bodily sensations related to feelings, and to interpret those feelings.

Body awareness has a complex connection to traumatic experience. For many trauma survivors, there is a greater sensitivity to bodily sensations—body awareness is acute—heightening interoception. This relates to hypervigilance to bodily sensations and coexisting increases in levels of stress and anxiety. Many trauma survivors reside in a state of constant activation of the sympathetic nervous system, which enhances the ability to perceive threat and identify danger.

For many trauma survivors, general life stressors elicit or trigger bodily sensations consistent with a trauma response because the stress response system is in a state of constant activation. The overactive stress response system increases the likelihood of generic stress responses, which may look like hypersensitivity to social criticism or becoming overwhelmed by minor stressors. In contrast, some trauma survivors reside in a freeze response or numbness, related to overactivation of the parasympathetic nervous system and hyposensitivity of the stress response system (Price & Hooven, 2018). In the freeze response, there is little body awareness or a sense of disconnection from the body, often related to dissociative tendencies.

The types of trauma and developmental context in which trauma occurs are relevant to body awareness. Childhood abuse and neglect can interfere with the development of body awareness, particularly when children's physical needs are punished or neglected. Basic needs such as thirst, hunger, toileting, and sleep often are either overlooked by neglectful caregivers or punished by abusive caregivers. Neglectful caregivers may fail to provide adequate nutrition, initiate healthcare, or implement hygiene routines. The abusive caregiver will ignore acute or sustained injuries due to abuse, whereas the neglectful caregiver is likely not to notice if an injury does occur.

Emotionally neglectful caregivers may fail to identify how physical needs, such as the need for adequate sleep or nutrition, relate to a child's emotional expressions and related difficulties, such as the propensity for emotion dysregulation or aggression. As such, the child might not learn how to attend to the body to promote emotion regulation and interpersonal effectiveness. When caregivers fail to acknowledge or provide for a child's basic physical needs, the child misses an opportunity to learn how to nurture and care for their body, as well as how the body expresses needs via bodily sensations, such as fatigue, hunger, or pain.

Attachment style can influence body awareness as well. Individuals with an anxious attachment style have greater interoceptive awareness and display a greater range of emotional expressions compared to those with an avoidant style, who tend to show a disconnection between internal physiological responses and outward bodily cues relative to emotional experience (Oldroyd et al., 2019). This can mean that an avoidantly attached individual may appear calm when they are distressed. Individuals with this attachment style learn to suppress behavioral responses, in essence overregulating negative affect, which gives the appearance they are not affected by stressful situations (Oldroyd et al., 2019). Patterns of emotional suppression may lead to decreases in interoception and body awareness.

Trauma survivors can benefit from instruction related to somatic awareness—how emotional states such as sadness, anger, or disgust exist as sensations in the body. According to Rothschild (2000), clients can use bodily sensations as a gauge to tell us how they feel, such as tired, hungry, thirsty, cold, comfortable, happy, or sad. Some traumatized clients may fear or even wish they did not have bodily sensations. When this is the case, Rothschild encourages the client to consider how the absence of such information could have consequences. For example, "What would happen if you could not feel pain from a hot stove?" Traumatized clients learn that increased body awareness facilitates our understanding of how bodily sensations carry information to enhance safety and security.

Somatic awareness contributes to a sense of attunement with our bodies. This leads to the capacity for responsiveness (self-care) or the ability to respond to internal bodily states. Both can be as simple as allowing ourselves to take bathroom breaks as needed rather than ignoring sensations in efforts to be present for external obligations, such as work. For some survivors, their traumatic history involved learning to override their body's signals or needs (such as for toileting or hunger), suppressing feelings of pain, or developing maladaptive strategies to shift attention and body experience (such as self-harm). Noticing somatic information is a precursor to self-care. Difficulties with body awareness can be one reason why trauma survivors so often struggle in this area.

> Noticing somatic information is a precursor to self-care.

As discussed in chapter 1, the nature, extent, complexity, and developmental context of traumatic experiences influences the traumatized client's capacity for mindfulness and body awareness. The oscillation between states of under- or overarousal is particularly prominent among individuals exposed to complex developmental trauma, as is a state of internal numbness or feeling frozen. Yet, many trauma survivors have a predominant imprint of trauma on their body awareness, such that some individuals have a tendency toward hypersensitivity or a hyperfocus on bodily sensations, whereas others have difficulty noticing, experiencing, or interpreting bodily sensations. In this context, incorporating mindfulness for body awareness can be a core skill that facilitates the client's capacity to observe their internal states and learn skills for effective self-regulation, including emotion regulation.

Body Awareness-Related Disturbances in Trauma Survivors

The mindful trauma therapist is keenly aware of the traumagenic context in relation to the trauma survivor's experience of body awareness, whether it be heightened, diminished, or oscillating. Inherent in many traumagenic experiences is a lack of bodily control or a violation of the integrity of the body (for instance, sexual assault). This can entail the intentional degradation of the trauma survivor's body (such as shaming body shape or size) or a more subtle dismissing of the trauma survivor's needs with regard to the body (such as refusing to provide menstrual hygiene products).

Some forms of trauma, such as psychological abuse, involve an intentional dismissal of the bodily needs of the trauma survivor. In the traumagenic context, the survivor's pain, discomfort, or fear related to bodily sensations tend to be ignored, minimized, or ridiculed by the abuser. These negative bodily sensations are suppressed by the survivor as a means of survival. In this way, the trauma survivor experiences minimized or heightened body awareness in relation to particular traumagenic contexts.

Traumatic experiences negatively affect the survivor's sense of control and agency regarding the body, as well as recognizing one's bodily needs and preferences. Experiencing sexual victimization can have devastating consequences on the survivor's perceptions of the body. Sexual violence is associated with heightened body shame, bodily disgust, and sexual dysfunction. Making matters worse, some trauma survivors experience body betrayal, such as when their body experiences physiological arousal in the form of a physical orgasm (or erection) during a sexual assault. This confuses the survivor and emboldens the abuser to use this incident of body betrayal as evidence that the assault was consensual and desired.

For many reasons, body awareness is an important factor in patterns of psychological adaptation seen among trauma survivors, including body image and eating-related difficulties or disorders, dissociation, somatic or pain disorders, difficulties in sexual relating (such as sexual dysfunction or dysfunctional sexual behavior), body self-loathing, and body betrayal. At times, the direct connection between trauma and body-related difficulties is clear to the client and therapist; in other cases, the effects of trauma on body awareness occur through intermediary processes such as avoidance, suppression, alexithymia, or other aspects of psychological adaptation, for instance dissociation, making the connection more difficult to discern.

BODY IMAGE AND RELATED FACTORS

Interpersonal trauma, particularly emotional, sexual, or physical abuse in childhood, is associated with distortions in body image. Trauma survivors experience higher rates of eating disorders, including anorexia, bulimia, and binge eating disorder, and all types of abuse are associated with a higher body mass index (BMI). Moreover, childhood abuse is associated with changes in body function, increased body sensitivity, and having a negative body image (Idini et al., 2024).

The downstream effects of difficulties with body awareness on emotion regulation may explain the link between eating disorders and a history of interpersonal trauma. For instance, anorexia, bulimia, and binge eating disorder are associated with difficulties in emotional awareness. Aspects of emotion dysregulation, such as difficulties with emotional awareness, relate to disturbances in body awareness.

Patterns of psychological adaptation to trauma, such as rumination, suppression, and avoidance, are associated with eating disorders, particularly bulimia nervosa (Aldao et al., 2010).

Childhood maltreatment may also lead to adaptations that involve hypersensitivity or hyperawareness of the body. For instance, increased levels of bodily control involved in disordered eating may be used to minimize or shift negative emotions, such as shame, among survivors of childhood maltreatment (Madowitz et al., 2015).

PHYSICAL HEALTH AND SOMATIC DIFFICULTIES

There is extensive evidence that experiencing trauma, particularly interpersonal abuse, is linked to higher rates of physical health problems. The adverse childhood experiences (ACEs) investigation (Felitti, 2002) was a fundamental study demonstrating childhood maltreatment is associated with an increased risk for a range of health problems, including emphysema, stroke, cancer, heart disease, hepatitis, and skeletal fractures. In addition, childhood abuse is associated with unexplained physical symptoms and somatization disorders, and intimate partner violence is associated with more severe and a greater number of somatization symptoms (for a review, see López-Martínez et al., 2018). Moreover, cumulative trauma exposure, particularly exposure to interpersonal abuse (in childhood or adulthood), is associated with higher rates of medical care and medication use, independent of the effects of traumatic stress (López-Martínez et al., 2018).

The neurobiological effects of childhood trauma via a dysregulation of the stress response may increase the likelihood of numerous negative health outcomes, including somatization. Body awareness is related to alexithymia (difficulties identifying and labeling emotional experiences), which appears to explain why individuals exposed to betrayal trauma have more health problems (Goldsmith, 2012). Related, high levels of experiential avoidance (the desire to avoid negative or painful internal experiences) along with lower levels of mindfulness (nonjudgmental awareness) seems to explain why survivors of childhood trauma experience greater somatic problems (Kroska et al., 2018).

DISSOCIATION

Dissociation involves a detachment, separation, or estrangement from the body. This detachment involves an altered state of consciousness, a feeling of being separate from the body, others, and the surrounding world. It can feel as if one is in a dreamlike state, as if things outside oneself are unreal (derealization), or as if we are watching ourselves (depersonalization).

Difficulties with body awareness related to dissociation may include experiences of looking at the body from outside, sensations that the body feels frozen or numb, or feeling separated from the body in general or during sexual activity (Price & Thompson, 2007). Bodily dissociation is more common among individuals who experience sexual or physical abuse, and among trauma survivors. Further, it is associated with greater health problems.

When working with trauma survivors, we can describe detachment as an absence of connectedness, either from the self, in terms of depersonalization, or disconnectedness from others (or the world) in the case of derealization. Mindfulness skills can be used to return to the present moment in the context of dissociation (Zerubavel & Messman-Moore, 2015). For example, when the trauma survivor engages in dissociative detachment to avoid emotionally challenging experiences, such as feeling anger, mindfulness skills in body awareness can be leveraged to decrease dissociation. In this case, mindfulness can facilitate noticing physical sensations in the body and present-moment awareness, shifting a focus from rumination regarding the responsibility or blame for the incident that triggered the dissociative response.

Considerations for Work with Trauma Survivors

Individuals who experienced trauma, particularly specific forms of interpersonal violence such as sexual abuse, may experience difficulty engaging in some body-focused mindfulness exercises, such as meditation practice that involves a focus on the breath or the body scan; these are both common components of MBIs. In these cases, trauma-sensitive modifications facilitate the use of these mindfulness exercises in a safe manner for the trauma survivor.

Body awareness can in itself be useful in determining a client's sense of safety or overwhelm. As a therapeutic tool, body awareness communicated by the client provides the mindful trauma therapist with information relevant to navigating the therapeutic window (see chapter 2), helping the therapist determine when to slow down or attempt to halt traumatic hyperarousal. The therapist may guide the client in separating past from present and interpreting somatic memory (Rothschild, 2000).

Practices that increase mindful awareness of the body may also be useful as a grounding exercise, in which the ability to sense the body (for example, feel your feet on the floor, back against the chair) can elicit a sense of calm. Grounding can shift the client's physiology so they remain within the optimal therapeutic window. Using body awareness to enhance grounding can increase a traumatized client's sense of safety, calmness, and control when in overwhelm (Schwartz, 2016).

Clinical Applications: Cultivating Body Awareness with Trauma Survivors

In this section, we will provide examples of implementing a mindfulness practice as a therapeutic intervention with an emphasis on body awareness. The mindfulness practices that best cultivate body awareness leverage attentional capacities and focus them on body sensations and the fostering of interoception. The practices we recommend for cultivating body awareness are listed in the box and correspond to mindfulness scripts that are included in your online therapist materials ("Mindfulness of Breath," "Body Scan," "Mindfulness of Body Part: Soles of the Feet," "Progressive Muscle Release," and "Mindfulness of Walking;" http://www.newharbinger .com/54650). Some practices involve noticing body sensations in the context of stillness, and some involve noticing body sensations in the context of movement. For some trauma survivors, the combination of stillness and body awareness may be challenging; in those cases, it may be helpful to build capacities through an initial leveraging of movement, then integrating some stillness at the end of the practice or between movements.

Practices That Involve Stillness

The mindfulness practices that we recommend for cultivating body awareness through exercises that involve stillness are listed in the box. **Mindfulness of breath** is a practice that typically involves noticing the breath without trying to make it be a particular way. The practice offers the breath as a present-moment anchor that we access by focusing on the ever-changing sensations of breathing. The **body scan** is a practice that goes through the body, area by area, exploring sensations with curiosity. This practice was discussed prior as an attention regulation practice; however, in the context of body awareness, the body scan focuses on sensing experientially. Although trauma survivors may have difficulty with the body scan's attention to body parts, Magyari (2016) noted that in her many years of running MBI groups for trauma survivors, they have not struggled notably with this practice. That said, if a client has a particular body part that leads to dysregulation because informal exposure is not effective in a state of overwhelm, we may choose to omit highly trauma-cued areas until greater capacities are available (Frewen & Lanius, 2015).

> **Mindfulness Practices That Cultivate Body Awareness**
>
> 1. Practices that involve stillness
>   - Mindfulness of breath
>   - Body scan
>   - Mindfulness of body part: Soles of the feet
> 2. Practices that involve movement
>   - Progressive muscle release
>   - Walking meditation

Finally, **mindfulness of body part** often involves the hands or feet but can focus on other parts like the face or the spine. Our handout example is a soles of the feet anchoring practice. This practice focuses on sensing into a particular body part, focusing all awareness on this part. It may also involve thinking about the functions that the body part serves on a regular basis and perhaps an invitation toward gratitude for the functions served by the body part. This can also be done with a body part that evokes a painful emotion, such as a part that elicits shame or self-loathing; in such cases, we recommend incorporating self-compassion (see chapter 10).

Stillness can be challenging for some trauma survivors, as avoided material can seem to rush in when things are quiet or less busy. There may be some agitation or restlessness, and there may be some distress or discomfort about the difference between the social messages about mindfulness (for example, it's relaxing, calming) and actual complex experiences of mindfulness. Through our introduction and our instructions during the practice, we emphasize that mindful body awareness involves a nonjudgmental, curious, caring attitude. We emphasize that intentional attention and curiosity about body sensations leads to increased attunement and awareness, listening to the somatically based information with care and receptivity. This sets up the opportunity for responsiveness, care, or nurturance that attends to essential needs (such as hydration, nourishment, rest). We contrast this with neglect or abuse and highlight how those experiences can lead to the client not learning to engage in self-care or even to learning to suppress or reject self-care needs. We celebrate when the client notices somatic information, and we delight when they demonstrate responsiveness.

Our working definition of self-care is attunement plus responsiveness. Thus, we tend toward encouraging clients to practice responsiveness to information gathered through body awareness, as this is a key element of self-care. For this reason, as discussed in chapter 6, we do not restrict form adjustments in practices involving stillness. For example, if we suggest sitting on the floor on a cushion, but the client wants to sit on a chair, we encourage that. Or if they adjust the way they are sitting by using a supportive bolster or adjusting their posture or leg position, we encourage the care and responsiveness to body needs.

Practices That Involve Movement

The mindfulness practices we recommend for cultivating body awareness that involve movement are listed in the box. **Progressive muscle release** is a practice that involves small movements with one muscle set at a time (for example, feet, legs, buttocks, abdomen). These are tensed, held, and then released in sequence. This practice is an adaptation (Coleman et al., 2024) of progressive muscle relaxation, an exercise you may be familiar with, which the client engages in with the goal of becoming more relaxed. In a mindfulness lens, the goal of relaxation makes this a striving practice, which is counter to the mindfulness pillar of nonstriving. Therefore, progressive muscle release allows the objective of the practice to be observing the process of tensing and releasing each muscle set rather than achieving a particular desired state (Coleman et al., 2024).

Mindful movement can involve a formal activity, such as an instructed or intentional yoga, tai chi, or qigong session, or it can involve an informal activity, such as gentle stretching with mindful intention and attention or some other slow and mindful movement (such as dancing or swaying). **Walking meditation** is a practice that focuses attention on the interoceptive changes that occur during walking—muscular changes, form changes (for instance, in the foot or leg), and processing proprioceptive and vestibular information (for instance, observing shifts in the balance process during walking).

Practices that involve movement emphasize turning the attention inward to attend to body sensations and sensory experience. Therefore, a walking practice will be focused on sensations through the body as one walks, not on listening to the birds and insects (although this is an appropriate attention regulation practice). Of course, that doesn't mean those things don't get noticed, but they are considered distractions from the formal walking practice. They may be pleasant distractions, and we may enjoy them, but they are noted as distractions nonetheless.

If you are providing instruction that involves movement in any more extensive physical manner (such as yoga or even gentle stretching), always include instruction that the client should privilege internal information over your instructions. We often introduce a movement practice by saying: "If I provide an instruction for something that doesn't feel right for your body—for example, it causes pain—prioritize your internal information, which is based on your body awareness, and modify so that it feels safe for your body. Mild discomfort may occur when we stretch or move, but let's not push through pain." This is an important message for trauma survivors, who have often had to practice ignoring somatically based information in the context of traumatic experiences and have often received messages endorsing the suppression and dismissing of pain. It also instills a message of caring about and responding to our somatic experiences. In addition, it is an important ethical and legal message to provide if you are not trained as a yoga instructor or exercise physiologist (or other similar role).

Instructions for Body Awareness

When we are using mindfulness practices to cultivate body awareness, our instructions emphasize the details and nuances of sensory experiences. As with all practices, the deeper our own practice of body awareness, the richer our instructions will be. If we attend only minimally to our body awareness, we likely have a poverty of language for describing sensory experience. You may find this list of sensation words helpful as a place to start. You can add many more words to this list. When providing instruction to cultivate body awareness, our use of rich sensory language helps invite the client to attend more richly to their experience. We often give options or contrasts as instructions, as this affirms that there is no right answer. For example: "Do those muscles feel relaxed or tense? Is the jaw clenched or soft? Does the skin feel warm or cold? Does it feel clammy or dry?"

Sensations Words				
Achy	Empty	Itchy	Pulsing	Strong
Bruised	Floating	Jittery	Rigid	Tender
Clammy	Flushed	Light	Shaky	Tense
Clenched	Grounded	Moist	Smooth	Thirsty
Cold	Goosebumps	Numb	Soft	Tight
Constricted	Heavy	Pain	Sore	Tingling
Dry	Hot	Pressure	Squirmy	Warm

OBSERVING SENSATIONS AS THEY ARE VERSUS INTERVENING TO SHIFT EXPERIENCE

One of the major dialectics in this work is that, on the one hand, we want to encourage acceptance of experience by allowing things to be as they are, while on the other hand, we want to encourage experimentation at how we can care for our bodies in ways that improve our somatic experience. We choose, based on case conceptualization and our clinical judgment or based on discussion with the client, what is the most helpful starting point between these practices.

> Some practices inherently involve changing the experience, whereas others involve strictly observing the experience. Some practices can be conducted in either manner.

Some practices, such as progressive muscle release, inherently involve changing the experience; other practices, such as the body scan, involve strictly observing the experience. Various other practices can be conducted in either manner. For example, mindfulness of the breath can be done as a strictly observing practice, simply noticing the breath just as it is without changing anything about it.

We can also do a modified version that involves elongating the exhalation, as we might do to help a client struggling with hyperarousal. This practice is called paced breathing in the context of dialectical behavior therapy (DBT) skills (Linehan, 2014). To address the dysregulation of the autonomic nervous system (ANS), we invite the client to explore the gentle elongation of the exhalation, which is the part of the breath cycle that facilitates parasympathetic activation (lowering physiological arousal). Another example is that the body scan, which is a practice in strictly observing, may include minimal instructions about loosening, such as those in MBCT: "…as best as you can, have a sense of (tense muscles) letting go, or releasing, on the out-breath" (Segal et al., 2013, p. 123).

ANXIETY ABOUT INTEROCEPTIVE EXPERIENCE

Among trauma survivors, anxiety about interoceptive experiences is not uncommon. It is helpful for us to consider, as we conceptualize this response, that these episodes typically involve escalations of anxiety or even panic. A typical occurrence may begin with hypervigilance over a particular body sensation (such as the heart rate or flushing), followed by anxiety, followed by worries about how it may worsen, followed by increased anxiety. As you can imagine, if this occurs with hypervigilance over the breath, then a practice such as mindfulness of breath may be quite challenging and aversive. In such a case, we can begin with gentler start-where-you-are practices, such as mindful movement or mindful walking.

At the same time, we want to explain to the client that shifting this hypervigilant monitoring of the challenging sensation is an important goal for further exploration. This is a great opportunity to apply change in perspective skills. It also often makes sense to build further capacities via mindfulness practice to scaffold acceptance and nonreactive observation

Mindfulness, Body Awareness, and Trauma

(decentering; see chapter 10). Then, the client may be much better able to tolerate mindfulness of breath or whatever the difficult interoceptive object of attention was.

Sometimes the anxiety is not quite as intense, and the client can tolerate it. In those circumstances, we use inquiry to process how the client responded to the anxiety about interoception. In the following example, the client reports anxiety about her interoceptive experience, and the therapist uses the inquiry process to facilitate new therapeutic perspectives on her anxiety. In this example, the sensations also have a specific association to the client's trauma history, therefore it is helpful to provide relevant trauma-related information.

Note that below we will describe historical trauma events that may be disturbing to read; we will describe only briefly and with only necessary detail relevant to her experience of shortness of breath (consistent with low-impact debriefing, see Mathieu, 2012; described in detail in chapter 11). In this example, the client has a history of trauma that involved her sister, who shared a room with her. The sister physically abused her at night by stuffing her under her blanket and not allowing her out while the client would feel she was suffocating under her blanket and would experience panic.

It is not atypical for the threatening physical sensations to be associated with a trauma event, and we repeatedly explore the relationship of clinical material to the client's trauma history. The client's symptoms meet criteria for PTSD, and she has intense anxiety over somatic sensations associated with the feeling she is losing her breath (anxiety over interoception of breath). She avoids exercise—if she has to take the stairs, she takes them slowly—and worries about something going wrong with her heart. The context here is in session, conducting inquiry following in session practice of mindfulness of breath.

Example Script: *Client Reports Experiencing Anxiety During Mindfulness of Breath*

Therapist: What did you observe during the mindfulness of breath practice? What sensations were you aware of in your body?

Client: I noticed that my breathing was jagged. I experienced a lot of anxiety about my shortness of breath and lots of worries about whether there is something wrong with my breathing.

Therapist: Beautiful. You noticed sensations of the breath, the emotion of anxiety, and thoughts that were worries about your breath. (Client nods.) What happened next?

Client: I guess it depends. There were a few different rounds of this kind of anxiety. Sometimes I focused on it, and other times I was able to calm myself down.

Therapist: When you would focus on it, how would that influence your experience?

Client: I started to notice more about my breathing not being smooth enough, and I started to panic. My breath got shorter and felt even more uncomfortable. I wondered if I needed to end the practice—I started thinking that I need to stand up and pace, and what will you say if I do that? It feels almost unbearable, like if this gets worse, I could die.

Therapist: So when you would focus on it, the anxiety would escalate, there were catastrophic thoughts or predictions, and you would begin to panic. What about the times when you were able to calm yourself down?

Client: I think those were times when I was really curious about the rhythm of the breathing. At one point, I was listening really closely to what you were saying about the movement between the lower belly and the upper chest, and I felt this rhythm that felt really soothing.

Therapist: What emotions were present then?

Client: I think I just felt really peaceful. I don't feel that very often. I wish I could hold on to it longer.

Therapist: It sounds beautiful, and it brings a wistfulness with it of wanting more.

Client: It does.

Therapist: I wonder if now that you know about that, you might be able to drop into that rhythm more easily? Are you curious about that?

Client: I am. I just get really stressed thinking about the other part. What if I have more of those moments of panic?

Therapist: Yes, how will you respond if that happens? What do you think you would say is most helpful at such times, based on what you are noticing?

(Some silence while the client considers.)

Client: I guess it would be something like, *See if you can settle into the rhythm.* And also it was helpful when I noticed the sensations changing across the lower belly and the upper chest.

Therapist: Beautiful. And are there any pieces of wisdom about what patterns to avoid falling into?

Client: Don't get fixated on some aspect of the breath that isn't right and start panicking.

Therapist: Yes, that's great wisdom. And if you notice an unhelpful pattern occurring, your job is to pivot.

Client: I see that.

Therapist: How is this different or similar to how you usually experience noticing your breath?

Client: I usually only go the panic route, and I don't really have that other way we were talking about. Sometimes, if it gets harder to breathe, I might even have a full-blown panic attack—I get really anxious about not being able to breathe.

Therapist: So this is a very different way of responding to anxiety about sensations of the breath or shortness of breath.

Client: It is.

Therapist: I wonder, when you think of this difficulty around not being able to breathe, do you relate it to your trauma history? I notice that I have some associations with your trauma experiences.

Client: (tears well up) I can't believe I never thought about that. It's exactly how I would feel when my sister would smother me. (Client cries, nodding periodically; therapist accompanies in compassionate silence.)

Therapist: Does seeing that help you to shift anything in how you are looking at your experience during mindfulness of breath? Or other times when you experience this anxiety about sensations of shortness of breath or uneven breathing?

Client: I guess it just really snaps things into focus. Like, I'm just stuck in that and reliving it.

Therapist: How organizing to put that back in its place in time. Especially the thought that you could die—there were times where perhaps that seemed like a real possibility, and you were trapped. That's an old thought associated with these sensations.

Client: I see that. I can remind myself that I am not going to die because I'm doing mindfulness of breath here.

Therapist: Lovely! So you are already walking us into the next part—how will you take this with you? How does this apply to taking care of yourself in the face of your difficulties?

Client: I am more capable than I have ever been before. There were times in my childhood when I felt really powerless. I don't have to feel that way anymore. Maybe I can start having a new way of thinking about my breath that isn't so caught up in those traumatic nights.

Therapist: I think that's really inviting. And you have these doorways that you found today—the rhythm, the changing sensations of the lower belly and the upper chest.

Client: I definitely want to keep working on this practice.

Therapist: Wonderful, great openness. So, if your home practice will be mindfulness of breath, how often do you think it would be helpful to do it? Guided or self-guided? For how long?

Client: Maybe daily, self-guided, for about ten minutes.

Therapist: Beautiful. I look forward to hearing about your practices.

Past-Present Discernment

One of the most important applications of body awareness is using sensory experience to establish information about the present-moment context. When working with trauma survivors who experience flashbacks or other intrusions as leading to confusing the past with the present, mindful awareness of sensory information (body awareness) is a core essential skill. Body awareness practices with an emphasis on sensory experience help differentiate present-moment awareness from past overlay (intrusion). Because intrusions are conceptualized as dissociative phenomena, practices that involve muscular engagement and movement (such as mindful movement, walking meditation, and progressive muscle release) may be particularly helpful.

As discernment between the past and present is a critical aspect of reducing traumatic responses and is a key element in responding to intrusions, we have scaffolded this skill using a worksheet: "Past-Present Discernment" (client worksheet: http://www.newharbinger.com/54650). The handout is made to help the client use this skill for home practice when experiencing a flashback or other intrusions. Some clients have a hard time remembering what they practiced in session, and in that case you might invite your client to write down the skill components and their responses as you do this practice together.

The following example demonstrates the therapist integrating this skill in session following an intrusive memory. Note that the exchange includes description of client's abusive context, but not of specific abuse events. The client is a middle-aged man who experiences intense and disruptive intrusive symptoms. He struggles immensely with anxiety, particularly as related to safety versus danger or harm. His childhood was marked by traumatic events of his father's rage episodes, involving verbal and physical abuse directed at him and his brother. The client has frequent flashbacks where he feels like he is back inside a memory of such a rage episode. The example script context is in session, and the client is visibly distressed and has just shared that he is currently having a flashback.

Example Script: *Therapist Introduces Past-Present Discernment Skill*

Client: I feel like I'm back in it again. I feel the panic rising; I feel like my father is going to jump out from around this corner and find me, and he is mad. I can smell his cologne. I feel like I have to hide.

Therapist:	I'm so glad that you let me know; I saw your expression change, but I wasn't sure what had happened. It sounds like you are having a flashback, where it feels like you are back in a past trauma, or like a trauma from the past is happening in the present.
Client:	Exactly. I feel like I'm back inside the memory.
Therapist:	Would you like me to walk you through a skill for flashbacks? You can use this whenever you feel that the past overlays the present moment? The essence of it is sorting out what is from the past and what is from the present. We can walk through it together.
Client:	Yes, that sounds helpful. Let's try that.
Therapist:	Great. I encourage you to write this down as we do it so that you can remind yourself how to use this skill in your home practice. We can begin by acknowledging and validating how painful or scary (you can note for yourself if there are other relevant emotions) it truly is to experience intrusive memories from these parts of your history.
	(Client sighs.)
Therapist:	What does the sigh express?
Client:	Feeling sad for myself about how scary he could be. How he terrorized me and my brother.
Therapist:	That is profoundly sad. (Nods, allows silence for integration.) Okay, the next step is to identify what elements of your current experience are from the past.
Client:	What do you mean?
Therapist:	What are the parts of what you're experiencing that you think are from the past; that is, they're not actually happening now? There may be some parts you're uncertain about, but are there any sensations you are certain are from the past and are not actually occurring right now?
Client:	The sense that my dad is around the corner. I know there is no way he is actually here.
Therapist:	Fantastic. That feels very clear to you. I agree. Do you think I can smell his cologne?
Client:	No, that's definitely from the past too. And there's a sense of noise in my head; that's old too. And feeling like I have to hide—I don't need to hide anymore.

Therapist: That's right—you don't need to hide anymore. That's from the past. What else?

Client: I guess I feel small and powerless—that's from the past. I think that's it.

Therapist: What are the parts of what you are experiencing that you think are from the present; that is, they are happening right now?

Client: The things that you are saying. You being here. Your office. That painting behind you.

Therapist: Lovely. You're using visual sensory input to let you know what is present at this time. Anything you notice based on touch sensation?

Client: I can feel the fabric of my pants, the skin of my arms against the arms of the chair.

Therapist: Are there any parts you are unsure of? They might be from the past or present?

Client: I guess the anxiety, the sense of panic.

Therapist: Were you feeling anxious or panicked then?

Client: Yeah, definitely.

Therapist: Are you feeling anxious or panicked now?

Client: I feel anxious but not really panicked.

Therapist: I wonder if that might be anxiety but not fear?

Client: Absolutely. I know I'm safe with you. I really wasn't safe then, so I was afraid.

Therapist: Okay, so also in your list of things from the past goes *true danger*. As you are discerning between past and present, it sounds like you would put anxiety in both present *and* past, and then fear or panic will go in past but not present, is that right?

Client: That feels exactly right.

Therapist: Great, we've sorted out so much here. And at this point, you can look at the list of things in the past—your father's presence around the corner, the cologne smell, having to hide, feeling small and powerless, anxiety, panic, and fear from feeling unsafe in the presence of true danger—and you can remind yourself that you have already survived all of the parts that are just in the past.

Client: Seriously. Wow. That feels really settling. Everything gets a little bit quieter inside.

Therapist: Beautiful. Now you have a way to take care of yourself when you experience intrusions.

Client: How can it seem so real?

Therapist: It's a perceptual process. I like to think about how it's like when you are on a train. Have you ever been on a stopped train and another train starts moving, and it seems like you are moving even if you clearly know that you are stopped and will be stopped for another ten minutes?

Client: Yeah, I've definitely had that experience. It really feels like you are moving, even if you know you are not.

Therapist: So I think it's similar to that, and this skill of past-present discernment can help you leverage other aspects of knowing so that the intrusion isn't as destabilizing for you. You're grounding and orienting using present-moment awareness with an emphasis on your sensory experience.

Client: I think this will be really helpful when I'm at work. Sometimes I can lose an hour or more after a flashback like this. I just get so disoriented, confused, and my body is in such a stress state. Maybe I can just take a few minutes to do this and get back on track more quickly?

Therapist: That's exactly how I hope you will use this. I'll give you a handout that walks you through what we did together today.

Note that some of these questions call for reality testing. Most of the time, clients will not have difficulty with this. However, sometimes this practice will bring to your attention that during the flashback, they in fact had difficulty with reality testing (for example, thought maybe the voice was audible to others, thought others could see a person or image from the event), and this is important information. This may occur even if most of the time the client's reality testing is very sound. We would treat concerns of this type by engaging in further clinical assessment, as it could possibly be a sign of more complex dissociative symptoms.

Clinical Application Summary

The mindfulness practices that best cultivate body awareness emphasize nonjudgmentally observing body sensations and fostering interoception. We include language that guides intentional direction of attention into sensory information; we privilege sensing into the experience over thinking about the experience.

The practices to build body awareness are split into two categories: those that involve noticing body sensations during stillness, and those that involve noticing body sensations during movement. The practices can also be differentiated by whether we observe the body experience as it is, focusing on acceptance, or whether we offer invitations toward shifting experience (for instance, softening muscles or elongating the exhalation).

We notice the choice point between observing the experience and responding to sensory information, for example, if the legs or back start to hurt in the position after being held for some time. In general, we encourage clients to practice responsiveness to information gathered through body awareness, emphasizing that this is a key element of self-care. We encourage the awareness of body sensations to be held in attitudes of nonjudgment, curiosity, and interest. We support the generalization of the body awareness skills within the client's daily life through home practice assignments that may include either or both formal mindfulness practices and off the cushion uses of mindfulness skills in noticing body sensations, gathering information, and practicing responsiveness.

CHAPTER 9

Mindfulness, Emotion Regulation, and Trauma

Emotion regulation is an important mechanism of mindfulness for trauma survivors. It interacts with the other overarching mindfulness mechanisms—attention regulation, body awareness, and changes in perspective—in a way that contributes to self-regulation (Hölzel et al., 2011). Emotion regulation is a frequent topic of discussion in the clinical literature, especially given that many psychological disorders involve difficulties in this domain. Some therapeutic approaches conceptualize emotion dysregulation as a core issue or source of difficulty associated with specific problems, such as anxiety, depression, or addiction.

Attention regulation, a mechanism of mindfulness discussed earlier (see chapter 7), is useful to enhance emotion regulation through emotional awareness and clarity. Another mechanism of mindfulness, body awareness (see chapter 8), is a key aspect of the context in which we experience emotional or affective responses. When practicing mindfulness, we notice and label these sensations. Body awareness permits the identification of sensations that signal the presence of specific emotions, increasing emotional awareness. In this way, emotion regulation develops in relation to attention regulation and increased awareness of bodily responses to emotionally provocative events or situations. When cultivating emotion regulation, we leverage the accurate detection and evaluation of cues related to physiological states and add strategies to modify the emotional response.

The current chapter will focus on emotion regulation in relation to integrating mindfulness into intervention for trauma. It consists of two parts. The first part, "Background," will go into detail about how emotion regulation relates to mindfulness and the relevance of emotion regulation to traumagenic contexts and trauma sequelae. In the second part, "Clinical Applications," we will discuss how the mindful therapist can utilize mindfulness practices to enhance development of emotion regulation and how these practices may be relevant to address specific types of trauma-related adaptations in clients.

Background: Emotion Regulation in Mindfulness and Trauma

It is important to note that most models of emotion regulation emphasize the shifting, control of, or changing of the emotional experience or response motivated by a preferred behavioral experience or outcome. Numerous cognitive behavioral treatment approaches integrate skills training in emotion regulation, often with the goal of reducing unpleasant emotional experiences. This stands in stark contrast to a mindfulness framework, which would discourage striving toward a particular response, behavior, or experience. Suppression (one type of emotion regulation strategy) is antithetical to mindful awareness and nonreactivity. In our work, we focus on emotion regulation as a pivotal process cultivated through mindfulness, rather than a goal toward which our clients should be striving. We see mindfulness as a means of enhancing emotion regulation skills and our clients' capacity to experience and tolerate distress, widening the window of tolerance.

> Emotion regulation increases the capacity to tolerate unpleasant emotions and leads to new ways of responding to emotions.

Emotion regulation relates to mindfulness in several ways. Mindfulness can promote emotion regulation through its facilitative impact on attention regulation (see chapter 7) and body awareness (see chapter 8). The process of emotion regulation can be enhanced by mindfulness due to its effects on increasing emotional awareness and emotional clarity. Mindfulness can enhance cognitive flexibility, facilitating cognitive reappraisal of threatening or other emotionally evocative experiences. The attitudinal approach of mindfulness emphasizing nonjudgment, nonreactivity, and self-compassion contributes to the capacity for emotion regulation. Mindfulness can enhance the capacity to tolerate emotional distress and facilitate psychotherapy through widening the window of tolerance (see chapter 2). Further, mindfulness enhances the willingness to experience unpleasant or painful emotional (or physical) states, which decreases avoidance. Thus, mindfulness may shift habitual responses characterized by avoidance through increasing acceptance (Chambers et al., 2009).

Mindfulness can facilitate what we call informal exposure (in contrast to a formal protocol of exposure), such as exposure to unpleasant emotional experiences that often trigger avoidant responses in trauma survivors. This increased capacity to tolerate unpleasant emotional states or experiences can lead to the development of new ways of responding to emotions. The mindfulness facet of nonreactivity further facilitates emotion regulation by enhancing the trauma survivor's capacity to examine behaviors and thought processes in a less biased manner while allowing physiological and emotional responses to dissipate (Chambers et al., 2009).

Emotion Regulation

We conceptualize emotion regulation as the process of modulating aspects of emotional experience, expression, or response. This distinguishes between behavioral regulation, which includes choosing between various expressions of emotion, and cognitive regulation, which involves selective inattention (Hölzel et al., 2011). When problems with emotion regulation occur, this may happen in terms of difficulties modulating emotional experience (and expression) and automatic or deliberate attempts to control (or suppress) emotional experience and expression, such as intellectualizing an emotional experience to reduce discomfort (Cicchetti et al., 1995).

Emotion regulation can include bottom-up (such as perceptual) processes and top-down (such as cognitive) processes (Chambers et al., 2009). Mindfulness can play a key role in enhancing both bottom-up and top-down processes, as well as making these processes conscious and deliberate so that they can be applied as skills.

Emotion dysregulation involves the breakdown of emotion regulation in some capacity. This typically involves any of the following: excessive emotional reactivity, dysregulated emotional intensity and expression (either excessive or overcontrolled), and deficits in emotional awareness and clarity, such as difficulties in the ability to identify and label emotional states (alexithymia). Emotionally dysregulated behavior includes various forms of impulsivity, such as negative urgency, inappropriate display of affect, and externalizing behavior such as aggression (Kim & Cicchetti, 2010). Ineffective emotion regulation strategies are common among clients who struggle with experiential avoidance, suppression, and rumination (Aldao et al., 2010).

> Emotion dysregulation includes:
> - excessive emotional reactivity
> - excessive (or overcontrolled) emotional intensity and expression
> - deficits in emotional awareness and clarity.

One common problematic emotion regulation strategy among trauma survivors is suppression. When chronic, suppression is a form of avoidance that actually underlies or maintains psychopathology ranging from depression to anxiety to substance use disorders (SUDs). Further, expressive suppression is associated with negative health impacts, including on the immune and cardiovascular systems. In contrast to its (likely) intended effect, expressive suppression *does not* decrease the experience of negative emotions, but instead decreases the experience of *positive* emotions.

> Paradoxically, suppression actually decreases the experience of positive, rather than negative emotions.

Expressive suppression is associated with difficulties in recall of information, disruption in social communication, and rumination (Chambers et al., 2009). Not surprisingly, suppression is a common emotion regulation strategy among survivors of trauma, given its connection to experiential avoidance. Thinking about this with our trauma-informed case conceptualization lens, it may be because the original traumagenic context constrained the development or efficacy of other more adaptive emotion regulation strategies.

Mindfulness and Emotion Regulation

Mindfulness meditation improves emotion regulation among mindfulness practitioners, including healthy novices and experienced practitioners (Hölzel et al., 2011). Mindfulness training is associated with reductions in emotional and physiological reactivity, decreased negative mood states, reduced distracting and ruminative thoughts and behaviors, and improved positive mood states. In particular, mindful breathing may be useful in reducing reactivity to repetitive thoughts. Overall, research suggests that mindfulness practice positively influences physiology, resulting in positive emotional experiences. Experienced meditators show a less severe startle response and a faster return to baseline when exposed to aversive stimuli, as well as a less severe startle response in general (Hölzel et al., 2011).

Mindfulness appears to affect neural mechanisms associated with emotion regulation. In particular, mindfulness meditation is associated with positive impacts on the prefrontal cortex and the amygdala (Hölzel et al., 2011). The prefrontal cortex is associated with selective attention and working memory, response inhibition, and monitoring emotional states, whereas the amygdala is associated with detecting threat. Mindfulness meditation increases activity in the prefrontal cortex, which inhibits activity in the amygdala, ultimately decreasing sensations of threat and fear. Emotion regulation is positively affected by mindfulness practice through the enhanced capacity for two adaptive emotion regulation strategies, reappraisal and extinction, which are discussed at length below.

MINDFULNESS AND REAPPRAISAL

Reappraisal is a cognitive emotion regulation strategy that involves shifting or reinterpreting the meaning of an event or experience to change one's emotional response to it (Hölzel et al., 2011). Positive reappraisal involves a process in which a stressful event is reexamined in a way to find benefit, find meaning, or perceive it as less threatening and more benign than it was initially. Dispositional mindfulness and mindfulness practice are associated with increases in positive reappraisal, which is associated with decreased levels of stress (Garland et al., 2011).

> Reappraisal increases openness to alternatives, clarifying available choices for responding. Ultimately, this can enhance the clients' ability to make intentional choices.

Reappraisal can be useful for trauma survivors when it is used to develop greater awareness of habitual patterns (for example, avoidance-based cognitions or other maladaptive cognitions), and learning what psychological adaptation patterns are helpful versus unhelpful. Reappraisal can facilitate cognitive flexibility and help trauma survivors shift attributions of responsibility, resulting in lower levels of self-blame.

MINDFULNESS, EXPOSURE, EXTINCTION, AND RECONSOLIDATION

Mindfulness practice involves exposure to negative, unpleasant, or unwanted experiences. The practice of mindfulness facilitates exposure to such experiences in the context of acceptance, in which we turn toward unpleasant sensations or emotions, rather than turning away. Over time, the unpleasant sensations or emotions pass, giving way to a sense of safety or wellbeing (Hölzel et al., 2011). This process involves informal exposure to unpleasant stimuli, similar to the process of exposure therapy, in which the client is exposed to fear-provoking stimuli and *prevented* from the typical response (usually escape or avoidance) to acquire a sense of safety in the presence of the previously feared stimuli.

Extinction is a process that allows the trauma survivor to learn not to have a fear response to neutral (not trauma-related) stimuli when there is no adaptive function for that response. It is related to the mindfulness facet of nonreactivity, which emerges from mindfulness practice, and involves an unlearning of previous connections between stimuli and fear (for instance, extinction and reconsolidation) that breaks ties to habitual emotional and behavioral reactions. It is important to note that the extinction of fear does not involve the erasing of the conditioned fear response, but involves the formation of a new memory or a modification of the old memory, which is reconsolidated with new contextual associations (Hölzel et al., 2011; Visser et al., 2018).

> Nonreactivity helps to break ties between habitual emotional and behavioral reactions.

Not surprisingly, the brain regions involved in mindfulness meditation are the same as those involved in fear extinction. The prefrontal cortex works with the hippocampus during extinction recall to inhibit fear. Research in this area suggests that mindfulness meditation may increase one's capacity to extinguish conditioned fear by enhancing aspects of the brain network involved in signaling safety (Hölzel et al., 2011). Mindfulness practices that relate to exposure and extinction may be useful for trauma survivors to help them build the capacity to tolerate and welcome emotions, to practice investigating emotions, and to learn responsiveness to emotion-based information. Mindfulness practice leads to increased self-efficacy and distress tolerance, knowing that one can experience distressing thoughts or images and just notice them without reacting.

Aspects of Emotion Regulation

Emotion regulation involves the anticipation of emotionally evocative events (such as appraisal) and responding to emotionally distressing situations when such events cannot be avoided (such as allowing emotion). When working with trauma survivors, it can be useful to consider other aspects of emotion regulation that we can incorporate into therapy with our clients. A trauma-informed, educational approach can facilitate the development of emotion regulation skills. Our goal is to ascertain our client's level of knowledge about their emotional experiences—exploring and perhaps gently correcting (mis)conceptions about emotions—using mindfulness.

We take steps to help the trauma survivor increase emotional awareness, fostering an understanding of the connections between emotional experiences and their motivations for behavior. The following section discusses some common approaches to emotion regulation work with clients, with suggestions or considerations for how we might incorporate adaptations for their work with trauma survivors.

EDUCATION AND DISPUTING EMOTION MYTHS

Many people who have experienced trauma adhere to incorrect beliefs or notions about emotions or "emotion myths" (Leahy et al., 2011), which often originate from the traumatic environment of their childhood. When key figures such as caregivers ignore or invalidate emotional experiences, trauma survivors tend to ignore or dismiss their own emotional experiences, may feel guilty or selfish for expressing emotions to others, or may believe that emotions are harmful.

> The mindful trauma therapist adopts a mindset of both teaching and witnessing the self-discovery of the client, offering empowerment rather than taking the role of the expert.

We can adopt a mindset that involves both teaching and witnessing the self-discovery of the client in this regard. A key distinction here is that our approach is trauma-informed, offering empowerment and collaboration. We do not take on the role of expert, telling the trauma survivor what their experience is or should be, instead helping the trauma survivor understand their experience by providing a guiding framework and apply that knowledge to themselves.

OBSERVING AND DESCRIBING EMOTIONS

The first step of emotion regulation involves the awareness of emotional experience. We teach the client how mindful awareness of emotional states (and thoughts) provides the foundation for emotion regulation. This awareness is a prerequisite for making intentional choices about how to handle or respond to that emotional state.

Emotional awareness is best cultivated through engaging in intentional exercises to observe and describe one's emotional experiences. Many individuals who experience trauma might struggle with this task. For one, difficulties identifying emotional states will be related to difficulties with body awareness (see chapter 8) and attention regulation (see chapter 7), but may also be related to conditions such as alexithymia, in which there is difficulty identifying and naming emotional states. Dissociation can also interfere with emotional awareness.

NONJUDGMENTAL STANCE TOWARD EMOTIONS

A key feature of the mindfulness approach to emotion regulation is that present-moment awareness occurs with an attitude of nonjudgment. Likewise, as the trauma survivor more deeply examines their emotional experiences, we encourage self-compassion and nonjudgment, specifically nonjudgment of the trauma survivor's emotional experiences. We refrain from judging emotions as good, bad, right, or wrong, given the impact of the traumagenic context on the trauma survivor's attitude toward emotions.

> Nonjudgment of emotional experiences involves refraining from judging emotions as good or bad or right or wrong.

It is likely that the invalidating environment in which trauma was experienced included explicit judgment and criticism of the trauma survivor's emotional experiences, so adopting a stance of nonjudgment is likely challenging for many survivors. In such cases, it is helpful to explore this explicitly, with questions about whether they want to carry that judgmental, critical stance forward.

ALLOWING AND WILLINGNESS

Mindfulness includes acceptance and willingness, which is a way one can relate to experiences (such as thoughts, emotions, or sensations). Willingness involves an intentional choice to decide to experience fully (rather than suppress) an event or sensation. In its most basic form, acceptance of emotional experiences is akin to *allowing* such experiences. Acceptance is a complex topic that we will discuss further as a shift in perspective (see chapter 10).

> Willingness involves an intentional choice to decide to experience fully (rather than suppress) an event or sensation.

The concept of allowing can be complicated and even confusing, especially for trauma survivors who wrestle with self-blame or survivor guilt. It is important that we communicate clearly to the client that allowing and willingness do not involve the act of endorsing a particular situation or seeking out unpleasant experiences. Rather, allowing refers to a willingness to recognize the reality of circumstances and experiences as they exist, rather than what we want them to be. Another perspective is that allowing means the absence of *fighting against* the reality of one's experience. This creates an opportunity for the trauma survivor to examine their experience in the wake of that reality and decide how they want to respond to it.

Emotion Regulation in Trauma

As discussed in chapter 3 (see Appendix 1; http://www.newharbinger.com/54650), many survivors will show psychological adaptations to trauma in the form of emotion dysregulation, detachment processes, and difficulties with particular emotions. Moreover, trauma survivors who present for therapy will often be eager to receive support to cope with emotion-related difficulties connected to their suffering and, potentially, for problematic maladaptive coping responses. It is common for trauma survivors to have difficulty modulating the intensity of emotions, either in general or with specific emotions, which can manifest either as an underregulated emotion (such as overwhelm) or difficulties related to an overcontrolled emotion (such as restrictive eating). Importantly, the mindful trauma therapist is aware that trauma survivors can experience dysregulation of positive emotions (for example, anhedonia).

Childhood maltreatment or a chaotic early home environment can disrupt the development of emotion regulation skills by reducing children's access to positive attachment figures and the modeling of adaptive emotional labeling, expression, and regulation behaviors (Dunn et al., 2018). Experiencing trauma, particularly when interpersonal in nature, chronic, and beginning prior to adolescence, is associated with greater difficulties in emotion regulation. Not surprisingly, childhood neglect, as well as emotional, physical, and sexual abuse are risk factors for emotion dysregulation. The extent, severity, and number of traumatic experiences across the lifespan affect trauma's impact on emotion dysregulation, with more chronic or frequent childhood maltreatment associated with significantly worse problems.

As discussed in chapter 2, the nature, extent, complexity, and developmental context of traumatic experiences influences the traumatized client's capacity for mindfulness emotion regulation. It is common for trauma survivors to experience difficulties maintaining optimal arousal and, instead, oscillate between states of under- and overarousal (Treleaven, 2018). This is particularly prominent among individuals exposed to complex developmental trauma. Mindfulness facilitates an expansion of the window of tolerance (for further discussion, see chapters 2 and 6), increasing the trauma survivor's capacity for trauma-focused therapy by enhancing emotion regulation.

Emotion Regulation-Related Disturbances in Trauma Survivors

The mindful trauma therapist is keenly aware of the traumagenic context in relation to the trauma survivor's capacity for emotion regulation. Emotion, one of several domains within the trauma-adaptation model (McCann et al., 1988), includes a range of feelings typically experienced negatively, such as fear, anger and rage, guilt, regret, sadness, grief or loss, disgust, and shame. Trauma survivors also experience emotional numbing, feelings of emptiness, or detachment. Emotion dysregulation is a component of most trauma-related syndromes and aspects of psychological adaptation, including anxiety disorders, depression, and nonsuicidal self-injury, as well as post-traumatic stress disorder (PTSD) and its variants. Emotion dysregulation explains common PTSD comorbidities (such as substance use, eating disorders, and borderline personality disorder [BPD]) partly because numerous disorders involve reliance on problematic emotion regulation strategies, including suppression, avoidance, and rumination (Aldao et al., 2010). We will discuss this further below.

PTSD, CPTSD, AND BPD

In the various trauma syndromes—PTSD, complex PTSD (CPTSD), and borderline personality disorder (BPD)—emotion regulation is affected differently. In the case of PTSD, emotion dysregulation typically is limited to persistent fear and physiological hyperarousal and, in some cases, dissociative symptoms. In the case of CPTSD, chronic difficulties with self-soothing lead to feeling worthless, shame, or guilt, emotional numbing or intense, diffuse emotional distress, and dissociation. For CPTSD with BPD, profound emotion dysregulation is present in the form of intense emotional lability, extreme uncontrolled anger, and volatile relational anxiety and hostility. Preexisting difficulties in emotion regulation play a prominent role in the development and maintenance of PTSD symptoms (Lee et al., 2015).

Maladaptive emotion regulation strategies, such as thought suppression, expressive suppression, experiential avoidance, and rumination, are associated with more severe PTSD symptoms. Different facets of mindfulness may be relevant to emotion regulation in these conditions. Emotional avoidance in the context of PTSD may benefit from an emphasis on mindfulness via acceptance as well as observing and describing the experience. Emotional avoidance and negative self-perceptions in CPTSD may respond well to facilitating mindful nonjudgment, whereas enhancing skills in mindful nonreactivity may be relevant to BPD.

SUBSTANCE USE DISORDERS

As mentioned in chapter 3, problematic or maladaptive substance use can serve different functions, including avoidance or numbing, which fall under the umbrella of emotion regulation. The literature is replete with evidence linking emotion regulation problems to a range of difficulties related to substance use, from hazardous or problematic use to outright SUDs.

Using the trauma-informed lens, we are cognizant of the link between PTSD and the elevated risk of developing SUDs in adults. In most cases, the SUD is more likely to follow the onset of PTSD, rather than to develop concurrently or prior to PTSD (see Messman-Moore & Bhuptani, 2017, for a review). This PTSD–SUD comorbidity can lead to more severe avoidance and arousal PTSD symptoms, especially with difficulties sleeping, and is more likely to occur among individuals who experienced childhood maltreatment. Maladaptive emotion regulation strategies, such as heightened levels of avoidance and rumination, explain the link between trauma exposure and increased risk for substance problems and more severe SUDs (Aldao et al., 2010; Messman-Moore & Bhuptani, 2017).

Some research suggests that the association is more common among women, which may be due to women's higher levels of rumination, a risk factor for SUDs. Mindfulness strategies, such as urge surfing, can help with the discomfort associated with cravings or in the context of reducing or eliminating substance use or other related behaviors (such as binge eating) that might serve the function of self-soothing for the trauma survivor.

DISORDERED EATING

Trauma survivors often struggle with disordered eating, which may include food restriction, emotional eating, overeating (including binge eating), or compensatory behaviors (such as purging or overexercising). In many cases of emotional eating or binge eating, emotion dysregulation is an underlying issue. Binge eating often serves a primary emotion regulation function among trauma survivors as a means of self-soothing to obtain comfort or blunt emotional intensity. Behavioral overcontrol in the form of restricted eating also is a means of emotion regulation.

Individuals who experience childhood maltreatment tend to believe that their emotions are overwhelming and uncontrollable. These beliefs are linked to greater levels of uncontrolled eating (the tendency to lose control of eating when hungry) and emotional eating (the tendency to overeat in response to negative mood states).

In contrast, beliefs that emotions are damaging, shameful, or irrational may instead lead to more restraint, controlling food intake to influence body weight or shape among survivors of childhood physical and emotional maltreatment (Strodl & Wylie, 2020). Food restriction can involve efforts to inhibit or suppress emotion (a form of emotion regulation) and attempts to regain control. In many cases, these patterns are unconscious in nature, and mindfulness skills can allow the trauma survivor to become more fully aware of emotional states in relation to such behavior and note any connections between such behavior and their traumatic past.

Clinical Applications: Cultivating Emotion Regulation with Trauma Survivors

When we target emotion regulation processes, we are working with one of three central techniques: 1) appraisal techniques, 2) exposure techniques, and 3) amplifying and cultivating positive emotions. We begin work with emotion regulation by highlighting the importance of how we respond to our emotions, which we will look at through the lens of cognitive responses (appraisal) and behavioral responses (suppression, overwhelm, panic, aggression). We set a tone of curiosity regarding noticing habitual cognitive and behavioral responses to emotion and learning more about *how* those responses impact the emotional experience. In addition, we implement practices that emphasize positive emotions, building capacities for noticing and experiencing these emotions through mindful awareness, amplifying when helpful and teaching savoring.

Appraisal and exposure techniques build clients' capacities to shift interpretations and tolerate painful emotions. The positive emotion techniques are *not* reappraisal practices; rather, they are resilience-enhancing practices that develop the client's capacity to notice, amplify, and savor positive emotions. This is crucial, as trying to instruct someone to feel differently about the situation (if that doesn't emerge naturally through shifts in appraisal; see below and chapter 10 concerning perception) is inconsistent with mindfulness—it is more consistent with what people sometimes call *toxic positivity* because it is often experienced as painfully invalidating. All of the suggested practices widen the client's window of tolerance through increased emotion regulation capacities. The practices for each emotion regulation process are mentioned in the boxes, and the practices themselves are included in your online therapist materials ("Kōan: The Story of Maybe," Mindfulness of Thoughts," "Gratitude for Exceptions to the Rule," "Mindfulness of Emotion," "Working with Difficulty," Looking at a Glass Jar," "Gratitude Practice;" http://www.newharbinger.com/54650).

We highlight that trauma adaptations (symptoms) show up in the context of painful and dysregulated emotions when we are on *automatic pilot* or when we don't have *alternative skills or resources*. Because these are habitual cognitive and behavioral processes, we must step out of automatic pilot to intervene. Therefore, the first skill we teach is "Pause and Consider" (client worksheet: http://www.newharbinger.com/54650).

In this skill, the client pauses when they are aware of an intense emotion, thereby interrupting the habitual process. Next, they notice and describe the emotional experience nonjudgmentally (see "Appraisal Techniques" below). They now have a *choice point*—the choice point involves possibilities of habitual responses and a myriad of alternative responses; the client considers their options for how to respond. Finally, they make a mindful choice consistent with what feels wise, skillful, helpful, or upholds their personal values.

> **Pause and Consider**
> 1. Pause.
> 2. Nonjudgmentally notice and describe.
> 3. Consider the choice point and all the options.
> 4. Make a mindful choice.

Through use of the pause and consider skill across time, we learn about the client's habitual responses to challenging emotional experiences (enrich case formulation) and get a better idea of whether cognitive or behavioral emotion regulation interventions are indicated (inform treatment planning). This skill is particularly crucial for trauma survivors who struggle with impulsive problematic behaviors.

In terms of treatment planning, appraisal techniques are the cognitive tools and exposure techniques are the behavioral tools. Appraisal techniques help the client look at how they are making sense of and responding to their experiences and how this drives their emotional reactions. Exposure techniques work differently, facilitating changes in the client's relationship to a particular emotion through creating new experiences with it. Amplifying positive emotion techniques builds resilience and emotional well-being. We will delve further into the application of each below.

If you are uncertain which type of emotion regulation process to lead with, you may find it helpful to start with nonevaluative awareness (nonjudgmental stance), which is also applied in the exposure techniques. If there is clinical value, client interest, and time in the client's course of therapy, many clients benefit from all sets of skills.

Appraisal Techniques: Cognitive Emotion Regulation

Mindfulness Practices That Cultivate Emotion Regulation Through Appraisal

- Kōan: the story of maybe
- Mindfulness of thoughts
- Gratitude for exceptions to the rule

When we strengthen appraisal capacities through mindfulness practice, we cultivate skills across the continuum of acceptance and change. On the acceptance side of mindfulness-based appraisal techniques, we practice nonevaluative awareness, learn to observe thought processes, and notice unhelpful thought patterns; on the change side, we use reappraisal. In between those polarities, we use appraisal techniques of cognitive flexibility and dialectical thinking.

NONEVALUATIVE AWARENESS

We begin by building *nonevaluative awareness*. This is a central application of a nonjudgmental stance and one of the best practices to help clients investigate the influence of judgments on emotions. We are often building here on nonevaluative awareness of body sensations from body awareness mindfulness practices. We focus attention on how the client responds to their emotions.

To engage in deliberate practice to scaffold this skill, we typically start with practicing *nonjudgmental description* as an informal mindful practice throughout session and in the client's life for home practice. To practice nonjudgmental description, rather than labeling something good or bad (or boring or stupid), we ask clients to label their feelings using nonevaluative description (in dialectical behavior therapy [DBT], this is the mindfulness skills of describing nonjudgmentally; Linehan, 2014). The goal is not to become free of judgments, but to learn to shift them to nonjudgmental descriptions for emotion regulation functions (with benefits to interpersonal functions). See the following example exchange, which occurs early in session, as the client shares how their week has been.

Example Script: *Facilitating Nonevaluative Awareness via Nonjudgmental Description*

Client: I keep feeling like a loser and thinking, *I'll never find love. I'm the worst. Yet another relationship destroyed by my stupidity and my rants and tantrums.* Basically, I act like a jerk.

Therapist: I can tell this is really distressing for you. I'm hearing some judgmental and evaluative words. Can you try to nonjudgmentally describe the situation?

Client:	I start thinking about him leaving me and then about all the people who have left me. I think about how when I'm upset, I get so emotional and angry; I do lots of blaming and accusing, and it pushes everyone away. I get stuck thinking how I'm going to end up alone.
Therapist:	Thank you, that was a skillful nonjudgmental description, and it sounded very different to me. You describe some thought processes, some emotions, and then some behaviors, and some outcomes of those behaviors that concern you. You also noted some distressing future predictions. Did that feel any different from the first statement with the judgments?
Client:	First way, I felt a lot of anger and disappointment in myself; the second way made me feel like I need to figure out how to do better.
Therapist:	So describing nonjudgmentally fostered a more constructive attitude and reduced anger and disappointment in yourself.
Client:	Yeah… I'd like to find that attitude more often.
Therapist:	The best way to do that is deliberate practice. Let's keep practicing describing nonjudgmentally as we talk more about this. (Client nods.) And maybe this would be a helpful home practice to try this week? You'll also have to practice catching judgments to know when to practice!
Client:	I think that would be helpful.
Therapist:	Okay, tell me more about what happened this weekend that stirred up intense emotions.

Nonevaluative awareness also includes accepting and acknowledging the uncertainty of outcomes, which is why it is not helpful to label things as good or bad. Our judgments actually introduce inaccuracy because we do not know yet how things will unfold. This is most evident in clients who escalate emotion dysregulation by catastrophizing (*It is bad because I will lose everything*) about problems that may or may not occur, often leading to overwhelming anxiety or panic.

One of our favorite ways to work on holding the not knowing of an outcome is with a kōan (mindfulness practice with a parable and space to contemplate the teaching), an old Chinese story called "The Story of Maybe."

The Story of Maybe

Once upon a time, there was an old farmer who had toiled over his crops for many years. One day, his horse suddenly ran away. When his neighbors heard the news, they came to visit him. "Such bad luck," they said with concern.

"Maybe," the farmer replied.

The next morning the horse returned, bringing with it three other wild horses. "How wonderful," the neighbors called out in joy.

"Maybe," answered the farmer.

The following day, the farmer's son was trying to tame one of the wild horses by riding it, was thrown off the horse, and broke his leg. The neighbors again tried to offer their sympathy for his hardship. "How awful," they said.

"Maybe," replied the farmer.

The day after, military officials arrived at the village to draft all of the young men into the army. Because the farmer's son's leg was broken, they passed over him, and he was not drafted. The neighbors congratulated the farmer on his good fortune.

"Maybe," said the farmer.

After sharing the kōan, our instructions invite mindful contemplation of how this "maybe" attitude applies to situations in their lives. The mindfulness practice is followed by inquiry (see chapter 6) for consolidation and generalization purposes.

Another practice for appraisal skills, **mindfulness of thoughts**, involves observing thoughts as passing mental events. The key to this practice is that we are not interacting with the *content* of thoughts, but rather noting thoughts as they arise and noticing any associated shifts in emotions, sensations, thoughts, or urges. As clients observe their thoughts, they begin to notice recurrent problematic processes (such as worry, rumination, self-criticism, and self-doubt). Noticing *habitual cognitive patterns* is important, providing key information to elaborate case conceptualization. In inquiry, we discuss how they responded and the subsequent shifts, over time helping the client identify which responses are problematic and which are helpful.

COGNITIVE FLEXIBILITY

Another important building block in appraisal-based emotion regulation capacities is *cognitive flexibility*, the ability to look at the same thing in different ways. This improves our ability to 1) consider that the first way we looked at something is not the only way to look at it, and 2) explore possibilities of other ways of looking at it. Note that for cognitive flexibility, we are not asking the client to change their thought, only to consider the possibility of alternatives (selection of an alternative thought is the change-based strategy of reappraisal). The following is an example script of facilitating nonevaluative awareness and building onto that by fostering cognitive flexibility in session, in response to content that the client brings in.

Example Script: *Facilitating Nonevaluative Awareness and Fostering Cognitive Flexibility*

Client: I can't stop thinking about the house that I didn't get. I missed the window and someone else made the offer first—because they can make decisions—and now the door is closed. I keep going through it in my head, stuck in a loop, ending with my failure.

Therapist: You describe that you are ruminating about the lost house; so, first of all, great job noticing! You say to yourself: 'Okay, right here is a spot where I inadvertently increase my suffering.' You created such an opportunity. So how are you responding when you notice?

Client: Sometimes I just get stuck in the thought—I'll be so mad at myself for hours. Sometimes I try to shift out of it by distracting myself with a TV show or something.

Therapist: Sounds like sometimes you intervene and opt out of rumination by shifting your attention and sometimes you stay in it, is that right? Let's gather what you are learning from these different options. What do you find when you let yourself ruminate?

Client: When I stay in it, I get more and more upset. Then I start thinking about all the different times that I struggled to make big decisions and missed out on opportunities because of it. Last night, I got into a fight with my partner because I was so agitated from the tour of my failures.

Therapist: What do you find when you intervene and shift your attention?

Client: When I redirect my attention away, I feel less distressed. I remember that my life is more than the house I don't have. I notice that other things matter too, some of them matter even more, and that puts my letdown in perspective.

Therapist: What emotions do you notice? Are you pining with sadness and longing, berating yourself in anger, or marking lessons learned with regret?

Client: Most of the time, I'm so mad at myself—that comes in a stream of self-criticism. The thoughts are all about how I mess everything up.

Therapist: So, the feeling is primarily anger. And it goes with failure/mess-everything-up thoughts. And we were just discussing that this particular blend of emotions and thoughts creates a lot of distress. Are there other ways of looking at it?

Client: (pauses to consider) Well, the house had its flaws, and that's why I wasn't sure about making an offer. There were some problems—including a structural issue—that felt really scary and made me unsure about making an offer.

Therapist: Hmm! That's a very different way of looking at these events. It removes the hindsight bias and reminds you of what was going on when you were in that period of uncertainty. Are there other ways of looking at it?

Client: Well, I guess everyone says that this is the process. There aren't a lot of houses on the market, and they go pretty quickly. Everyone I talked to had stories like this too.

Therapist: A few ways to look at this! A big mistake, a problematic house that requires deep consideration, and it's part of the process to consider places that other people end up buying.

Client: Pretty much. Yeah, that's helpful.

Therapist: How do you know it's helpful?

Client: My heart rate slowed, and I felt calm.

Therapist: So lovely that you're noticing these things. I'm glad this is resourcing… Do you notice how you turned on yourself when you actually had some sound reasoning?

Client: (eyes well up) That's exactly what I did. It makes me feel really sad.

Therapist: What would responsiveness to the sadness look like?

Client: Trying not to turn on myself with all that anger… And thinking of other ways of looking at it.

Therapist: Lovely. I'm appreciating how effectively you've practiced both nonjudgmental description and trying other ways of looking at things. What would be a helpful home practice?

Client: I can try to walk myself through this whenever thoughts about the house kick up. I'll definitely have opportunities to practice.

Therapist: That's wonderful. I appreciate your willingness to greet it differently; I'm looking forward to hearing more about how that goes.

REAPPRAISAL

Reappraisal is the skill in which the client chooses another way of thinking about the situation and decides to shift their appraisal. Fostering cognitive flexibility sometimes leads naturally to reappraisal because one of the options is particularly convincing or helpful to the client. Sometimes we select a reappraisal more deliberately, perhaps not because the client is convinced but because they believe it is more helpful. This is especially relevant in the case of interpersonal problems, which are typically present-day manifestations of trauma adaptations. The client may consistently appraise others as trying to exploit or take advantage of them or as disregarding of them, and this may be more of a historical echo than a present-day truth. In such cases, deliberate reappraisal may be very helpful.

Our favorite tool for reappraisal is the kōan. In particular, we like using Valerie Cox's poem titled "The Cookie Thief," which you can find easily on the internet if you search for it. Similarly to the format used in the prior kōan example, after reading the poem, provide a meditative space for contemplation about the teaching and its relevance to the client.

DIALECTICAL THINKING

The final appraisal skill is *dialectical thinking,* which involves considering opposing or contradictory perspectives and reconciling them by finding a synthesis or integration of both perspectives. In this process, we also explore what is being left out of the current discussion on both sides. The synthesis of seemingly opposite perspectives is understood to provide a more complete, integrated viewpoint. This way of thinking is rooted in ancient Greek philosophy and has been codified into psychotherapy in DBT (Linehan, 2014).

We often begin developing dialectical thinking informally in session in discussions and for home practice. One way of promoting dialectical thinking in informal mindfulness practice is to notice conjunctions, catch "or," "but," and other contrasting conjunctions, and replace them with additive conjunctions (such as "and," "also," and "in addition;" Linehan, 2014). Clients can also practice dialectical thinking by articulating both sides or perspectives on a topic (for instance, "On the one hand…, and on the other hand…"). You can also model these skills, correcting your own "or" and "but" conjunctions to "and" or other additive conjunctions or framing both sides that you see.

When a client brings in a situation with opposite perspectives, such as an argument with their partner or a disagreement with a coworker, it's a great opportunity for engaging dialectics. You can ask dialectical questions, such as "How might both perspectives be right?" The client's answer to that, or one that you develop together, is a dialectical synthesis. Another way to practice is to notice extreme one-sided statements and invite dialectical thinking. For example, if your client is convinced that their child going to camp would be terrible, you might ask, "Could the opposite be true?" Another way to ask this is, "Might there be any silver linings?"

Another way to engage dialectical thinking is through silver linings related to painful experiences, which you might consider discussing using self-disclosure about a personal experience of failure or other adversity that had profound silver linings. Since most therapists do not disclose much about their histories, clients often pay close attention when they do. Always begin a self-disclosure by checking with the client to see if they are open to hearing about your experience, and letting the client know why you are sharing it (because it is relevant to experiences of failure).

After sharing your story, ask the client what they take from it. You might talk about how silver linings are often not visible from the place of disappointment. We might discuss the concept of dialectics, highlighting that something can at once be absolutely devastating and, at the same time, be an opportunity for whatever emerges or is pursued next. The story does not have to be about failure; it can also show dialectics through other concepts, such as resilience in the face of adversity or important growth through an experience of hardship. If you do not have a personal story that you feel comfortable disclosing, you can use an example from a famous person (for example, Helen Keller, Frederick Douglass, or Oprah Winfrey). Any of these options help the client explore a new narrative that incorporates not knowing the outcome and possibilities of different outcomes.

One mindfulness practice that we find particularly helpful in dialectical thinking is one that we developed for our clients, **gratitude for the exception to the rule**. This practice is helpful when a client is making global, negative statements that are devastating to them. We request that they identify an exception (or a few) to the belief. After they are identified, we guide a practice of experiencing gratitude for these exceptions to the negative belief, amplifying awareness of these counterexamples and what it feels like when they experience (both cognitively and emotionally) that the belief is not globally true.

For example, a client may say after a series of unpleasant dates and conflict with a friend, "I am too much. No one wants to put up with someone who has as many problems as I have." In such a case, you begin by acknowledging that you see they feel very alone, given the recent dating disappointments and conflict with a friend. You follow this with asking for counterexamples: "Who does want you around? Who treats you like you are not too much?" Exceptions may be domain-wide (problems at home but not at work or vice versa) or specific, which may include their children, an old friend (even if they don't talk often), or people in their religious or cultural community. Importantly, you yourself will often be an exception.

Once an exception, or preferably multiple exceptions, are identified, you begin the mindfulness practice of inviting gratitude for the identified exception. We instruct observing feelings, sensations, thoughts, urges, and images that arise in response to focusing on gratitude for the exception. During inquiry, we emphasize experiential markers of positive emotions and, if available, consolidate that through deliberate attention to the exception, the belief may seem slightly less compelling (reducing the conviction in a problematic or distorted trauma-related belief).

Exposure Techniques: Behavioral Emotion Regulation

Exposure techniques help clients change their relationship to a particular emotion through practicing tolerating it and creating new experiences with that emotion. These practices widen the client's window of tolerance for particularly challenging trauma-related emotions. Exposure involves habituation or inhibitory learning. Habituation occurs through repeated experiences tolerating emotions that were previously experienced as intolerable or overwhelming. Inhibitory learning occurs through experiencing emotions in new ways, facilitated by having novel ways of responding to historically dysregulated or prohibited emotions.

For most of our clients, mindfulness skills of nonevaluative awareness of emotions (see above, "Appraisal Techniques"), self-compassion toward painful emotions (see chapter 10), and cultivating responsiveness to emotions are new ways of responding that can create changes in emotional experiencing and reduce levels of

> **Mindfulness Practices That Cultivate Emotion Regulation Through Exposure**
> - Mindfulness of emotion
> - Working with difficulty
> - Looking at a glass jar

distress, with consolidation and repetition leading to inhibitory learning. All exposure benefits from repetition via *deliberate practice*.

The type of exposure we are using in mindfulness practice is *informal exposure*. Here, we use exposure *processes* (applying principles) rather than an exposure *protocol* (formal exposure). We leverage opportunities in session to replace avoidance with approach behavior as they arise. Leading up to this point in our work with the client, we will have already identified emotional avoidance (for instance, suppression, dissociation, or avoidance of cues that prompt particular emotions) and explored the relationship between avoidance and increased symptoms, reduced quality of life, and missing out on valued experiences. We consistently communicate the importance of promoting approach behavior in place of avoidance, highlighting the client's ability to tolerate aversive, painful, or uncomfortable emotions.

When a situation occurs in which there is a recognized challenging emotion arising in therapy, we can drop into emotional experiencing. By doing this, we create two important opportunities: to practice tolerating aversive and painful emotions (habituation), and to facilitate a new experience of the emotion by cultivating new responses such as acceptance or self-compassion (inhibitory learning). The new responses are also enhanced by practices directly targeting shifts in perspective (see "Self-Compassion" and "Cognitive Defusion" in chapter 10).

A foundational practice for allowing emotional experiencing is **mindfulness of emotion**, which comes from Buddhist recognition practice (observing and noticing). This mindfulness practice emphasizes noticing emotion and allowing it to be there without engaging in habitual avoidance reactions. The instructions include guidance on not avoiding, allowing emotional experiencing, and not intensifying or holding on to the emotion (Linehan, 2014). The function of this exercise is to practice allowing, tolerating, and being curious about challenging emotions. Inquiry emphasizes consolidation of experiencing challenging emotions as tolerable and manageable.

One of our favorites for cultivating new experiences of emotions is **working with difficulty**. This practice emphasizes supporting oneself through difficulty by responding gently, tenderly, and with curiosity to emotions (Segal et al., 2013). We will discuss in chapter 10 how this practice pairs emotional acceptance with cognitive defusion. The instructions emphasize releasing the focus on review of (rumination on) events by de-emphasizing attention to the story of what happened and shifting the focus to emotion and tending to emotional experiencing. Pema Chödrön (2007) summarizes this beautifully in the mindfulness phrase "drop the story and feel the feeling." Using the working with difficulty practice, we guide clients in how to consider responding to painful emotional experiences with tenderness, care, and exploration of responsiveness. This exposure practice generates new experiences that, with repetition, lead to inhibitory learning (new associations).

For some trauma survivors, there may be particularly challenging emotions for which these exposure practices may be outside of the window of their tolerance. There might be a particular emotion—a typical one for trauma survivors is shame—that is absolutely flooding for your client when at high intensity. Due to shame-related schemas that are common trauma adaptations, they may frequently experience high-intensity shame and associated dysregulation, making it a treatment priority. In such cases, if mindfulness of emotion and working with difficulty are too overwhelming, we can titrate the intensity by introducing deliberate layers of distance. By doing this, we are engaging *deliberate, volitional detachment* to reduce the intensity of exposure as an alternative to dysregulation leading to dissociative detachment.

A helpful practice for a titrated distance is "Looking at a Glass Jar" (Lamagna, 2017). The following example is an introduction to this practice following flooding in response to talking about childhood ritual sexual abuse experiences. Notice that within the example, the therapist also briefly integrates skills of labeling emotions and past-present discernment (chapter 8).

Example Script: *Introducing Looking at a Glass Jar for Titration*

Client:	(sobbing) "It's overwhelming! I feel like I'm stained by my abuse. I don't want to talk about this anymore—it's too much!
Therapist:	Would you be willing to pause and put words to what emotion you are feeling?
Client:	I guess it's shame. I feel like I just want to hide or even leave our session. And fear, too, like it's not okay for us to talk about this.
Therapist:	That's so helpful when you share that. Shame. I understand better what you are feeling, and you are bringing your prefrontal cortex online by labeling emotions, helping yourself regulate overwhelming emotions. It makes sense that you have urges to hide or leave, since those are shame-related urges. Are you willing and able to stay with me here to practice tolerating shame? (Client nods.) Can you clarify more about the fear?
Client:	The fear has two parts. One is that it's really hard to talk about, and I'm afraid that I can't handle it. The other is that something terrible will happen.
Therapist:	For that second part, what is the source of that message? Where did it come from?
Client:	My parents always said, after every one of those awful experiences, that terrible things would happen if I talked about it.
Therapist:	Do you think of the fear as a piece that is about the past or about the present?
Client:	It's totally from the past.
Therapist:	Okay, great clarity there, then keep reminding yourself that the fear is old, and comes from threats, which are perpetrator strategies.
Client:	That's really powerful.
Therapist:	I'm glad that's helpful… Looking at you, you seem a little more settled, and your breathing is slower. Are you back in your window of tolerance?

Client: Yeah, I am.

Therapist: This would be a great time, if you were willing, to try a mindfulness practice that allows us to lower the intensity of contact with this memory and the shame associated with it by putting it in a glass jar. Would you be willing to put the memory and the shame associated with it in a glass jar as I lead you through a mindfulness practice where we just observe the glass jar from the outside? We could imagine that it is over there, (gestures to a coffee table) and we can keep the lid closed. How does that sound?

Client: I think I can do that.

Therapist: Thank you for your willingness. I believe this might help you build important capacities. Keep remembering that *you have already survived* the experience in the memory. If at any point you need a bit more distance, you can just let me know. Will you be able to let me know verbally or might it be more accessible to give a hand gesture?

Client: I'll either tell you or wave my hand.

Therapist: Great. Okay, take a comfortable position in your chair...

See the online therapist materials to continue into full practice script (http://www.newharbinger.com/54650).

Cultivating and Amplifying Positive Emotions: Emotion-Varying Emotion Regulation

Trauma-informed practice emphasizes enhancing resilience. In emotion regulation, this involves learning to be present with painful or challenging emotions as well as with pleasant or positively experienced emotions, including joy, pride, hope, gratitude, awe, and inspiration, among others. Many trauma survivors have significant deficits in positive emotions, perhaps due to the inadvertent effects of deliberately suppressing painful emotions (given nonselective strategies that suppress all emotions except at breakthrough intensities, when they are often dysregulated), dissociation, or behavioral avoidance. Cultivating and amplifying positive emotions is therefore an important emotion regulation skill that helps enhance resilience.

There are two general categories of techniques for amplifying positive emotions: 1) responding to emotions that are naturally occurring, and 2) inviting positive emotions through mindfulness practices. For practices with naturally occurring emotion, the client may arrive into session with a positive emotion or it

> **Mindfulness Practices That Cultivate and Amplify Positive Emotions**
> - Mindfulness of emotion
> - Gratitude practice

may arise during session, and we immediately focus on tasks of *noticing* and *amplifying* via mindfulness practice. For practices that invite positive emotions, you will introduce a practice that elicits attention to a positive emotion and instruct noticing and experiencing the emotion.

Both of these types of practice are, in essence, teaching *savoring*. This allows us to amplify experiencing and appreciating positive emotions, as well as to reexperience positive emotions after the moment that produced them has passed. This is an extraordinary tool for trauma survivors, who often carry the past with them in the most painful ways, helping them learn to revisit the past in ways that are emotional enhancing. Sometimes people are confused about how this is mindfulness of the present moment; we are practicing focusing on the way the present-moment experience is influenced by wherever our attention is resting. We are practicing cultivating positive emotion in the present moment through attentional prompts, highlighting that continued intentional practice will foster resilience.

MINDFULNESS PRACTICE WITH NATURALLY OCCURRING POSITIVE EMOTION

We often begin by doing this practice informally when positive emotions arise in session, (including through savoring past experiences): noticing, amplifying by attending deeply to body awareness, and allowing emotional experiencing. We are explicit in the processing of these experiences via brief inquiry. If the client is uncomfortable with positive emotion and deflects or pushes it away, we take an interest. This is often a trauma adaptation formed because either it is so painful to desire positive emotion or the positive emotion was historically directly attacked or punished (particularly when incongruous with parental mood or emotion). Through inquiry, we emphasize the resilience-enhancing qualities of positive emotion and the idea that we can generate and amplify positive emotion as a form of self-care.

We can also do this through formal mindfulness practice, using **mindfulness of emotion** (discussed above, "Exposure Techniques: Behavioral Emotion Regulation"). This practice emphasizes nonevaluative observation, body awareness, and allowing emotional experiencing. Used in this context, the practice focuses on the present positive emotion and guides the client through experiencing the emotion. If we are addressing deficit (positive emotions are blunted), we also amplify the emotion. As always, practice is followed by inquiry to facilitate consolidation and generalization.

MINDFULNESS PRACTICE INVITING AND EXPERIENCING POSITIVE EMOTION

For practices that invite positive emotions, you are eliciting an emotion that is not currently present; this requires great sensitivity as it can be perceived as invalidating of current painful emotions. We emphasize that these practices are resilience enhancing, allowing us to tap into the upward spirals of positive emotion (Garland et al., 2011). We highlight that having positive emotions does not negate the pain and suffering. Experiencing positive emotions *is not meant to fix or lessen* the pain that is present; it is also not a reappraisal or suppression strategy. Rather, it is meant to sit alongside this pain.

Our favorite way to explain this is to introduce the concept of an *antidote*. An antidote does not eliminate a toxin; instead, it neutralizes or disrupts its harmful effects. Consistent with this idea, positive emotions are antidotes to corresponding painful emotions (see "Antidote Table"). Perhaps for a brief period the sharpness of the pain is softened, although we validate that it is still there.

Antidote Table	
Painful Emotion	**Corresponding Emotion Antidote**
Sadness	Joy
Shame	Pride, dignity
Guilt	Self-compassion (see chapter 10)
Hopelessness	Hope
Loneliness	Gratitude, love, interconnectedness
Boredom	Awe/wonder
Moral disgust	Inspiration/moral elevation
Anger	Compassion (see chapter 10)

We select the emotion based on current relevance (antidote to current emotional difficulty) or case conceptualization (antidote for the most painful or dysregulated emotion that the client struggles with). We lead mindfulness of emotion, inviting the client to bring to mind a situation in which the antidote emotion was felt. Instructions emphasize noticing the experience of the emotion (body sensations, urges) and allowing emotional experiencing. In inquiry following practice, we attend to thoughts and internal responses, particularly to highlight differences from habitual ways of responding to positive emotion.

Because moral distress and moral injury can be enduring reactions to trauma, moral elevation is an important antidote to consider. Moral elevation involves *inspiration*; it is experienced by being aware of morally inspiring acts by another person. This is particularly powerful when it's current (thus offering the potential to follow a thought leader or join a movement), although it can also be historical. We assign the client home practice of finding inspiring individuals or groups relevant to the client's moral distress. After they tell us about the inspiring figure(s), we engage in mindfulness of emotion, focused on emotion of inspiration.

Although most of the time we apply mindfulness of emotion to the relevant emotion, we have included a separate practice for **gratitude practice** to emphasize that it involves a circumstance of feeling cared for, supported, helped, or nurtured in some way. Receiving nurturance can be meaningful for trauma survivors, especially those who experienced emotional neglect. These practices are sometimes called benefactor practices, highlighting the relational nurturance aspect. Gratitude can also generate a sense of connection, which can be fostered further using interconnectedness practices (see chapter 10).

Finally, when positive emotions arise, both informally during sessions and through the formal practices discussed and provided in the therapist materials, we are attending and amplifying for resilience-enhancing functions (savoring). We call this *blowing on embers* and encourage our clients to notice and be mindful of positive emotions throughout their daily lives as an informal practice, emphasizing blowing on embers.

Clinical Application Summary

In developing emotion regulation capacities, we are applying appraisal techniques and exposure techniques and cultivating positive emotions. Appraisal techniques focus on targeting cognitions (in particular, interpretations); they include nonevaluative awareness (encompassing a nonjudgmental stance and not knowing of outcomes), cognitive flexibility, reappraisal, and dialectical thinking. Exposure techniques focus on building capacity for emotional experiencing; they include leveraging both distress tolerance (habituation) and new ways of responding to emotions (inhibitory learning) to expand the client's window of tolerance. Techniques for cultivating positive emotions include attending to naturally occurring positive emotions with noticing, amplifying, and savoring, as well as inviting emotions that are not currently present via mindfulness practices that invite a focal cue that elicits a particular positive emotion.

CHAPTER 10

Mindfulness, Changes in Perspective, and Trauma

Changes in perspective interact with the other overarching mindfulness mechanisms—attention regulation, body awareness, and emotion regulation—in a way that contributes to self-regulation (Hölzel et al., 2011). This change in perspective involves the observer perspective, which occurs when the self becomes detached from experience. It can emerge as a shift in the appraisal of the self, such as self-concept, or in events outside the self, including the self in relation to others. Ultimately, changes in perspective alter subjective experience.

Attention regulation (see chapter 7) is useful to facilitate changes in perspective through deliberate direction of awareness (such as noticing thoughts, feelings, and sensations). Body awareness (see chapter 8) provides clues or evidence that shifts are taking place, as we notice changes in our physiology or body sensations, such as dissipation of arousal as a result of decentering. Emotion regulation (see chapter 9) may be a precursor to or occur in parallel with changes in perspective related to heightened emotional awareness and diminished reactivity. As we engage in mindfulness practices consistently, changes in perspective will develop over time.

The current chapter will focus on changes in perspective and its relevance to integrating mindfulness into intervention for trauma. This chapter is divided into two parts. In the first part, "Background," we will discuss how mindfulness can elicit changes in perspective and the relevance of such changes to traumagenic contexts and trauma sequelae. The second part, "Clinical Applications," details how the mindful therapist can introduce mindfulness practices that may enhance the emergent processes that result from changes in perspective and how these practices may be relevant to address specific types of trauma-related adaptations in clients.

Background: Changes in Perspective in Mindfulness and Trauma

Changes in perspective involve mindfulness concepts that relate to changes in how we perceive our experiences or the world, including changes in the relationship we have with our thoughts and emotions. Changes in perspective emerge from regular, continued contact with mindfulness practice. Such changes are emergent because they develop from consistent, ongoing mindfulness practice, rather than skills that are trained directly. Although we guide our clients in cultivating these processes or skills, the meaningful development of these capacities emerges through experiential processes facilitated by mindfulness practice.

Mindfulness changes the perception and relation to one's internal and external experiences. Although changes in perspective related to mindfulness are diverse, we organize them into three general areas: 1) the experience of our thoughts, 2) mindset, and 3) relation to others and ourselves. Changes in perspective happen when we experience our thoughts, including our thoughts in general, about the self, and about others as separate from ourselves—as something that can be observed. They also involve significant shifts in our mindset, such as radical acceptance. Lastly, changes in perspective transform how we see and relate to others and ourselves, including that we are deserving of self-care and kindness. Below we highlight some key concepts relevant to integrating mindfulness into psychotherapy with trauma survivors.

Key Areas Related to Changes in Perspective

1. Thoughts
2. Mindset
3. Relation to self and others

Mindfulness and Change in Perspective: Thought

In mindfulness approaches, thought (and its processes) is a mental event that is separate from the self who experiences them. Extended mindfulness practice, whether formal meditation practices or informal practices, connects to emergent experiences in which we experience our thoughts as outside of the self. Mindfulness promotes a metacognitive processing mode that involves perceiving thoughts as transient rather than an aspect of reality.

Importantly, this process develops detachment from thoughts (and other experiences), which enhances flexibility and facilitates changes in perspective. This phenomenon, which has been referred to as cognitive defusion, reperceiving, decentering, and the observer perspective, involves taking a step back and observing one's thoughts and feelings from an objective perspective, as mental events that are a product of the mind rather than facts, truth, or reality. A key behavior in decentering involves noticing thoughts, observing the body, and bringing attention to the present moment. Related, the observer perspective takes a nonjudgmental stance, observing thoughts (or emotions, and so forth) as they are, noticing their relation to other experiences (such as urges), and connecting such experiences to internal or external stimuli.

Cognitive fusion involves a sense of attachment to inner experience such that there is no separation between experiences (such as thoughts) and the self. In this way, thoughts become reality, which may interfere with well-being. Cognitive fusion creates problems for trauma survivors in terms of negative beliefs related to trauma, such as self-blame, or distorted or magical thinking.

Cognitive defusion involves decentering and taking the observer perspective, witnessing thoughts as mental events, observing thoughts without getting caught up in the content, and reminding oneself that all thoughts are not necessarily true. This can be helpful in addressing problematic thought patterns that are common psychological adaptations to trauma, such as rumination and worry. We can explain the concepts of decentering, observer perspective, and cognitive (de)fusion while providing techniques to promote defusion, such as labeling thoughts as descriptive or evaluative, adding the phrase "I notice I am having the thought…" or more imaginal mindfulness exercises such leaves on a stream.

> Cognitive defusion involves witnessing thoughts as mental events without getting caught up in the content.

Mindfulness and Change in Perspective: Mindset

Mindfulness can transform the experience of trauma survivors by changing perspectives in mindset, which involves a way of being that influences behavior and the qualities that the trauma survivors carry within themselves. This mindset includes equanimity, psychological flexibility, and radical acceptance.

EQUANIMITY

Equanimity is an emergent mental state that arises from ongoing mindfulness meditation practices, which involves psychological stability and composure that is unwavering or undisturbed in the context of stress, emotional states, or pain. It involves a balanced response to extreme emotions, such as joy or misery—a neutral emotion or feeling that is neither pleasant nor unpleasant, which also involves neither intensifying nor deepening mental states (Desbordes et al., 2015). In essence, it is a sense of balance that arises from mindfulness practices facilitating nonreactivity in the face of negative stimuli.

Equanimity also involves impartiality; you experience unpleasant thoughts (or emotions) without reaction (such as repressing or judging). Rather than a behavioral act or strategy, which is associated with emotion regulation, equanimity involves a state of being that can be experienced. Equanimity involves a sense of steadiness, clarity, and grounding. It is a capacity that enhances distress tolerance, nonreactivity, and intentional choice. The even-minded attitude of equanimity is essential for the trauma survivor to witness their experiences (for example, emotions, thoughts, behaviors, and sensations) without judgment. Although equanimity is not formally or explicitly taught in psychotherapy, it relates to attitudes from mindfulness-based interventions (MBIs; such as acceptance and commitment therapy [ACT], dialectical behavior therapy [DBT], or mindfulness-based cognitive therapy [MBCT]), including nonjudgment, nonaversion, nonattachment (or letting go), and acceptance (Desbordes et al., 2015).

VALUES

Changes in perspective and mindset often focus on living a meaningful life despite one's challenges (trauma included), which means shifting focus from what we cannot control (including what has happened in the past) to what we value, what is important to us, and how we can live a life consistent with those values. In this way, mindfulness promotes psychological flexibility through changes in perspective. The concept of psychological flexibility is associated with the ACT model (Harris, 2021), which argues that psychological health is based on the ability to behave in accordance with goals or values instead of in response to thoughts, feelings, or sensations (whether wanted or unwanted). In this model, psychological flexibility involves maintaining full contact with the present moment, including our thoughts and feelings, without engaging in behavior to change those experiences.

> Focusing on values is a key element of trauma therapy because survivors cannot control or change their traumatic past.

Value-driven behavior involves engaging in behavior consistent with one's values so unwanted or unpleasant experiences (such as a trauma cue) will not interfere with behavior or the pursuit of goals (for example, fear of scathing criticism not interfering with giving an important presentation at work). Focusing on values is a key element of trauma therapy, given that survivors may not be able to control or change their current circumstances and certainly not their traumatic past.

We can help trauma survivors in values clarification, which involves an exploration to reconnect with what is personally meaningful. This helps with motivation, intrusive thoughts, and avoidant behaviors. This facilitates a sense of direction that can guide the trauma survivor when developing goals and choosing intentional, value-driven responses to current life circumstances, including patterns of psychological adaptation, such as symptoms of anxiety or depression. In addition to values work, mindfulness enhances the capacity for radical acceptance. Radical acceptance is a key component of this movement toward living a life worth living, and thus a fundamental skill for trauma recovery.

RADICAL ACCEPTANCE

Acceptance is a complex topic (mentioned in chapter 3 and chapter 9), akin to *allowing* emotional experiences. It involves a willingness to experience unwanted thoughts, emotions, or sensations (internal experiences) in order to pursue one's values and goals (Bond et al., 2011). Radical acceptance is based on the idea that suffering comes not directly from pain but from our response to it, and the idea that acceptance is the first step toward change (Brach, 2004).

Radical acceptance is a valuable response to situations that cannot be changed or controlled, especially past experiences of trauma (Brach, 2004). A key response when there are circumstances or factors outside of our control, radical acceptance helps to prevent being "stuck" in unhappiness, bitterness, or anger. This would lead to suffering, which arises from experiencing pain (in whatever form: physical, emotional, or spiritual) in a context of nonacceptance.

Because acceptance can be an especially sensitive area for trauma survivors, who may have experienced invalidation from family members (or even well-meaning therapists) who call on them to "forgive" their perpetrator, it is important for us to clarify that radical acceptance is not forgiveness, approval, agreement, or resignation. Instead, we are accepting, *completely*, that what currently exists in the present and the past cannot be changed, even though we do not like it.

When the trauma survivor manages to engage in radical acceptance, they are letting go of fighting reality, instead acknowledging things as they are.

For many, radical acceptance can involve a sudden change in perspective, a "light bulb moment." Radical acceptance creates a space and opportunity to respond to difficult circumstances with change (Brach, 2004). In our framework, we see radical acceptance as an emergent phenomenon that cannot be forced in an intellectual, intentional manner. However, we can help the trauma survivor move toward radical acceptance by being on the lookout for signs of struggling with acceptance, including thoughts such as *This shouldn't be happening*, or *This is not fair*. Radical acceptance of experiences such as abuse can be pivotal in psychotherapy with survivors because this change in perspective can motivate changes in how they respond to the current circumstances.

> Radical acceptance creates a space and opportunity to respond to difficult circumstances with change.

Mindfulness and Change in Perspective: Relation to Self and Others

The changes in perspective discussed previously—related to thought, metacognition, and changes in mindset—closely connect to the changes in perspective in relation to the self and others. When taking on the perspective of the observer self, the mindfulness practitioner not only experiences their own thoughts in a different way, they also experience others in a completely different way, making space to extend compassion and loving-kindness to others.

Changes in perspective involve the witnessing of thoughts, self-talk, and the origin of those beliefs. In many cases, the trauma survivor can trace the origin of negative beliefs about the self to the source—an abusive or absent parent figure or caregiver. Changes in perspective then permit the next level of understanding: that such thoughts and behaviors of the parent figure do not indicate truth, but it is their perspective. This realization can be a transformative experience, helping the survivor examine their trauma history from a different perspective.

SELF-REFERENTIAL THINKING

Self-referential processing or thinking includes thoughts about the self, how others evaluate the self, and exaggerated self-focus. It involves engaging with or relating to experience through its connection to the self. This can result in judgment of experiences in the context of self-relevance, such as liking an experience or labeling it good or bad. Self-referential processes characterized by negative cognitive biases, repetitive thought patterns (rumination), and overgeneralized recall of autobiographical memories increase negative emotional states and exacerbate internalizing symptoms, such as depression and anxiety (Lin et al., 2018).

Mindfulness practices can reduce self-referential processing and negative self-evaluation, move attention away from a narrative (autobiographical) self-focus, and increase experiential or interoceptive functioning (Farb et al., 2007). Mindfulness shifts attention to the present rather than self-referential memories and focuses on awareness of experience rather than its relevance to the self. These processes may be partly responsible for reducing levels of internalizing symptoms following mindfulness training.

COMPASSION AND LOVING-KINDNESS

Compassion involves the capacity for empathy or witnessing the suffering of another, along with the desire to alleviate it. Loving-kindness is a mindset in which we desire happiness for others and oneself. Compassion is a skill that we can teach through specific practices, just like mindfulness. Loving-kindness meditation (LKM), or *metta*, usually involves a practice of first directing loving-kindness toward the self and then to others. These meditations use phrases and imagery, which can be personalized. In a randomized clinical trial in which LKM was compared to cognitive processing therapy (CPT), a gold standard trauma-focused treatment, it demonstrated noninferior reductions in post-traumatic stress disorder (PTSD) symptoms and greater reductions in depressive symptoms (Kearney et al., 2021).

Compassion and loving-kindness bring a quality of warmth, tenderness, and connection to the experience of mindfulness, facilitating the capacity for self-soothing behavior. Such qualities are particularly important for trauma survivors. Compassion-based approaches are relevant to trauma adaptations, such as shame and self-criticism (for instance, self-compassion), and anger, resentment, or hostility (for instance, LKM toward others). We can model compassion and loving-kindness to our clients through our attitude and teach specific skills through mindfulness practices.

> Compassion and loving-kindness bring a quality of warmth, tenderness, and connection to the experience of mindfulness.

Self-compassion is an active stance in which we seek to understand and ameliorate our own suffering. It involves treating oneself kindly in times of difficulty, recognizing that we are not unique in our difficulties but that pain is a universal part of being human; holding difficulty with mindful awareness so that we can observe but not become fused with our pain (Germer & Neff, 2015). There is extensive research on self-compassion and related practices for trauma survivors. Self-compassion can serve to buffer against the effects of trauma exposure, both in the short and long term (Seligowski et al., 2015). Yet, many survivors of child maltreatment experience lower levels of self-compassion, which is linked to emotion dysregulation. Thus, enhancing self-compassion can promote trauma recovery by enhancing emotion regulation and reducing symptoms of PTSD.

Practices that enhance self-compassion help to deactivate the threat system associated with autonomic arousal and insecure attachment by increasing parasympathetic activity, heart rate variability, and feelings of safety (Strand & Stige, 2021). Self-compassion increases in response to MBIs, either through general mindfulness practices or with specific interventions focused on LKM or self-compassion.

We should be conscious of the double-edged sword associated with compassion work in trauma survivors (Germer & Neff, 2015). All trauma-focused therapy opens up the pain of the past, but mindfulness enhances awareness of this pain and privileges remaining in contact with it. Although compassion-based intervention provides an important opportunity for healing among trauma survivors, it can be challenging, given such exercises can activate needs for social connection and attachment, as well as traumatic memories associated with them.

Generating feelings associated with connectedness and attachment may be triggering for trauma survivors, requiring attunement from the therapist to assist the client in anticipating this possibility and working through this difficulty (Strand & Stige, 2021). Survivors may experience memories of being abused, neglected, or shamed by significant others, making it difficult for them to direct compassion to the self and others and to receive compassion, increasing their distress, a phenomenon called *backdraft* (Germer & Neff, 2015). During inquiry, we explore how backdraft may have come up and, if relevant and resourcing, provide brief psychoeducation about the concept.

Changes in Perspective in Trauma

As mentioned in chapter 1, trauma changes beliefs about the self, others, and the world. Such changes may be imperceptible when developmental trauma occurs, as the self is forming around that experience. In contrast, adult-onset traumas, particularly impersonal traumas, typically result in minimal changes to perspectives on the self (and others). The mindfulness framework facilitates a compassionate mindset for the client. Importantly, we help to model a compassionate response when we note traumagenic beliefs. Moreover, mindfulness widens the window of tolerance when the trauma survivor steps into observer mode; this involves a healthy state of decentering from such a vulnerable state while experiencing the painful beliefs and emotions, which accompany such fixed beliefs.

We should be on the lookout for challenges connected to perspective on the self and look for opportunities when mindfulness may help release such difficulty. Psychological rigidity is a sign of difficulty taking perspective and decentering from the self. Another sign of such problems is the recurrence of trauma-related themes or beliefs, which relates to the sensation of feeling stuck. This involves a strongly held (inflexible) traumagenic belief associated with heightened emotional distress (Resick et al., 2016). Many traumagenic stuck points involve the integration and assimilation of psychological abuse, which can look like self-hatred and self-blame. Trauma survivors frequently believe that they are worthless and are to blame for abuse, having absorbed such messages from their abuser.

Mindfulness facilitates examination of the stuck point by helping the trauma survivor decenter from the belief. Take, for example, the belief, *I am worthless. I am dirty and ruined—no one will love me since I was sexually molested.* With a change in perspective (decentering), *I am having a thought that I am worthless because of my abuse*; then, *I am having the thought that my worthlessness is related to the loss of virginity from abuse.* In this case, the observer perspective allows the survivor to examine the truthfulness and adaptiveness of the beliefs while deepening the understanding of the traumagenic and societal context in which the beliefs formed. The trauma survivor comes to witness the thought as an experience to be observed (rather than accepted as truth or reality) in a context of self-compassion, nonjudgment, and curiosity.

Disturbances Related to Change in Perspective Among Trauma Survivors

The mindful trauma therapist is keenly aware of how an individual accommodates to their traumatic past. The traumagenic context is the backdrop against which the trauma survivor comes to define their sense of self, relationships, and beliefs about the world, whether benevolent or malevolent. In the case of child maltreatment, the trauma will literally shape the child into the person they are to become. Mindfulness practices lead to emerging shifts in perspectives on the self, which can affect perceptions of the self as bad, powerless, or deserving of abuse. We discuss these shifts in perspective related to psychological adaptation of trauma survivors further below.

INTERNALIZED STIGMA AND POWERLESSNESS

Experiences of interpersonal trauma, particularly child maltreatment, are associated with powerlessness and the internalization of stigma from the abuse that occurred (Finkelhor & Browne, 1985). Survivors of childhood maltreatment often may experience themselves as disgusting, struggle with guilt and shame, and feel that they do not fit in. The child also internalizes stigma associated with trauma, such as childhood sexual abuse, or feels powerless when they cannot fend off, fight back, or escape the abuse.

The internalization of stigma and powerlessness occurs within many aspects of the psychological adaptation model, including shifts in beliefs (such as self-blame or self-hatred), rumination, obsessive thinking, or worry. Feelings of powerlessness connect to self-doubt, low levels of self-efficacy, or having an external locus of control, with many trauma survivors feeling that they do not have the power to change their life. Changes in perspective of the self may shift some of these strongly held traumagenic beliefs.

Mindfulness skills help the trauma survivor engage in cognitive defusion, decentering from their experience and observing their mind (thoughts), body (sensations), and behavior to choose how to respond. At times, we can help the trauma survivor navigate an upsurge of negative or painful feelings and thoughts (backdraft) when they make attempts at self-compassion or when they turn toward rather than away from their traumatic memories.

DISTURBANCES IN SELF AND IDENTITY

Traumatic experiences, especially those during early childhood that involve attachment (with caregivers) and development, often negatively affect the sense of self. Trauma survivors may come to believe that there is something inherent in them that makes them flawed and thus not worthy of love or respect. They may feel defective in some way or not good enough (Courtois,

2014). Abuse by a caregiver creates a dilemma for the child—how to maintain connection to this primary attachment figure despite their fear or feelings of rejection. Clearing the attachment figure and perpetrator of blame, which involves rationalizing the abuse via self-blame, can preserve this connection. This process, called *doublethink*, involves generating a negative view of the self as deserving abuse or neglect so the child becomes all bad and the parent can remain all good. In other cases, the child may dissociate and compartmentalize traumatic experiences, resulting in a *double self* where memories of abuse are not easily accessed (Herman, 2015). These two processes can result in a stable negative self-concept (the former case) or a fragmented sense of self (the latter case).

Radical acceptance helps the trauma survivor release these perspectives on the self so that the abuse or neglect is no longer the victim's responsibility. As the trauma survivor comes to radically accept that their experience was abusive and that they coped with the most effective adaptations they had available at the time, their perspective on the trauma changes, altering the sense of self-blame, lifting the sense of deservedness, and improving the self-concept.

Survivors of childhood trauma have a tendency to overfocus on significant others, typically caregivers, a process called *other-directedness* (Briere & Scott, 2015). This is a survival strategy adaptive in the traumagenic context, which involves privileging the experiences and needs of the powerful other (typically a caregiver) at the expense of noticing one's own reality, needs, or experiences. As a result, the trauma survivor has difficulty determining their own needs and engaging in self-soothing behavior due to a lack of *internal reference* when experiencing strong emotions (Briere & Scott, 2015). This may involve having a less coherent sense of self and difficulties with self-monitoring internal states that inform one's physical or psychological needs.

Identity difficulties interfere with interpreting thoughts, feelings, and bodily sensations and translating internal experience into motivation for behavior. In this context, we engage in behavior that validates and accepts the needs of the client, thus communicating clearly through our responsiveness the importance of the trauma survivor's needs.

DISTURBANCES IN RELATEDNESS

Developmental trauma can cause disturbances in relationships. These problems can arise from disturbances in identity, difficulties with emotion regulation, and fear of abandonment. Interpersonal difficulties may lead to highly conflictual or chaotic relationships and experiencing difficulty forming healthy intimate adult attachments. Adaptation to trauma may result in the forming of relational patterns emphasizing dominance and control or submissiveness and subjugation.

Mistrust, paranoia, and fear can lead to anger or rage, hostility, and aggression. Fear of reprisal may instead lead to patterns of fawning and difficulties with assertiveness. In many situations, changes in perspective related to cognitive defusion may shift the understanding of potential (unwarranted) threats, which may mitigate anger or aggression. Similarly, self-compassion may provide the impetus to shift patterns of subjugation and increase assertiveness.

When to Focus on Change in Perspective

Most clients, including trauma survivors, benefit from psychotherapy that teaches skills that change perspective. Traditional cognitive behavioral therapy (CBT) models do this indirectly through skills training in cognitive restructuring, which focuses on controlling the content of one's thoughts to shift emotional states and behavior. In contrast, mindfulness approaches aim to change perspective directly. Consistent with third-wave (mindfulness- and acceptance-based) behavioral therapies, mindfulness involves changing the client's relationship to their thoughts and beliefs, which increases cognitive flexibility.

Cognitive or psychological flexibility is a hallmark of adaptive psychological functioning and helps to address rumination, worry, and obsessive thinking commonly seen in survivors of trauma. They can get entrenched in habitual thought patterns and hypervigilance, focusing on cues of danger or other traumagenic themes in a fixed rather than flexible perspective. This fixedness on danger, hurt, or trauma increases the likelihood of malevolent interpretations of neutral or benign events, perpetuating experiences of anxiety, mistrust, or shame. Mindfulness facilitates psychological flexibility by providing a foundation for trauma survivors to unpack their responses to particular events, determine the appropriateness of their emotional states, and consider whether their attributions or appraisals are adaptive in the current (rather than a past traumagenic) context.

In psychotherapy with most trauma survivors, a change in perspective is relevant to the case conceptualization and treatment plan. In some cases, changes in perspective unfold or emerge in a developmental process across ongoing psychotherapy, after an initial focus on attention processes, then body awareness, and then emotion regulation. In other cases, we may choose to infuse the concepts of changes in perspective (such as radical acceptance) throughout the work with the survivor earlier in treatment, in all stages of trauma therapy.

By its very nature, approaches related to changes in perspective can be challenging because it involves fundamental changes to the concept of the self, others, or the world. Further, although many trauma survivors can intellectually grasp the concepts of acceptance or self-compassion, frequently they have trouble implementing behavioral changes due to inadequate modeling, extreme discomfort, or the interference of antithetical beliefs or feelings (such as self-loathing or shame). As such, we must consider how to introduce concepts in a compassionate manner that reduces the survivor's reactivity and discomfort (to maintain the window of tolerance).

Clinical Applications: Cultivating Changes in Perspective with Trauma Survivors

We apply these concepts with clients as relevant to present-day challenges or treatment plan, selecting those processes that are most fundamentally linked with resolving current distress or impairment. The better you understand the concepts, as described in the first part of this chapter, the better you can identify what kind of change in perspective would be helpful.

If you want to emphasize changes in perspective and are uncertain what type to target, we recommend starting with a change in perspective on thoughts, as clients find this relatively straightforward compared to the emotional complexity involved in the other practices. We often see notable changes in levels of distress and reactivity because all of the practices widen the client's window of tolerance through increased emotional and cognitive capacities. Suggested practices are in the box for each type of change in perspective, and practice scripts are included in the online therapist materials ("Ocean Waves on a Stormy Day," "Mindfulness of Emotion," "Choiceless Awareness," "Noting Practice," "Mindfulness of Thoughts," and "Working with Difficulty," "RAIN," "Kōan: Muddy Road," "Tree with Deep Roots," "Tenderness and Self-Compassion," "Self-Compassionate Body Scan," "Loving-Kindness," "Compassion for Others' Hardships," and "Tonglen;" http://www.newharbinger.com/54650).

Mindfulness Practices That Cultivate Change in Perspective: Thought

When inviting change in perspective on thoughts, our mindfulness practices emphasize decentering and cognitive defusion. These practices are helpful in many contexts when the client is overidentified with thoughts, emotions, or memories. The aim of these practices is to see the self as separate from those experiences or as the self that is having those experiences pass through. This is not meant to be invalidating; we acknowledge in our guidance that there may be very painful, convincing elements that draw us into habitual reactivity.

> **Mindfulness Practices That Cultivate Change in Perspective: Thought**
>
> **Decentering**
> - Ocean waves on a stormy day
> - Mindfulness of emotion
> - Choiceless awareness (open monitoring)
> - Noting practice
>
> **Cognitive Defusion**
> - Mindfulness of thoughts
> - Working with difficulty

DECENTERING

When a client is struggling with intense reactivity to a thought (for instance, *I am permanently damaged from my abuse experiences*), an emotion (such as shame, anger, or sadness), or a sensation (such as back pain or full stomach sensations), decentering may be helpful. These practices focus on observing emotions, thoughts, and sensations as they pass by, without viewing emotions as essential aspects of the self or thoughts as truths or realities.

Instructions emphasize that our experiences are passing events we can observe in a nonreactive, nonjudgmental stance. We often use metaphors to convey decentering, suggesting clients view experiences as *trees on a landscape, leaves on a stream,* or *clouds moving slowly in the sky*. Although we tend to favor nature metaphors, MBCT instructions also provide the useful metaphor of observing thoughts as though watching projections on a cinema screen (Segal et al., 2013).

Ocean waves on a stormy day is a decentering practice we developed in response to the imagery our clients found helpful. The instructions emphasize viewing experiences as individual large waves in a larger ocean. We provide imagery of a stormy context paired with guidance about passing through the storm. Then, we invite clients to observe thoughts, emotions, and sensations as they arise and release them to dissolve into the larger ocean. Finally, we remind them that the ocean will soon be calm again as the storm passes on. This is similar to the well-known *leaves on a stream* practice; however, it has a rough and more activated context, which can suit the tumultuous emotions many trauma survivors have.

Nevertheless, clients who experience emotional blunting and persistent anhedonia may prefer one of the other quieter imagery metaphors listed above. Also, clients with tumultuous emotions may benefit from quiet imagery for balance, so experiment to find what imagery resonates and feels useful for your client.

One of our favorite cognitive defusion practices is **noting practice** (also referred to as mental labeling). It emphasizes open awareness and applying categorical labels mentally to stimuli that arise—*thoughts, emotions, sensations, images,* and *urges*—with a nonreactive, nonjudgmental mindset. When the client notices a dry mouth, they mentally note *sensation*; when wanting to scratch an itch, *urge*; when feeling annoyed, *emotion*; when they think they are stupid, *thought*. This detaches the client from the content of the experience and reduces reactivity, allowing for a different relationship to the relevant stimuli.

When this skill is well established, you can use a more detailed version. Here, the client notes by labeling with greater specificity but still at a high level. When the client notices thoughts that maybe their partner will leave them, they note *worry*; when feeling unlovable, *shame*; when thinking about dinner, *planning*; when hearing traffic sounds, *hearing*; when judging themselves for practicing inadequately, *self-criticism*. This practice helps the client notice patterns, such as having a lot of planning thoughts or that worry thoughts are followed by feelings of hopelessness and sensations of nausea. The following example is of inquiry following a detailed version of the noting practice.

Example Script: *Facilitating Decentering and Cognitive Defusion*

Therapist: What did you notice during the noting practice?

Client: (sighs) It was relentless judgments, mostly self-criticism. And I can just feel how the shame and anger at myself follow. It was a hard practice.

Therapist: How was the tone of noting—harsh or gentle, jarring or quiet, judgmental or accepting?

Client: Harsh, critical… I guess it felt contemptuous.

Therapist: How did you experience that?

Client: I go right to shame, feeling like I'm not good enough.

Therapist: That sounds painful… In what ways was your experience of that different during this practice from your everyday experience?

Client: I think most of the time I don't even notice the stream of critical commentary. I really noticed in this practice… I felt it.

Therapist: What happens when you notice it and feel it in this way?

Client: I guess it makes me sad. I hear echoes of my dad and his endless ranting about our mistakes and our flaws.

Therapist: Yes, you learned and internalized that way of treating yourself. Are there other ways it was different in this practice?

Client: Yeah, when you were talking about the tenderness of a wound that hasn't quite healed, that really hit a chord. I teared up… for me, for all I went through.

Therapist: I'm really hearing a softening.

Client: (tears in eyes) I think if I can remember that feeling of care, knowing I hurt like that for all those years, I think I would treat myself differently. Maybe a little more gentle.

Therapist: I'm moved to hear you say that. I am so curious how you will carry this with you in the upcoming week.

Another decentering practice we recommend is **choiceless awareness** (also referred to as open monitoring). In this practice, we guide the client in moving from focused awareness at the start of the practice to open, spacious awareness in which they observe passing stimuli (internal and external) without getting caught up in content or storyline. If the client finds this practice challenging, return to the noting practice for a slightly more active mental task as related to the stimuli that arise and decreased emphasis on spacious awareness.

For an emphasis on decentering from emotions, **mindfulness of emotion** (from chapter 9) cultivates decentering by observing an emotional experience without reacting to it, judging it, or amplifying it. We guide the client to avoid going back to the storyline about why the emotion is there, instead focusing on noticing the emotion with nonreactivity, nonjudgment, and allowing it to be there because it already is.

COGNITIVE DEFUSION

For an emphasis on decentering from thought, we use cognitive defusion practices. We find that cognitive defusion is the most accessible of the changing perspectives skills for many of our clients, as people understand the idea that sometimes our thoughts are not factual (like when we are wrong or misunderstand something). We can apply **mindfulness of thoughts** (from chapter 9) as a cognitive defusion practice. It focuses on observing thoughts as mental events without reacting to them, judging them, believing them, or needing to act on them. We guide the client to step back from engaging with the thought, letting it pass by like a leaf on a stream. Any of the decentering practices can be used for cognitive defusion when they specifically emphasize thoughts. In addition, **working with difficulty**, which is discussed below, leverages cognitive defusion paired with acceptance.

Mindfulness Practices That Cultivate Change in Perspective: Mindset

We invite a change in perspective on mindset through mindfulness practices emphasizing acceptance, values clarification, and equanimity. The aim of these practices is to change the client's relationship to the difficulty by changing how they approach and interact with it. The client engages in experiential learning of new ways of relating to pain and hardship.

> **Mindfulness Practices That Cultivate Change in Perspective: Mindset**
>
> **Radical Acceptance**
> - Working with difficulty
> - RAIN
>
> **Values Clarification**
> - Working with difficulty with values emphasis
> - Kōan: "Muddy Road"
> - LKM phrase selection
>
> **Equanimity**
> - Tree with deep roots
> - Choiceless awareness

RADICAL ACCEPTANCE

We find that practices in radical acceptance are particularly helpful for trauma survivors because there may be extensive nonacceptance around the trauma history. Nonacceptance can manifest as getting stuck in *why* questions (*Why did they do that to me?*), ruminating on the unfairness or injustice of the trauma, or obsessing about how the trauma could have been averted (counterfactuals: *If only I hadn't gone there that night...*). Radical acceptance may be applied to many areas of difficulty related to trauma adaptations, such as chronic pain difficulties, fear of abandonment, painful emotions, and distressing memories.

We started working with acceptance through an emphasis on *allowing* in emotion regulation processes (chapter 9), which is a gentle step. Radical acceptance takes the full leap—it begins with allowing and involves us fully accepting the reality we are currently in. We relinquish fighting against what is, noticing all the resources that we reclaim by letting go of that struggle. Fundamentally, our clients must accept that it is a complicated and messy world, with things happening all around us that are difficult, terrifying, tragic, beautiful, surprising, inspiring, joyous, strange, and boring; further, there will always be some things that are out of our control and some that are in our control. This is not meant to be minimizing or invalidating, it is meant to acknowledge the true, inescapable messiness of this world.

Many clients will express concern that nothing will ever change if they stop fighting. This is particularly painful as related to social justice issues that are sources of or contributors to traumatic stress, such as problematic practices in law enforcement and the legal system, or institutional betrayal and moral injury in hostile, exploitative, or negligent systems. In such cases, we find psychoeducation is helpful. We explain, "You are so right to want to fight for something better in the future. I am all for that! I want to highlight that *acceptance is not resignation*—I am not inviting you to enroll for a future that looks just like this. Instead, you accept that right now, we live with some really broken systems. That is already true. The future is not determined yet." Then we invite the client to reflect on differentiating acceptance from resignation in their situation.

Working with difficulty (Segal et al., 2013) is a very helpful practice for cultivating radical acceptance. This practice (from chapter 9) is used to facilitate a change in perspective by engaging radical acceptance of emotional experiencing paired with cognitive defusion from the storyline of what created the difficulty, thereby experientially practicing the guidance *drop the story and feel the feeling* (Chödrön, 2007). It profoundly facilitates radical acceptance of painful emotions, disentanglement from ruminative processes via cognitive defusion, and developing new ways of responding to painful experiences.

One of our favorite radical acceptance practices is Tara Brach's **RAIN** practice. The four steps of RAIN are 1) recognizing what is happening using mindful, nonjudgmental awareness, 2) allowing life to be just as it is, letting things be, 3) investigating with a gentle, curious stance emphasizing somatic awareness, and 4) nurture with loving presence, offering care and tenderness (Brach, 2019). One of the things that happens when we radically accept and stop struggling against what is happening (or has happened) is that we can then use those resources to better take care of ourselves—the nurture aspect of the RAIN practice captures this element.

VALUES CLARIFICATION

Mindfulness practices can also facilitate a change in perspective through an emphasis on values, primarily through values clarification. During mindfulness practices such as choiceless awareness or mindfulness of thoughts, clients may notice certain themes that elicit intense emotions, specifically because those things matter to them. When the client discovers what is meaningful to them, it provides scaffolding for developing and strengthening a sense of identity. Clarifying values also involves identifying internalized values from others that aren't consistent with the client's true values. Values clarification also gives clients information on how to prioritize competing values when relevant situations arise.

We have discussed working with difficulty, which integrates cognitive defusion and radical acceptance; when we guide with a *values emphasis*, we reengage cognitions lightly. We add instructions: "Noticing that the thoughts and emotions that capture our attention do so because they touch on something that matters deeply to us." We invite investigation of the relevant values. Often much more intense reactions manifest when the value feels threatened, so we recommend noting the value with its polar opposite: belonging and exclusion, approval and rejection, connection and disconnection, validation and invalidation, control and freedom, and self-care and self-neglect.

These themes may be strongly related to problem behaviors or other current difficulties the client is experiencing and readily applied, facilitating a change in perspective. For example, a trauma survivor who has restricted eating for decades as a way of controlling dysregulation may identify central values of self-care, modeling healthy behaviors for their children, and freedom. If we unpack freedom, we might emphasize concepts like *food freedom* (letting go of restrictive food rules). A focus on values means that even if the client still struggles with a negative body image of their nourished body, they focus on the values that matter to them and feel clarity that these matter more than their body shape dissatisfaction.

Another helpful way to engage in values clarification is through a kōan. One of our favorites for values clarification involving moral complexity (competing values) is the old Zen kōan, "Muddy Road." This is helpful when moral issues are at the heart of therapy, as they are for clients who experienced perpetration-type moral injury (such as witnessing abuse of others and staying silent). It is helpful if they can recognize and have compassion for the other values they were protecting and that they may now have new or increased capacities to engage the values that were not upheld during the traumagenic period, countering hindsight bias and outcome-based reasoning. "Muddy Road" articulates the moral complexity involved when a rule is broken for a higher value.

Muddy Road

Tanzan and Ekido were once traveling together down a muddy road. A heavy rain was still falling. Coming around a bend, they met a lovely girl in a silk kimono and sash, unable to cross the intersection.

"Come on, girl," said Tanzan at once. Lifting her in his arms, he carried her over the mud.

Ekido did not speak again until that night when they reached a lodging temple. Then he no longer could restrain himself.

"We monks don't go near females," he told Tanzan, "especially not young and lovely ones. It is dangerous. Why did you do that?"

"I left the girl there," said Tanzan. "Are you still carrying her?"

Muddy Road's teaching on the complexity of morality can be particularly meaningful when trauma survivors were told they deserved abuse (typically physical and psychological abuse) due to their "bad" or "wrong" behavior, which often leads to self-blame. Understanding the complexity of values and morality can help the client recognize that, in fact, the behavior was serving safety, protection, or other higher values than the rules.

For example, a client whose mother physically assaulted her after she emptied her mother's bottle of alcohol because "that's not allowed" may reconceptualize that event based on emergent value themes of compliance and defiance or preoccupation and disregard for health behaviors. Clients have profound changes in perspective through thinking about the complexity of morality and comparing rules (even rules with strong rationale) to their higher values, as well as the notion that sometimes one value is discounted to promote another more meaningful or essential value.

Finally, LKM can also be engaged as a values clarification practice. Here, we emphasize the phrase selection as a distinct phase of the process, creating space for the client to identify what matters to them to offer as well-wishes when we invite them to choose their phrases for the practice. During inquiry, we explore how it felt to use these personally chosen phrases.

EQUANIMITY

Practices that enhance equanimity cultivate a change in perspective through shifting into a mindset of mental calmness and stability. This type of change in perspective involves perceiving the self as steady and stable even during great challenges. During times of adversity, hardship, and pain, equanimity practices allow clients to experience an inner steadiness and composure that is powerfully stabilizing. In more neutral or mild emotional contexts, equanimity practices promote a sense of calm and contentment, sometimes described as inner peace. This has a subdued quality, typically involving regulated physiological arousal (center of window of tolerance).

We are interested in cultivating equanimity to enhance well-being as it can be relatively stable, in contrast to pleasure, which occurs in response to certain conditions and is therefore fleeting and impermanent. Finally, equanimity also enhances resilience by allowing clients to experience that although they may not be able to control events that occur or the actions of others, they do have control over how they respond (Salzberg, 2020).

Choiceless awareness, which we discussed above as a decentering practice, is also a lovely practice for cultivating equanimity. It involves observing arising stimuli from a decentered, nonreactive perspective. The central task of the practice is decentering—to notice arising stimuli (thoughts, emotions, sensations) without engaging in thinking about the stimulus, instead simply observing it and then releasing attention from it, without pushing it away. As an emergent process that is not directly instructed or targeted in this practice, equanimity often arises in the context of such decentering.

Imagery practices can be helpful for inviting equanimity. The mindfulness element is the sensory embodiment of the imagery or the emotional experience of the imagery. The most well-recognized is mountain meditation, in which the guided imagery of the mountain stays constant through weather and seasons and various conditions, unfazed by the profound changes around it (Kabat-Zinn, 1994). The embodiment is guided in the practice (bringing the mountain into your own body) by imagining the legs as the base of the mountain and head as the peak. Another metaphor you might use for a practice is the sky as a constant behind the clouds—we look up and see the clouds, but behind that the sky itself remains unchanged.

Another imagery-based equanimity practice is the **tree with deep roots**. This is a practice we developed in response to how strongly our trauma survivor clients resonate with tree imagery. The guided imagery emphasizes how deep the roots go, steadying the tree in high winds and storms, and how the tree resources from the earth and sun for restorative processes. We note that the tree may have burls—knotty parts that signify locations of injury to the tree from environmental damage, disease, or insect attack, and we highlight the beauty of these burls to passersby and artisans. We borrow Kabat-Zinn's (1994) use of humorous wisdom, noting that the tree does not refuse rain or snow (acceptance) or push away supportive admirers (receiving social support), or feel unworthy of awe or appreciation (dignity).

Mindfulness Practices That Cultivate Change in Perspective: Self and Other

The practices that cultivate change in perspective on self and other are antidote practices (see discussion and table in chapter 9). As a reminder, an antidote relieves or counteracts a poison, and we conceptualize antidotes as neutralizing, reducing, or disrupting a painful or problematic emotional or cognitive process. These practices facilitate changes in perspective through teaching us new ways of relating to difficulties within ourselves or in our relationships with others. We are deeply affected by how we treat ourselves and others and by whether we perceive ourselves as having some connection broadly with all other beings.

> Mindfulness Practices That Cultivate Change in Perspective: Self and Other
>
> **Self-Compassion**
> - Tenderness and self-compassion
> - Self-compassionate body scan
> - Loving-kindness
>
> **Compassion**
> - Loving-kindness
> - Compassion for others' hardships
> - Tonglen
>
> **Interconnectedness**
> - Loving-kindness with emphasis on common humanity
> - Tonglen

SELF-COMPASSION

Self-compassion is an antidote to self-berating, self-loathing, and self-destructive behaviors. For some clients, self-compassion creates a shift in perspective around the ways that they want to treat themselves and speak to themselves internally, while for others, the shift is how they relate to and feel toward their bodies and taking care of their bodies. As discussed earlier in the chapter, remember to anticipate backdraft and discuss it during inquiry following practice.

For clients with harsh self-criticism, it is a new way of approaching hardships where there are things to learn, compassionately present with the parts that are painful and still able to take lessons learned for the future (note the integration of dialectical thinking). Because self-criticism typically serves the purpose of ensuring one remembers for next time, we emphasize the importance of gently helping oneself gather lessons learned, highlighting this is a future-focused alternative to self-berating for past mistakes or failures.

For clients who experience self-loathing, self-compassion is extremely challenging but also, when accessible, exceptionally healing. Clients may have generalized self-loathing but also often have specific self-loathing. For these clients, self-compassion practices should be introduced by first focusing on compassion for aspects of the self that are not loathed, if available. Then parts that are loathed can be integrated into existing self-compassion practices focused on neutral aspects, and finally practices that focus on self-compassion for loathed aspects.

If a client finds self-compassion inaccessible, bolstering is needed. Our go-to strategy is encouraging the client to find a picture of themselves when they were young—ideally, one in which they look sad, confused, or scared—and bring it into session. We then guide a practice in self-compassion for the young self, keeping the eyes open during the practice to look at the picture or closing the eyes and opening them to look at it when helpful. This is typically quite powerful. If needed, the picture can be used during standard self-compassion practices (below) as well.

Self-compassion is transformative for clients whose psychological adaptations included behaviors that provided short-term relief (or control, self-validation of pain, and so forth) but in the long term were harmful to them (such as self-harm, food restriction, or addiction). These behaviors often occurred in the context of painful stimuli (as escape or control behaviors performing emotion regulation functions), and as part of maintaining these behaviors, they undervalued self-care and self-protection and overvalued immediate distance from the pain or distress. When clients develop increased self-compassion, they often feel they can begin to heal their relationships with their bodies. As related to current harmful behaviors (mental or behavioral), the more connected the client is to caring about themselves, the harder it is to engage in self-destructive behaviors, and the more invested they are in trying to develop new ways of relating to hardship.

We have some suggested practices here. Note that self-compassion can also be integrated into other practices by adding sentences in the guidance that invite self-compassion. For example, "Taking a moment, as we notice the pain or sadness that is here, to soften and perhaps offer some compassion toward yourself, knowing you endured all of that trauma or adversity and still carry pain or sadness from it."

A practice we often begin with is **tenderness and self-compassion**, which emphasizes fostering a tender and caring stance toward yourself. This practice leverages the multiple meanings of *tender*—it is both the painful quality of the wound (*it still feels tender*) and the soft, gentle stance toward it (*approaching it tenderly*). Because the tenderness of the wound is so salient in the moment, the pivot to a gentle, caring stance using the same word appears to become more available. The following example script is of inquiry following this practice.

Example Script: *Facilitating Inquiry Following Tenderness and Self-Compassion*

Therapist: What body sensations were you aware of during the practice?

Client: My dry mouth, the pain in my shoulder, a stirred up, uncomfortable feeling in my stomach.

Therapist: How did you respond to the body sensations that you noticed?

Client: I moved the way my arm was resting, and the pain lessened. I put my hand on my belly when you suggested that… that felt comforting. That surprised me.

Therapist: I'm moved to see your increased responsiveness; it's a lovely expression of self-compassion.

Client: I'm seeing that responsiveness helps me know *how* to take better care of myself. I want to practice listening and responding to my body.

Therapist: I'm enjoying your curiosity. How is this way of noticing different from your typical way?

Client: I feel more connected to myself when I'm responsive and not just ignoring my physical needs.

Therapist: How meaningful. This feels particularly recovery-oriented in the context of the neglect that you experienced as a child, and the ways you inadvertently maintained that as an adult.

Client: I see that. It's powerful to feel like I'm ready to take care of myself now.

Another practice we often integrate is the **self-compassionate body scan**. This practice is similar to the standard body scan from chapter 8; however, rather than emphasizing body awareness, the guidance in this practice focuses on acknowledging and recognizing ways that experiences have been hard on the body, ways that the body has suffered or endured hardship, and feeling compassion toward that hardship. If you are aware that the client has somatic trauma sequelae, you integrate that into the practice; for example, "Bringing awareness to the shoulder, especially the shoulder that your mother injured in her rage and violence. Offering compassion to the shoulder that still feels the legacy of chronic soreness and vulnerability from that injury."

Finally, the ultimate practice for changes in perspective on the self and other is **LKM**, as it incorporates self-compassion, compassion for others, and interconnectedness, making it potent for extensive changes in perspective. Our clients often describe perspective shifts cultivated by this practice as transformative; many also observe that LKM enhances equanimity (emergent process), consistent with traditional Buddhist conceptualization of the practice.

The LKM invites us to offer loving-kindness well-wishes (for example, *May I be safe, May I be happy, May I be healthy, May I live life with ease*) for a series of recipients, including ourselves;

phrases can be tailored, for example, trauma survivors may appreciate the traditional phrase, *May I be safe from danger.* We articulate that all these wishes are aspirational in a world where people are oppressed, exploited, and harmed by extreme violence (Salzberg, 2020).

The practice typically begins with application to oneself, then calling to mind someone who has supported or helped them, then a neutral acquaintance, then someone challenging, then all beings. However, we typically do not begin with self-compassion, as we find it is often the most challenging due to psychological adaptations to trauma and backdraft. Instead, we place it at the end, after all beings, with the guidance "… And one of these beings is you. Letting awareness rest here, turning these well-wishes toward ourselves."

Note that initially, we provide guidance that someone challenging should not be the perpetrator of abuse. Once they are comfortable with the practice, many clients do find it helpful, particularly in the common context that perpetrators of abuse are still part of the client's life. Nonetheless, we do not recommend starting with individuals who are also a trauma cue, as we are trying to help clients use these practices in their window of tolerance.

COMPASSION

Compassion for others is an antidote to anger, contempt, hatred, disappointment, and hurt, as it facilitates a change in perspective about another, which can soften hard feelings and (re) introduce some sense of care and shared common humanity. Willingness is essential; it would not be trauma-informed to apply these practices toward an object of compassion that the client feels reluctant to target. Thus, when introducing a contextually driven compassion practice, we ask, "Would it be helpful to use a compassion practice to bring some compassion for (person) into the mix?" Note that the "into the mix" framing communicates that this does not negate or invalidate the anger, disappointment, or hurt (dialectical thinking).

LKM emphasizes compassion for others in most of its targets (see details above). You can engage the full practice or a titrated form of LKM, **compassion for others' hardships,** which focuses on just one object of well-wishes. For this practice, the client chooses an object that they would like to offer compassion to (such as a friend experiencing adversity) or someone for whom compassion would be a helpful antidote to current emotions (such as a frustrating colleague or toddler with behavioral problems). We provide guidance that emphasizes recognition of this person's various hardships. We do this by having the client offer information about known hardship prior or during the practice and then we guide based on that. Clients often report feeling connected to beloved others who are struggling and having more dialectical emotions and softening toward challenging objects of compassion.

One of the more challenging and powerful practices is **tonglen**, a practice of inhaling pain or suffering and exhaling compassion as an offering for others. The object can be someone they care about who is struggling or a group that is struggling (such as a war-torn region or children experiencing abuse). This practice can be challenging the first time; however, often by the second practice the client begins to cultivate a change in the relationship to their sadness or pain about the suffering object, different from the client's habitual way of interacting with this content. This practice often reduces a client's sense of helplessness when loved ones are struggling.

INTERCONNECTEDNESS

Practices that cultivate interconnectedness facilitate changes in perspective on self and others by cultivating a sense of connection to all of humanity, nature, all sentient beings, and so forth. Interconnectedness can be an antidote to loneliness, disconnection from others, and hatred toward others. It can be unrelated to physical proximity or mutuality, which makes this a very accessible way to feel connected, even for clients whose trauma adaptations include severe interpersonal difficulties. To some clients, the concept of interconnectedness can sound esoteric and inaccurate, so we often give science-based metaphors from nature (for example, the oxygen we breathe comes from oceanic and land plant photosynthesis, or aspen groves with shared roots).

The practices we use to cultivate interconnectedness are the same as those described above for compassion. However, for interconnectedness practice, we emphasize common humanity aspects. For LKM, we may choose to only focus on the level of all beings or we may emphasize common humanity within the well-wishes by including guidance at the other person level, such as *She suffers like I suffer, She grieves like I grieve, She fears harm to her family like I fear harm to my family*, and similarly at the broader level of all beings by changing the pronoun to *they*.

For tonglen, we emphasize instruction on noticing that we can take on a practice that produces an offering for someone whom we are targeting. The nature metaphors discussed above are useful in discussing transformational aspects of tonglen, as they offer scientifically established analogous processes.

Clinical Application Summary

All of the changes in perspective can be profoundly transformative. These can be taught and discussed and yet experientially they are emergent, arising out of mindfulness practice—in particular continued formal mindfulness practice. They include shifts in perspective on one's thoughts, mindset, and relationship to self and others. Using case conceptualization, we identify the most helpful processes to target (corresponding to areas of greatest difficulty or impairment) and engage practices from that section to invite shifts in perspective for our clients. Note that these practices are quite abstract, and if clients struggle with them, it may be helpful to first build capacities using attention regulation or body awareness practices.

Part 4

Additional Considerations for the Mindful Trauma Therapist

CHAPTER 11

Therapists' Reactions to Working with Trauma

Working with trauma survivors inherently involves extensive therapist attention to trauma and its lasting legacy through trauma adaptations. Trauma itself—particularly interpersonal trauma with its intentionality—is horrific and disturbing at a deep, moral level. We come face-to-face with this over and over in our work, alongside the client's enduring suffering. Dialectically, beside that lies the power of resilience, the beauty of healing and recovery, and transformation through post-traumatic growth and meaning-making. We do our best to focus on the latter. Nonetheless, we can be affected by the malevolence, cruelty, and sadism we may be exposed to. Learning about symptoms that therapists may experience and how to respond to them is a crucial part of the mindful trauma therapist's professional development, and building these capacities becomes a cornerstone of a sustainable practice.

It is helpful to think of trauma therapists as professionals who experience indirect exposure to trauma. Depending on the specifics of our work, we may have a great deal of trauma exposure or just some. Frequency and detail level of exposure is linked to clinician trauma symptoms. It is helpful to think of this as an occupational challenge for all trauma therapists rather than a clinician-specific challenge. Trauma-informed approaches emphasize clinician wellness and integrate attention to secondary traumatic stress (STS), empathic strain, and burnout.

Trauma therapists are extra attentive to ethical issues, and our care for ourselves is a central ethical factor given that *we ourselves* are the instrument or tool we work with in psychotherapy.

> It is our responsibility to attend to difficulties when they arise, work on the areas that disrupt or impede our clinical abilities or inhibit our flexible behavioral repertoire in session, and to continuously and intentionally expand our window of tolerance.

Addressing relational trauma involves relational healing, thus psychotherapy with survivors of interpersonal trauma requires special attention to relational elements. We need to be psychologically healthy to do our best work. Moreover, trauma survivors have often adapted to be highly emotionally attuned; those who lived with unpredictable, unreliable, and sometimes abusive attachment figures may hypermonitor a therapist's nonverbal responses. Our struggles with our own wellness may inadvertently be visible at times.

It is not our responsibility to never struggle. STS is an inherent risk involved in working with trauma. Instead, it is our responsibility to attend to difficulties when they arise, work on the areas that disrupt or impede our clinical abilities or inhibit our flexible behavioral repertoire in session, and to continuously and intentionally expand our own window of tolerance. This means we have an ethical commitment to *trauma stewardship*, building our capacity to tolerate, accept, and process painful emotions in ourselves and others. Trauma stewardship is the daily practice of tending to hardship, pain, or trauma, tending to and responsibly guiding those who are struggling without taking their hardships on as our own, and continuously developing our ability to be fully present in our experience, even (or perhaps especially) when difficult (van Dernoot Lipsky & Burk, 2009).

Manifestations of Therapist Difficulties

Therapist difficulties may manifest as STS, empathic strain, and burnout. Each of these are distinct constructs, and it is helpful for us to be aware of each of them, practice preventative measures, identify and monitor for warning signs, and intervene as needed.

One of the central ways that working with trauma can take a toll on therapists is *STS*, also referred to as vicarious traumatization. STS involves post-traumatic stress disorder (PTSD) from indirect trauma exposure to disturbing details (APA, 2013) in addition to alterations in personal and professional systems of meaning beyond PTSD (moral distress, decreased empathy, diminished professional self-efficacy, and feeling stigmatized; Sprang et al., 2019). These reactions are important if they affect clinician wellness and professional functioning, even if they are subthreshold of a PTSD diagnosis.

For example, clinicians might experience intrusive thoughts about a particular event that a client detailed, new mistrusting thoughts about others in their lives, increased worries about vulnerability to harm (such as yourself or your children), or intense moral distress about the cruelty that exists in our world. These symptoms of STS are important to notice and intervene on, even if a full-blown PTSD constellation is not present.

Empathic strain, also referred to as compassion fatigue, can occur when we begin to take our clients' difficulties on as our own. Empathy for pain involves emotionally participating in the pain of others and actually activates the same neural networks in the brain that control the direct experience of pain. In contrast, compassion involves the motivation to help by offering care and concern. Singer and Klimecki (2014) highlight that empathy is a self-oriented emotion that blurs self–other distinctions, whereas compassion is an other-oriented emotion with distinct self–other boundaries. This is even evident in our language: *empathy with* and *compassion for*. Further, neuroscience studies demonstrate that empathy and compassion training elicit changes in differential brain networks with an opposite affective experience. Empathy is associated with negative affect (like stress) and the urge to withdraw, while compassion is associated with positive affect (like love) and the urge to help.

Burnout is a prolonged response to chronic emotional and interpersonal stressors on the job; it is a *stress response*. However, burnout is not related specifically to trauma exposure. Rather, it is related to the fit between the clinician and their job or organization. Decades of research identified six positive aspects that promote engagement and well-being when there is strong job–therapist fit. These same factors contribute to burnout when fit is poor: 1) sustainable workload, 2) choice and control, 3) recognition and reward, 4) supportive work community, 5) fairness, respect, and social justice, and 6) clear values and meaningful work (Maslach, 2017).

For therapists, a problematic fit contributing to burnout may include high expected caseloads (unsustainable productivity demands), lack of control to set desired limits with clients, receiving only critical or corrective feedback, discrimination, or a cynical and pessimistic work community. The research highlights that burnout is the result of situational and environmental factors just as much as employee-level personal variables, and that social relationships in the work context can contribute to or mitigate problems through enhanced connection, support, and meaning (Maslach, 2017).

All of these factors intersect with other important dimensions of our own life experiences. These include our personal context and circumstances (such as stressors, family illness, or parenting challenges), sociocultural context and how it relates to aspects of our own identity (see chapter 1, "Traumatic Invalidation"), and personal trauma experiences. Contributing factors to our traumatic stress may include overt trauma and insidious or covert trauma experiences. Although true for all therapists, intersectionality—the interlocking oppressive forces that are associated with our various identities—creates social conditions of injustice that interact to compound traumagenic factors (Gómez, 2023). Therefore, traumatic invalidation, discrimination, tokenization, and other traumagenic experiences disproportionately impact therapists who identify as Black, Indigenous, and People of Color (BIPOC); lesbian, gay, bisexual, transgender, queer or questioning, intersex, and asexual, aromantic, or agender, and others (LGBTQIA+); ethnic minorities, immigrants, or stigmatized religious minorities; and so forth.

The contributors from our personal traumatic stress exposures are both a risk factor and, dialectically, a strength. Our experience of traumatic stress contributes to vulnerability of STS, and at the same time provides us with profound personal knowledge about the depth of pain and the extraordinary power of recovery processes and healing, which allows us to embody transformative qualities relevant to recovery processes (Zerubavel & Wright, 2012). Our professional identity may be directly linked to our own post-traumatic growth, a result of finding meaning and purpose through recovery from trauma. The more resolved our personal trauma-related reactions are, the more likely our history is resourcing rather than disadvantaging.

Furthermore, we must engage in appropriate self–other differentiation. We cannot assume that our recovery journey informs what others need for theirs. When clinical difficulties related to our trauma histories arise, we recommend consultation or supervision. We encourage having a trusted consultant, supervisor, or peer consultation group with expertise in trauma with whom you feel comfortable being vulnerable and sharing personal difficulties. For this, we recognize that our field needs to continue to improve in normalizing and destigmatizing therapists' personal trauma, consistent with how we approach client trauma with compassion and support (Zerubavel & Wright, 2012).

Getting Educated and Identifying Your Warning Signs

The best way to address therapist difficulties is through learning about STS, empathic strain, and burnout; engaging in prevention through capacity building; monitoring our own symptom levels; and intervening when needed. We can leverage our clinical knowledge to monitor our wellness and identify warning signs when we are struggling with STS, empathic strain, or burnout. Nonetheless, we may not do this. If we do have difficulty applying this knowledge to ourselves, let's become curious about that—*is it due to lack of self-awareness, lack of knowledge or recognition of these constructs as relevant to clinicians, or our self-neglect?*

We begin by learning more. We recommend two excellent resource collections on STS. The first is the National Child Traumatic Stress Network (NCTSN), whose STS collaborative group has disseminated helpful materials and fact sheets on this topic (http://www.nctsn.org/trauma-informed-care/secondary-traumatic-stress/nctsn-resources). The second is the Secondary Traumatic Stress Consortium, which offers information, resources, and training on STS (http://www.stsconsortium.com/free-resources). Their extensive resources include presentations, assessment tools, and recommended books, podcasts, and websites.

Self-Awareness and Self-Monitoring

In STS, the symptoms of PTSD are accompanied by changes in personal and professional systems of meaning such as moral distress, decreased empathy, diminished professional self-efficacy, and feeling stigmatized (Sprang et al., 2019). We encourage you to practice self-awareness and self-attunement, noting STS symptoms when and if they arise. The STS Consortium provides assessment tools for measuring STS and the Center for Victims of Torture provides the Professional Quality of Life: Health Worker (ProQol-H; Center for Victims of Torture, 2021) assessment with scales measuring STS, burnout, moral distress, perceived support, and compassion satisfaction (http://proqol.org/proqol-health-1).

Burnout includes symptoms in three areas: exhaustion, cynicism, and a decline in sense of professional efficacy (Maslach, 2017). You may attend to these factors in your work. Note that the ProQol-H described above includes a burnout scale, so this measure provides an effective way to monitor both STS and burnout, as well as other relevant dimensions. Remember that burnout is related to person–job or organization fit, so consider those elements as well when you are increasing self-awareness in this domain.

Empathic strain will be evident when you share your client's pain, struggle with self–other separation related to your client(s), and feel like you have nothing left to give (or no desire to give) to a particular client or clients in general. Empathic strain is marked by negative affect (likely resonant with a client's salient trauma-related affect) and the urge to withdraw. You may feel irritated by your client(s), frustrated, or resentful. We encourage you to pay attention to these signals, as empathic strain is emotionally depleting and impedes our therapeutic abilities.

Across time, if you are self-aware and monitoring your symptoms of STS, burnout, and empathic strain, you will learn more about how these therapist difficulties show up for you. We are particularly interested in identifying early warning signs, as it is always easier to intervene earlier than after symptoms have intensified. We recommend building our personal STS toolkit with personalized systems for monitoring early warning signs, applying routine prevention strategies, and implementing intervention plans.

Strategies for Prevention and Intervention

Our strategies can be used for both prevention and intervention related to STS, empathic strain, and burnout. When we use the skills on a regular basis, they can help decrease the likelihood of developing STS, empathic strain, and burnout. However, when increased symptom manifestations do occur, these same strategies may also act as intervention strategies, mitigating worsening or intensification of symptoms.

If you are struggling with intensifying symptoms, along with continuing to use helpful preventative strategies (for instance, self-care or Components for Enhancing Clinician Experience & Reducing Trauma [CE-CERT]), we encourage you to add additional intervention strategies. Of course, if you are using these interventions but experience continuing or worsening symptoms, or if your reactions are extremely intense or disruptive, then external resourcing may be needed or helpful. In this case, we encourage you to seek supervision or consultation (particularly with an STS specialist) or seek personal therapy focusing on the relevant difficulties with an STS-informed trauma therapist, especially if disruption is pervasive.

Frequency, Depth, and Pervasiveness of Trauma Exposure

The degree of trauma exposure we experience is a matter of frequency, depth, and pervasiveness. TEND Academy (2020) suggests assessing trauma exposure in our daily routines. First, consider how you start your day, what routines or habits are in place, and whether they involve disturbing images of pain and suffering and distressing or violent stories. Second, consider the frequency of trauma exposure at work: does it involve trauma details, is your caseload some or mostly trauma, and what contexts (for example, clinical services, team meetings, reviewing case files, or office drop-ins from colleagues) are the sources? Finally, consider evenings and weekends: are you consuming the news, and if watching TV or movies, are those violent or aggressive?

In our experience conducting trainings for established clinicians, it is astonishing how many clinicians who work with trauma go home and watch shows centered specifically on trauma (such as *Law & Order*). These questions are powerful because they bring into focus the extent of overall trauma exposure we have. Furthermore, they invite questions about pervasiveness. For example, would you like to have a part of your day or a day of your week that are not trauma-loaded? We begin to see that while some areas may be necessary and meaningful (such as clinical services), others may not be necessary or may be easily reducible if we choose to decrease overall trauma exposure.

In our direct clinical work, there is no question that we must build the capacities to stay present with the painful experiences that our clients have been through, including the agonizing emotions that may accompany them. In colleague debriefings, consultation team meetings, and case conferences, details of trauma can be effectively limited using the low-impact debriefing method described momentarily.

Bear in mind that supervisees who are in training (unlicensed) or are licensed but struggling with disruption to workplace functioning should be encouraged to debrief as fully as needed for them to process what they are reacting to in the material when in individual (not group) supervision. In such circumstances, the supervisor resources the supervisee by helping them hold horrific, unbearable, or devastating trauma content.

We can reduce unnecessary trauma exposure in highly trauma-exposed environments by practicing Mathieu's (2012) **low-impact debriefing**, which involves four steps to reduce the sharing of unnecessarily graphic details. The first step is *self-awareness* about context and appropriateness of trauma-related discussion as well as what one is seeking from the interaction and whether details (such as violent, gruesome, or

Low-Impact Debriefing
1. Self-awareness
2. Fair warning
3. Consent
4. Limited disclosure

psychologically disturbing elements) are at all relevant. Unless the consultation need is actually about the details (for instance, a mandated reporting question), then the details are unnecessary. Even in debriefing, our needs center on our emotions or thoughts, not the content of what we heard.

The second step is *fair warning*, which involves letting the other person(s) know that we are about to share a difficult or disturbing story. This orients them and gives them a chance to prepare themselves internally. The third step is *consent*, which involves asking for permission to proceed, awaiting affirmative consent before proceeding (silence is not a green light).

Finally, we share using limited disclosure without grotesque or particularly disturbing details. High-level or categorical descriptions (highly titrated versions) are extremely helpful here. For example, one might share, "I'm having a hard time getting details of a particularly violent trauma description out of my head." The details themselves are, in fact, not relevant at all to getting help with trauma-related intrusive thoughts, which is what is needed here. Just knowing there are intrusive thoughts is enough to allow colleagues to offer strategies for addressing intrusions, such as the cognitive task memory interference procedure discussed below, responding to painful emotions, and containment followed by emotional and cognitive processing in a resourcing context.

Most of the time it is not about the details, yet dialectically, occasionally it is. At those times, practice low-impact debriefing with an emphasis on fair warning, including if the story has violent or cruel details or describing as relevant for informed consent, still limiting to only necessary details. Low-impact debriefing is for colleagues, team spaces, and presentations, whereas in supervision (and with clients) we encourage open sharing of the details necessary for client or supervisee processing. This is a lovely way to help others in your environment limit their indirect trauma exposure. Encourage others to use this as well.

Responding to Indirect Trauma Exposure

Even as we find ways to limit the frequency and pervasiveness of our trauma exposure, we can still be exposed to graphic details of horrific, disturbing, or gory details of trauma events in our direct clinical service, in supervision, and sometimes in emails or voicemails from individuals seeking therapy. When this occurs, there are a variety of techniques to use that can help you prevent or reduce associated trauma symptoms.

Shift from empathy (with) to compassion (for). When you notice empathic strain, inhibit the urge to withdraw to protect yourself, and instead protect yourself by shifting to compassion, noticing how the urge shifts to motivate you to help alleviate suffering and shifts from negative to positive emotional valence. Try to prevent or interrupt mirroring of client gestures and facial expressions (Rothschild, 2000). Emphasize mental separation between self and other. Even as you hold compassion for the other; internally emphasize the self–other boundary rather than empathic resonance. Our manner does not need to be cold or detached to hold boundaries; rather, we remain warm and compassionate.

Avoid and disrupt visualization. As much as possible, avoid visualization and disrupt any that inadvertently occurs. Even in a treatment like prolonged exposure (PE), where we ask the client to visualize the event, the therapist does not need to participate in visualization. It is not our memory that is being reconsolidated through emotional processing. Instead, we are doing our therapist activities: observing the client signs of hyperarousal or hypoarousal, looking for hot spots, getting periodic distress and physiological arousal ratings, and listening for new information related to key trauma-related cognitions.

If visualization occurs, *create distance* by turning it to black-and-white or making it far away like a zoom lens zooming out farther and farther (Rothschild, 2022).

Disrupt consolidation of visual elements of memory. If you experience visualization of a client's trauma, you may be able disrupt the consolidation of this into an intrusive image through a simple visuospatial interference task (Tetris). This task interferes with the consolidation of sensory elements of memory associated with intrusions. *Do not use another game as other visuospatial games do not appear to serve the interference function.* Tetris appears to be particularly helpful due to the mental rotation involved. Results are impressive in reducing intrusions. For example, Iyadurai and colleagues (2023) found that engaging in this imagery-competing task intervention in COVID-19 intensive care staff reduced the baseline median of fourteen intrusive memories per day to *one* per day four weeks post intervention, compared to a control group with *ten* per day.

This procedure is ideally applied *within six hours* following the indirect trauma exposure that you feel may develop into intrusive symptoms. Engage the memory interference procedure. This can also be applied *after six hours* by adding an additional step of *waiting ten minutes* before playing Tetris for increased memory malleability (Iyadurai et al., 2023).

> **Memory Interference Procedure to Reduce Intrusive Memories**
>
> 1. Find a Tetris website or app (many free options).
> 2. Engage a memory reactivation method (written account or describing hot spots).
> 3. If it is > six hours since indirect trauma exposure, wait ten minutes. If it is < six hours, proceed to step 4.
> 4. Play Tetris for fifteen to twenty minutes, engaging mental rotation.

Skills for reducing STS. We recommend Brian Miller's (2021) book, *Reducing Secondary Traumatic Stress*, in which he offers a skills-based model called CE-CERT. His framework emphasizes that reducing STS cannot be targeted only through self-care strategies that are allotted to evenings and weekends. Instead, he emphasizes strategies for changing the experience of doing our work *during the workday*. He also emphasizes substituting active responses for passive responses to reduce therapist helplessness and overwhelm in the face of threat, which he conceptualizes as central contributors to STS.

CE-CERT targets five domains: 1) experiential engagement (countering avoidance), 2) reducing rumination (attentional strategies), 3) conscious narrative (intentional appraisal), 4) reducing emotional labor (decreasing emotional suppression), and 5) parasympathetic recovery (intentionally engaging skills to return to the window of tolerance throughout the day). As you can see, these skills are consistent with those we discussed in various chapters throughout the book, although here they are focused on therapist-centered applications.

Use safety-enhancing strategies as relevant. If we are in session, we try shifting our posture or position, using embodied processes to shift internal context. We engage in containment with a commitment to return in a more resourced context. Then, we anchor using our preferred anchor—somatosensory (breath in nostrils, chest, or belly; hands, feet), auditory, or visual. Finally, we integrate responsiveness to painful emotions by resourcing through learning or receiving support, engaging in restorative activities (self-care), self-soothing, and practicing self-compassion formally or informally.

Integrating Mindfulness Practices and Safety-Enhancing Strategies

As noted above, the techniques and strategies discussed throughout this book can also be applied to reduce our own difficulties and symptoms and enhance our resilience and well-being. The mindfulness practices are *capacity building*, helping us cultivate therapeutic qualities for sitting with and guiding people through deeply painful experiences and emotions. The change in perspective practices are useful to therapists in resourcing for the emotionally challenging landscape of trauma therapy. The safety-enhancing strategies help us remain in our window of tolerance (stabilizing throughout the day via intentional regulation of the autonomic nervous system [ANS]) and increasing therapist resilience (Miller, 2021).

> You can use the resources throughout this book to reduce your own symptoms, build your capacities, and enhance your resilience and well-being.

Safety-Enhancing Strategies. The safety-enhancing strategies have five functions relevant to our experience as therapists: 1) monitoring physiological arousal, 2) intentionally regulating the ANS to return to physiological equilibrium, 3) reducing emotional intensity, 4) staying in the present moment, and 5) responding to painful emotions. To monitor physiological arousal, we use body awareness and the physiological arousal scale. To regulate the nervous system intentionally, we use downregulating hyperarousal and upregulating hypoarousal strategies (select which based on your arousal experience). For high-intensity emotions, use the strategies to reduce emotional intensity (such as containment, labeling emotions, or anchoring). Use grounding techniques to stay in the present moment. To respond to painful emotions, use that category of strategies (resourcing, restorative activities, self-soothing, self-compassion).

> Therapist Uses of Safety-Enhancing Strategies
>
> 1. Monitoring physiological arousal.
> 2. Intentionally regulating the autonomic nervous system to return to physiological equilibrium.
> 3. Reducing emotional intensity.
> 4. Staying in the present moment.
> 5. Responding to painful emotions.

If you are using these strategies in session, you may do so silently and discreetly without your client's awareness; or, if suitable, you may choose to lead the strategy explicitly, integrating it into the session. For example: "Before we get started today, let's take a few minutes to do an auditory grounding practice," or "I just rushed from another building, and my physiological arousal is high, so would it be okay if we took a few minutes together for elongated exhalations to down-regulate arousal? And does that suit your physiology, or would it be better for you to do elongated inhalations for yourself?" This is simultaneously great therapist self-care and models integrations of these strategies into our daily lives. Our clients often express appreciation when they see us applying the strategies that we recommend to them.

Across time, use of these strategies allows us to expand our window of tolerance, build our capacities as clinicians, and enhance our resilience and well-being. The wider our own window of tolerance, the more capacities we are resourcing into the clinical work (Treleaven, 2018). Conversely, the narrower our window of tolerance, the more likely that it may constrain or limit our clinical work. Our expanded capacities help our clients grow and help us stay healthy in the process. Our enhanced resilience and well-being allow this to be sustainable across time while working with clients who may have very complex needs.

Mindfulness Practices. To support ourselves in times of difficulty, we turn to mindfulness practice for many of the same reasons we explain to our clients. We apply body awareness practices to become more embodied, attune to body sensations, and ground ourselves in the present moment. We apply emotion regulation practices to work with our appraisals or to build our capacity to tolerate particularly challenging emotions. We engage change in perspective practices to expand our capacities to hold space for unfathomable and devastating experiences (radical acceptance), to facilitate finding distance from the excruciating pain (decentering; compassion), and to cultivate steadiness within (equanimity).

As we have discussed throughout the book, we recommend you choose mindfulness practices thoughtfully rather than haphazardly, starting with the mechanism of mindfulness (attention, body awareness, emotion regulation, or change in perspective) you wish to target, and if relevant, identify the specific quality to cultivate and select a practice that fits the desired construct. Keep antidote practices in mind. For example, if you are experiencing empathic strain, choose compassion practices to cultivate this more helpful stance toward your clients. If you feel destabilized by the chaos in your clients' lives, choose equanimity practices to steady yourself.

Self-Compassion. In the face of painful emotions, hardship, mistakes, and failures, or when we feel our flaws are exposed, we emphasize *therapist self-compassion*. This is foundational in our intentional stance toward ourselves (Terri and Noga) and what we hope to foster in our workshops and trainings, therapy with therapist clients, consultations, and supervision. This is because self-compassion is an essential ingredient of our *willingness* to be attuned, responsive, nurturing, and caring toward ourselves. It replaces behaviors that contribute to therapist STS, such as pushing oneself past limits in times of struggle, perfectionism and unrelenting standards, harsh self-criticism or self-berating, and scathing self-judgment, with a constructive, gentle, kind alternative that can still involve commitment to doing better or differently in the future.

We may experience backdraft in response to self-compassion, as discussed in chapter 10. Try leaning in and working through your barriers. If you need further scaffolding, try using the strategy of finding a picture of yourself as a child, especially one with some sad or challenging quality or one from a difficult time, and see if that invites self-compassion. As an example, here are the ones that we (Noga and Terri) use for ourselves.

If it is hard to engage in self-compassion, you might try looking at the picture and saying the habitual things (such as self-berating or perfectionistic demands) and noticing how that feels. We can also explore self-care (attunement and responsiveness) as a behavioral form of self-compassion.

Conclusion

In this chapter, we provide resources for further education and assessment tools to enhance therapist self-awareness. We suggest ways to use the resources within this book for enhancing our own wellness and reducing symptoms in the context of work that may include extensive indirect trauma exposure. We encourage the use of mindfulness practices—particularly the change in perspective practices (acceptance, self-compassion, compassion, cognitive defusion, equanimity, and interconnectedness)—and safety-enhancing strategies to support therapist well-being and sustainable practice.

The landscape of trauma is aggression, victimization, violence, and cruelty. We bear witness to this, and across time, we may be changed by those experiences. We want to keep an eye on this. To the extent that this allows us to be profoundly dialectical, deeply acknowledging pain and suffering while also capable of compassion and hope, this can enhance our clinical abilities working with trauma. To the extent that this leads to our own distress, despair, or disruptions in functioning, this can be a real hazard in our occupation. As we have been discussing throughout the book, our responses influence the trajectory of symptoms, and this is where we concentrate our efforts when clinician difficulties arise. We encourage mindful trauma therapists to take care of themselves with intentionality, integrating self-compassion during times of difficulty, struggle, and painful emotions.

Conclusion

Our goal in writing this book was to provide a resource for clinicians who want to incorporate mindfulness practices into psychotherapy with trauma survivors in a safe, intentional manner. From the outset, we wanted to make explicit our values of integrating trauma-sensitive principles and the principles of mindfulness. The process-based approach enhances flexibility and choice so that the clinician can maximize responsiveness and the client has a sense of control and autonomy. We hope our framework will help clinicians thoughtfully engage in numerous mindfulness options based on case conceptualization and optimize choices for treatment planning that both enhance client empowerment and maximize safety. We can accomplish this when we, as clinicians, fully understand the mechanisms of mindfulness that underlie why and how mindfulness practices can benefit trauma survivors.

Although the process-based approach is not formulaic, it does have central tenets that permeate throughout the framework. First, our own mindfulness helps to create an atmosphere for integrating this into psychotherapy. As clinicians, we embody the key facets of mindfulness when working with trauma survivors, modeling curiosity and nonjudgment, openness and awareness, nonstriving, acceptance, equanimity, and compassion. We walk beside our clients on their journey, serving as a guide with expertise rather than as an expert. To do this, we use the method of inquiry to process mindfulness practices experientially to build client awareness, put observations in context, facilitate consolidation, and generate insight.

Engaging in mindfulness practices and participating in the process of inquiry creates the opportunity for trauma survivors to learn to trust their experiences, paving the road to recovery. Another central tenet of the process-based approach is our emphasis on flexibility and responsiveness. We are responsive to the client's needs when selecting and guiding the trauma survivor through mindfulness practices or trauma processing, helping to modulate or titrate client overwhelm in a way that promotes the expansion of the trauma survivor's window of tolerance while maintaining safety.

One of the central values in our framework is that of safety. Our process-based approach to integrating mindfulness into psychotherapy with trauma survivors emphasizes safety with regard to mindfulness practice, trauma processing, and by attending to trauma-sensitive principles. This approach promotes treatment flexibility, as we modulate the use of mindfulness skills and the amount of trauma processing for the client to stay physiologically regulated. We accomplish this through our focus on developing the client's ability to intentionally regulate ANS arousal. We can facilitate the maintenance of adaptive levels of physiological arousal through mindfulness and safety-enhancing strategies. We use the window of tolerance to help the client notice approaching overwhelm by assessing physiological arousal. We teach the skills in session, and through home practice, the trauma survivor generalizes the skills by independently engaging in responses to self-regulate outside of therapy. Our ongoing monitoring of arousal promotes therapist and client responsiveness, which helps the client stay in or return to the window of tolerance.

The process of engaging safely in mindfulness practice brings with it the opportunity for trauma survivors to observe their habitual reactions that developed in a traumagenic context. Conceptualizing current symptoms as trauma adaptations is powerful because the trauma survivor can see the function of their responses and recognize when and how they were adaptive, at least at one point in time. This concept of trauma adaptations opens the door to self-understanding and self-compassion for the traumatized self, creating an opportunity for the survivor to relate to their past traumatic experiences and their adaptations with compassion and understanding rather than judgment and self-criticism. This intersection is essential.

When we conceptualize trauma adaptations as functional with an attitude of mindfulness that includes warmth, self-compassion, nonjudgment, and acceptance, we reduce shame and self-blame and can destigmatize trauma adaptations. These capacities enhance the trauma survivor's ability to experience painful emotional states during trauma processing and promote healing.

We cannot forget that many of the difficulties our clients face originated from a traumagenic context. The experience of trauma, especially child abuse, neglect, or intimate partner violence, affects the sense of self and, importantly, the capacity for providing oneself compassion and self-care. We conceptualize responsiveness and self-care as a correction to the earlier experiences of abuse and neglect. In this act, the trauma survivor is both acknowledging and grieving what was lost and learning to provide for themselves the care they did not receive earlier. The mindfulness attitudes of acceptance and nonjudgment can carry the trauma survivor forward as they deepen their capacity for self-compassion.

This work of helping trauma survivors heal is inspiring, hope instilling, and deeply moving. This journey takes immense courage and requires vast resources, primarily internal and relational. As the therapist is the guide, the therapist ensures preparation of the resources and leads the way bravely. We trek with our clients into territories that they may have believed were far too dangerous to risk, and with the right resources, we find that we can be safe there.

Sometimes facilitating trauma recovery feels like a loving-kindness practice emphasizing the client. We wish our clients all the well-wishes of courageous healing and flourishing. We offer these wishes to all the trauma survivors who are suffering and searching for recovery and to all the extraordinary therapists who are building toolkits to guide them.

References

Aldao, A., Nolen-Hoeksema, S., & Schweizer, S. (2010). Emotion-regulation strategies across psychopathology: A meta-analytic review. *Clinical Psychology Review, 30*(2), 217–237. http://doi.org/10.1016/j.cpr.2009.11.004

American Psychiatric Association. (2013). *Diagnostic and Statistical Manual of Mental Disorders* (5th ed.). http://doi.org/10.1176/appi.books.9780890425596

Anderson, T., & Farb, N. A. S. (2018). Personalising practice using preferences for meditation anchor modality. *Frontiers in Psychology, 9,* 2521. http://doi.org/10.3389/fpsyg.2018.02521

Banks, K., Newman, E., & Saleem, J. (2015). An overview of the research on mindfulness-based interventions for treating symptoms of posttraumatic stress disorder: A systematic review. *Journal of Clinical Psychology, 71*(10), 935–963. http://doi.org/10.1002/jclp.22200

Barber, C. W., & Miller, M. J. (2014). Reducing a suicidal person's access to lethal means of suicide: A research agenda. *American Journal of Preventive Medicine, 47*(3 Suppl 2), S264–S272. http://doi.org/10.1016/j.amepre.2014.05.028

Benjet, C., Bromet, E., Karam, E. G., Kessler, R. C., McLaughlin, K. A., Ruscio, A. M., Shahly, V., et al. (2016). The epidemiology of traumatic event exposure worldwide: Results from the World Mental Health Survey Consortium. *Psychological Medicine, 46*(2), 327–343. http://doi.org/10.1017/S0033291715001981

Bodkin, J. A., Pope, H. J., Detke, M. J., & Hudson, J. I. (2007). Is PTSD caused by traumatic stress? *Journal of Anxiety Disorders, 21*(2), 176–182. http://doi.org/10.1016/j.janxdis.2006.09.004

Bond, F. W., Hayes, S. C., Baer, R. A., Carpenter, K. M., Guenole, N., Orcutt, H. K., Waltz, T., & Zettle, R. D. (2011). Preliminary psychometric properties of the Acceptance and Action Questionnaire-II: A revised measure of psychological inflexibility and experiential avoidance. *Behavior Therapy, 42*(4), 676–688. http://doi.org/10.1016/j.beth.2011.03.007

Brach, T. (2004). *Radical Acceptance: Embracing Your life with the Heart of a Buddha.* New York: Bantam.

Brach, T. (2019). *Radical Compassion: Learning to Love Yourself and Your World with the Practice of RAIN.* New York: Penguin Life.

Briere, J. N., & Scott, C. (2015). *Principles of Trauma Therapy: A Guide to Symptoms, Evaluation, and Treatment 2nd edition, DSM-5 Update.* Thousand Oaks: SAGE Publications.

Britton, W. B. (2016). Scientific literacy as a foundational competency for teachers of mindfulness-based interventions. In D. McCown, D. Reibel, & M. S. Miccozzi (Eds.), *Resources for Teaching Mindfulness: An International Handbook* (pp. 93–119). Springer International Publishing. http://doi.org/10.1007/978-3-319-30100-6_5

Britton, W. B. (2019). Can mindfulness be too much of a good thing? The value of a middle way. *Current Opinion in Psychology, 28,* 159–165. http://doi.org/10.1016/j.copsyc.2018.12.011

Bromberg, P. M. (2006). *Awakening the Dreamer: Clinical Journeys.* Mahwah, NJ: Analytic Press.

Center for Victims of Torture. (2021). *Professional Quality of Life Scale for Health Workers, Version 1.* http://proqol.org/proqol-health-1

Chambers, R., Gullone, E., & Allen, N. B. (2009). Mindful emotion regulation: An integrative review. *Clinical Psychology Review, 29*(6), 560–572. http://doi.org/10.1016/j.cpr.2009.06.005

Chödrön, P. (2007). *The Places That Scare You: A Guide to Fearlessness in Difficult Times.* Boulder, CO: Shambhala Publications.

Cicchetti, D., Ackerman, B. P., & Izard, C. E. (1995). Emotions and emotion regulation in developmental psychopathology. *Development and Psychopathology, 7*(1), 1–10. http://doi.org/10.1017/S0954579400006301

Clark, C., Classen, C. C., Fourt, A., & Shetty, M. (2015). *Treating the Trauma Survivor: An Essential Guide to Trauma-Informed Care.* Routledge/Taylor & Francis Group. http://doi.org/10.4324/9780203070628

Cloitre, M., Courtois, C. A., Ford, J. D., Green, B. L., Alexander, P., Briere, J., Herman, J. L., et al. (2012). The ISTSS Expert consensus treatment guidelines for complex PTSD in adults. Retrieved from: http://terrorvictimresponse.ca/wp-content/uploads/ISTSS-Expert-Concesnsus-Guidelines-for-Complex-PTSD-Updated-060315.pdf

Coleman, J. N., Arthur, S. S., Lachman, S. E., Choi, Y., Zerubavel, N., Davidson, B., Reese, J. B., & Shelby, R. A. (2024). Developing a cognitive behavioral intervention for gynecologic cancer survivors undergoing pelvic exams. *Women's Reproductive Health*, 1–24. http://doi.org/10.1080/23293691.2024.2363820

Corrigan, F. M., Fisher, J. J., & Nutt, D. J. (2011). Autonomic dysregulation and the Window of Tolerance model of the effects of complex emotional trauma. *Journal of Psychopharmacology*, 25(1), 17–25. http://doi.org/10.1177/0269881109354930

Courtois, C. A. (2014). *It's Not You, It's What Happened to You: Complex Trauma and Treatment*. Dublin, OH: Telemachus Press.

Courtois, C. A., & Ford J. D. (2016). *Treatment of Complex Trauma: A Sequenced, Relationship-Based Approach*. New York: Guilford Press.

Craig, A. D. (2015). *How Do You Feel? An Interoceptive Moment with Your Neurobiological Self*. Princeton: Princeton University Press.

Crane, R. (2009). *Mindfulness-Based Cognitive Therapy: Distinctive Features*. New York: Routledge/Taylor & Francis Group.

De Jongh, A., Resick, P. A., Zoellner, L. A., van Minnen, A., Lee, C. W., Monson, C. M., Foa, E. B., et al. (2016). Critical analysis of the current treatment guidelines for complex PTSD in adults. *Depression and Anxiety*, 33(5), 359–369. http://doi.org/10.1002/da.22469

Desbordes, G., Gard, T., Hoge, E. A., Hölzel, B. K., Kerr, C., Lazar, S. W., Olendzki, A., & Vago, D. (2015). Moving beyond mindfulness: Defining equanimity as an outcome measure in meditation and contemplative research. *Mindfulness*, 6(2), 356–372. http://doi.org/10.1007/s12671-013-0269-8.

Doyle, G. (2022, November 10). Trauma responses are reflexes, not choices. Think hot stove. *Use Your Damn Skills*. http://useyourdamnskills.com/2022/11/10/trauma-responses-are-reflexes-not-choices-think-hot-stove

Dunn, E., Nishimi, K., Gomez, S. H., Powers Lott, A., & Bradley, B. (2018). Developmental timing of trauma exposure and emotion dysregulation in adulthood: Are there sensitive periods when trauma is most harmful? *Journal of Affective Disorders*, 227, 867–877. http://doi.org/10.1016/j.jad.2017.10.045

Dutton, D. G., & Painter, S. (1993). Emotional attachments in abusive relationships: A test of traumatic bonding theory. *Violence and Victims*, 8(2), 105–120.

Farb, N. A. S., Segal, Z. V., Mayberg, H., Bean, J., McKeon, D., Fatima, Z., & Anderson, A. K. (2007). Attending to the present: Mindfulness meditation reveals distinct neural modes of self-reference. *Social Cognitive and Affective Neuroscience*, 2(4), 313–322. http://doi.org/10.1093/scan/nsm030

Felitti, V. J. (2002). The relation between adverse childhood experiences and adult health: Turning gold into lead. *The Permanente Journal*, 6(1), 44–47. http://doi.org/10.7812/TPP/02.994

Finkelhor, D., & Browne, A. (1985). The traumatic impact of child sexual abuse: A conceptualization. *American Journal of Orthopsychiatry*, 55(4), 530–541. http://doi.org/10.1111/j.1939-0025.1985.tb02703.x

Fitzgerald, M. (2022). Childhood maltreatment is associated with adult psychopathology through decreased dispositional mindfulness. *Journal of Aggression, Maltreatment & Trauma*, 31(10), 1263–1278. http://doi.org/10.1080/10926771.2022.2043971

Forbes, D., Bisson, J. I., Monson, C. M., & Berliner, L. (2020). Effective treatments for PTSD: Guiding current practice and future innovation. In D. Forbes, J. I. Bisson, C. M. Monson, & L. Berliner (Eds.), *Effective Treatments for PTSD: Practice Guidelines from the International Society for Traumatic Stress Studies* (3rd ed., pp. 3–12). Guilford Press.

Ford, J. D., & Courtois, C. A. (2021). Complex PTSD and borderline personality disorder. *Borderline Personality Disorder and Emotion Dysregulation*, 8, 16. http://doi.org/10.1186/s40479-021-00155-9

Forner, C. C. (2017). *Dissociation, Mindfulness, and Creative Meditations: Trauma-Informed Practices to Facilitate Growth*. Routledge/Taylor & Francis Group.

Freyd, J., & Birrell, P. (2013). *Blind to Betrayal: Why We Fool Ourselves We Aren't Being Fooled*. Trade Paper Press.

Frewen, P., & Lanius, R. (2015). *Healing the Traumatized Self: Consciousness, Neuroscience, Treatment.* New York: W. W. Norton & Company.

Fung, H. W., Chien, W. T., Lam, S. K. K., & Ross, C. A. (2023). The relationship between dissociation and complex post-traumatic stress disorder: A scoping review. *Trauma, Violence, & Abuse, 24*(5), 2966–2982. http://doi.org/10.1177/15248380221120835

Gallagos, A. M., Lytle, M. C., Moynihan, J. A., Talbot, N. L. (2015). Mindfulness-based stress reduction to enhance psychological functioning and improve inflammatory biomarkers in trauma-exposed women: A pilot study. *Psychological Trauma: Theory, Research, Practice and Policy, 7*(6), 525–532. http://doi.org/10.1037/tra0000053

Garland, E., Gaylord, S. A., Fredrickson, B. L. (2011). Positive reappraisal mediates the stress-reductive effects of mindfulness: An upward spiral process. *Mindfulness, 2*(1), 59–67. http://doi.org/10.1007/s12671-011-0043-8

Germer, C. K., & Neff, K. D. (2015). Cultivating self-compassion in trauma survivors. In V. M. Follette, J. Briere, D. Rozelle, J. W. Hopper, & D. I. Rome (Eds.), *Mindfulness-Oriented Interventions for Trauma: Integrating Contemplate Practices* (pp. 43–58). Guilford Press.

Goldberg, S. B., Lam, S. U., Britton, W. B., & Davidson, R. J. (2022). Prevalence of meditation-related adverse effects in a population-based sample in the United States. *Psychotherapy Research: Journal of the Society for Psychotherapy Research, 32*(3), 291–305. http://doi.org/10.1080/10503307.2021.1933646

Goldsmith, R. E., Freyd, J. J., & DePrince, A. P. (2012). Betrayal trauma: Associations with psychological and physical symptoms in young adults. *Journal of Interpersonal Violence, 27*(3), 547–567. http://doi.org/10.1177/0886260511421672

Goldsmith, R. E., Gerhart, J. I., Chesney, S. A., Burns, J. W., Kleinman, B., & Hood, M. M. (2014). Mindfulness-based stress reduction for posttraumatic stress symptoms: Building acceptance and decreasing shame. *Journal of Evidence-Based Complementary & Alternative Medicine, 19*(4), 227–234. http://doi.org/10.1177/2156587214533703

Gómez, J. M. (2023). *The Cultural Betrayal of Black Women and Girls: A Black Feminist Approach to Healing from Sexual Abuse.* American Psychological Association. http://doi.org/10.1037/0000362-000

Harned, M. S. (2022). *Treating Trauma in Dialectical Behavior Therapy: The DBT Prolonged Exposure Protocol (DBT PE).* Guilford Press.

Harned, M. S., Korslund, K. E., Foa, E. B., & Linehan, M. M. (2012). Treating PTSD in suicidal and self-injuring women with borderline personality disorder: Development and preliminary evaluation of a Dialectical Behavior Therapy Prolonged Exposure Protocol. *Behaviour Research and Therapy, 50*(6), 381–386. http://doi.org/10.1016/j.brat.2012.02.011

Harper, L., Jones, A., Goodwin, L., & Gillespie, S. (2022). Association between trait mindfulness and symptoms of post-traumatic stress: A meta-analysis. *Journal of Psychiatric Research, 152*, 233–241. http://doi.org/10.1016/j.jpsychires.2022.05.027

Harris, R. (2021). *Trauma-Focused ACT: A Practitioner's Guide to Working with Mind, Body, and Emotion Using Acceptance and Commitment Therapy.* New York: Context Press.

Hayes, S. C., Strosahl, K. D., & Wilson, K. G. (1999). *Acceptance and Commitment Therapy: An Experiential Approach to Behavior Change.* Guilford Press.

Herman, J. L. (2015). *Trauma and Recovery: The Aftermath of Violence—From Domestic Abuse to Political Terror.* New York: Basic Books.

Hölzel, B. K., Lazar, S. W., Gard, T., Schuman-Olivier, Z., Vago, D. R., & Ott, U. (2011). How does mindfulness meditation work? Proposing mechanisms of action from a conceptual and neural perspective. *Perspectives on Psychological Science: A Journal of the Association for Psychological Science, 6*(6), 537–559. http://doi.org/10.1177/1745691611419671

Idini, E., Paredes-Carreño, P., Navarro-Gil, M., Barceló-Soler, A., Valera-Ceamanos, D., & Garcia-Campayo, J. (2024). Age of traumatic experience as a predictor of distorted body image in patients with eating disorders. *Clinical Child Psychology and Psychiatry, 29*(3), 1043–1057. http://doi.org/10.1177/13591045241251902

Iyadurai, L., Highfield, J., Kanstrup, M., Markham, A., Ramineni, V., Guo, B., Jaki, T., et al. (2023). Reducing intrusive memories after trauma via an imagery-competing task intervention in COVID-19 intensive care staff: A randomised controlled trial. *Translational Psychiatry, 13*, 290. http://doi.org/10.1038/s41398-023-02578-0

Janoff-Bulman, R. (1992). *Shattered Assumptions: Towards a New Psychology of Trauma.* New York: Free Press.

Jasbi, M., Bahmani, D. S., Karami, G., Omidbeygi, M., Peyravi, M., Panahi, A., Mirzaee, J., Holsboer-Trachsler, E., & Brand, S. (2018). Influence of adjuvant mindfulness-based cognitive therapy (MBCT) on symptoms of post-traumatic stress disorder (PTSD) in veterans - results from a randomized control study. *Cognitive Behaviour Therapy, 47*(5), 431–446. http://doi.org/10.1080/16506073.2018.1445773

Kabat-Zinn, J. (1990). *Full Catastrophe Living: Using the Wisdom of Your Body and Mind to Face Stress, Pain, and Illness.* New York: Delacorte Press.

Kabat-Zinn, J. (1994). *Wherever You Go, There You Are: Mindfulness Meditation in Everyday Life.* Hyperion.

Kabat-Zinn, J. (2003). Mindfulness-based interventions in context: Past, present, and future. *Clinical Psychology: Science and Practice, 10*(2), 144–156.

Kearney, D. J., Malte, C. A., Storms, M., Simpson, T. L. (2021). Loving-kindness meditation vs cognitive processing therapy for posttraumatic stress disorder among veterans: A randomized clinical trial. *JAMA Network Open, 4*(4), e216604. http://doi.org/10.1001/jamanetworkopen.2021.6604

Kelly, A, & Garland, E. (2016). Trauma-informed mindfulness-based stress reduction for female survivors of interpersonal violence: Results from a stage I RCT. *Journal of Clinical Psychology, 72*(4), 311–328. http://doi.org/10.1002/jclp.22273

Kim, J., & Cicchetti, D. (2010). Longitudinal pathways linking child maltreatment, emotion regulation, peer relations, and psychopathology. *Journal of Child Psychology and Psychiatry, 51*(6), 706–716. http://doi.org/10.1111/j.1469-7610.2009.02202.x

Kroska, E. B., Roche, A. I., & O'Hara, M. W. (2018). Childhood trauma and somatization: Identifying mechanisms for targeted intervention. *Mindfulness, 9,* 1845–1856. http://doi.org/10.1007/s12671-018-0927-y

Lamagna, J. (2017, June 14). *Using Parts Work in AEDP* [Retreat presentation]. AEDP Essential Skills Retreat, Durham, NC, United States.

Larsen, S. E., Stirman, S. W., Smith, B. N., & Resick, P. A. (2016). Symptom exacerbations in trauma-focused treatments: Associations with treatment outcome and non-completion. *Behaviour Research and Therapy, 77,* 68–77. http://doi.org/10.1016/j.brat.2015.12.009

Leahy, R. L., Tirch, D., & Napolitano, L. A. (2011). *Emotion Regulation in Psychotherapy: A Practitioner's Guide.* New York: Guilford Press.

Lee, D. J., Witte, T. K., Weathers, F. W., & Davis, M. T. (2015). Emotion regulation strategy use and posttraumatic stress disorder: Associations between multiple strategies and specific symptom clusters. *Journal of Psychopathology and Behavioral Assessment, 37*(3), 533–544. http://doi.org/10.1007/s10862-014-9477-3

Lin, Y., Callahan, C. P., & Moser, J. S. (2018). A mind full of self: Self-referential processing as a mechanism underlying the therapeutic effects of mindfulness training on internalizing disorders. *Neuroscience and Biobehavioral Reviews, 92,* 172–186. http://doi.org/10.1016/j.neubiorev.2018.06.007

Lindahl, J. R., Britton, W. B., Cooper, D. J., & Kirmayer, L. J. (2019). Challenging and adverse meditation experiences: Toward a person-centered approach. In M. Farias, D. Brazier, & M. Lalljee (Eds.), *The Oxford Handbook of Meditation* (pp. 841–864). Oxford University Press. http://doi.org/10.1093/oxfordhb/9780198808640.013.51

Lindahl, J. R., Cooper, D. J., Fisher, N. E., Kirmayer, L. J., & Britton, W. B. (2020). Progress or pathology? Differential diagnosis and intervention criteria for meditation-related challenges: Perspectives from Buddhist meditation teachers and practitioners. *Frontiers in Psychology, 11,* 1905. http://doi.org/10.3389/fpsyg.2020.01905

Lindahl, J. R., Fisher, N. E., Cooper, D. J., Rosen, R. K., & Britton, W. B. (2017). The varieties of contemplative experience: A mixed-methods study of meditation-related challenges in western Buddhists. *PLOS One, 12*(5), e0176239. http://doi.org/10.1371/journal.pone.0176239

Lindahl, J. R., Kaplan, C. T., Winget, E. M., & Britton, W. B. (2014). A phenomenology of meditation-induced light experiences: Traditional Buddhist and neurobiological perspectives. *Frontiers in Psychology, 4,* 973. http://doi.org/10.3389/fpsyg.2013.00973

Linehan, M. M. (1993). *Cognitive-Behavioral Treatment of Borderline Personality Disorder.* New York: Guilford Press.

Linehan, M. M. (2014). *DBT Skills Training Manual.* New York: Guilford Publications.

Lodha, S., & Gupta, R. (2022). Mindfulness, attentional networks, and executive functioning: A review of interventions and long-term meditation practice. *Journal of Cognitive Enhancement*, 6, 531–548. http://doi.org/10.1007/s41465-022-00254-7

López-Martínez, A. E., Serrano-Ibáñez, E. R., Ruiz-Párraga, G. T., Gómez-Pérez, L., Ramírez-Maestre, C., & Esteve, R. (2018). Physical health consequences of interpersonal trauma: A systematic review of the role of psychological variables. *Trauma, Violence & Abuse*, 19(3), 305–322. http://doi.org/10.1177/1524838016659488

Lutz, A., Slagter, H. A., Dunne, J. D., & Davidson, R. J. (2008). Attention regulation and monitoring in meditation. *Trends in Cognitive Sciences*, 12(4), 163–169. http://doi.org/10.1016/j.tics.2008.01.005

Madowitz, J., Matheson, B. E., & Liang, J. (2015). The relationship between eating disorders and sexual trauma. *Eating and Weight Disorders*, 20(3), 281–293. http://doi.org/10.1007/s40519-015-0195-y

Magyari, T. (2016). Teaching individuals with traumatic stress. In D. McCown, D. Reibel, & M. S. Micozzi (Eds.), *Resources for Teaching Mindfulness* (pp. 339–358). Springer.

Maslach, C. (2017). Finding solutions to the problem of burnout. *Consulting Psychology Journal: Practice and Research*, 69(2), 143-152. http://doi.org/10.1037/cpb0000090

Mathieu, F. (2012). *The Compassion Fatigue Workbook: Creative Tools for transforming Compassion Fatigue and Vicarious Traumatization*. Routledge/Taylor & Francis Group.

McCann, I. L., Sakheim, D. K., & Abrahamson, D. J. (1988). Trauma and victimization: A model of psychological adaptation. *The Counseling Psychologist*, 16(4), 531–594. http://doi.org/10.1177/0011000008816400

Medeiros, G., Prueitt, W. L., Minhajuddin, A., Patel, S. S., Czysz, A. H., Furman, J. L., Mason, B. L., Rush, A. J., Jha, M. K., & Trivedi, M. H. (2020). Childhood maltreatment and impact on clinical features of major depression in adults. *Psychiatry Research*, 293, 113412. http://doi.org/10.1016/j.psychres.2020.113412

Messman-Moore, T. L., & Bhuptani, P. H. (2017). A review of the long-term impact of child maltreatment on posttraumatic stress disorder and its comorbidities: An emotion dysregulation perspective. *Clinical Psychology: Science and Practice*, 24(2), 154–169. http://doi.org/10.1111/cpsp.12193

Miller, B. C. (2021). *Reducing Secondary Traumatic Stress: Skills for sustaining a Career in the Helping Professions*. Routledge/Taylor & Francis Group.

Miyake, A., Friedman, N. P., Emerson, M. J., Witzki, A. H., Howerter, A., & Wager, T. D. (2000). The unity and diversity of executive functions and their contributions to complex "Frontal Lobe" tasks: A latent variable analysis. *Cognitive Psychology*, 41(1), 49–100. http://doi.org/10.1006/cogp.1999.0734

Ogden, P. (2010). Modulation, mindfulness, and movement in the treatment of trauma-related depression. In M. Kerman (Ed.), *Clinical Pearls of Wisdom: Twenty-One Leading Therapists Share Their Key Insights* (pp. 1–13). W. W. Norton & Company.

Oldroyd, K., Pasupathi, M., & Wainryb, C. (2019). Social antecedents to the development of interoception: Attachment related processes are associated with interoception. *Frontiers in Psychology*, 10, 712. http://doi.org/10.3389/fpsyg.2019.00712

Paterniti, S., Raab, K., Sterner, I., Collimore, K. C., Dalton, C., & Bisserbe, J.-C. (2022). Individual mindfulness-based cognitive therapy in major depression: A feasibility study. *Mindfulness*, 13, 2845–2856. http://doi.org/10.1007/s12671-022-02000-8

Pérez-Peña, M., Notermans, J., Desmedt, O., Van der Gucht, K., & Philippot, P. (2022). Mindfulness-based interventions and body awareness. *Brain Science*, 12(2), 285. http://doi.org/10.3390/brainsci12020285

Pollak, S. M. (2013). Teaching mindfulness in therapy. In C. K. Germer, R. D. Siegel, & P. R. Fulton (Eds.), *Mindfulness and Psychotherapy* (2nd ed., pp. 133–147). New York: Guilford Press.

Posner, M. I., & Petersen, S. E. (1990). The attention system of the human brain. *Annual Review of Neuroscience*, 13, 25–42. http://doi.org/10.1146/annurev.ne.13.030190.000325

Price, C. J., & Hooven, C. (2018). Interoceptive awareness skills for emotion regulation: Theory and approach of mindful awareness in body-oriented therapy (MABT). *Frontiers in Psychology*, 9, 798. http://doi.org/10.3389/fpsyg.2018.00798

Price, C. J., & Thompson, E. A. (2007). Measuring dimensions of body connection: Body awareness and bodily dissociation. *The Journal of Alternative and Complementary Medicine*, 13(9), 945–953. http://doi.org/10.1089/acm.2007.0537

Punski-Hoogervorst, J. L., Engel-Yeger, B., Avital, A. (2023). Attention deficits as a key player in the symptomatology of posttraumatic stress disorder: A review. *Journal of Neuroscience Research, 101*(7), 1068–1085. http://doi.org/10.1002/jnr.25177

Resick, P. A., Monson, C. M., & Chard, K. M. (2016). *Cognitive Processing Therapy for PTSD: A Comprehensive Manual*. New York: Guilford Press.

Resick, P. A., Williams, L. F., Suvak, M. K., Monson, C. M., & Gradus, J. L. (2012). Long-term outcomes of cognitive-behavioral treatments for posttraumatic stress disorder among female rape survivors. *Journal of Consulting and Clinical Psychology, 80*(2), 201–210. http://doi.org/10.1037/a0026602

Reyes, A. T., Bhatta, T. R., Muthukumar, V., & Gangozo, W. J. (2020). Testing the acceptability and initial efficacy of a smartphone-app mindfulness intervention for college student veterans with PTSD. *Archives of Psychiatric Nursing, 34*(2), 58–66. http://doi.org/10.1016/j.apnu.2020.02.004

Roemer, L., & Orsillo, S. M. (2020). *Acceptance-Based Behavioral Therapy: Treating Anxiety and Related Challenges*. New York: Guilford Press.

Rothschild, B. (2000). *The Body Remembers: The Psychophysiology of Trauma and Trauma Treatment*. W. W. Norton & Company.

Rothschild, B. (2022). *Help for the Helper: Preventing Compassion Fatigue and Vicarious Trauma in an Ever-Changing World: Updated + Expanded* (2nd ed.). New York: W. W. Norton & Company.

Salzberg, S. (2020). *Lovingkindness: The Revolutionary Art of Happiness*. Shambhala.

Schiavone, F. L., Frewen, P., McKinnon, M., & Lanius, R. A. (2018). The dissociative subtype of PTSD: An update of the literature. *PTSD Research Quarterly, 29*(3), 1–4.

Schielke, H. J., Brand, B. L., & Lanius, R. A. (2022). *The Finding Solid Ground Program Workbook: Overcoming Obstacles in Trauma Recovery*. Oxford University Press. http://doi.org/10.1093/med-psych/9780197629031.001.0001

Schwartz, A. (2017). *The Complex PTSD Workbook: A Mind-Body Approach to Regaining Emotional Control and Becoming Whole*. San Antonio, TX: Althea Press.

Segal, Z. V., Williams, J. M. G., & Teasdale, J. D. (2013). *Mindfulness-Based Cognitive Therapy for Depression* (2nd ed.). New York: Guilford Press.

Seligowski, A. V., Miron, L. R., & Orcutt, H. K. (2015). Relations among self-compassion, PTSD symptoms, and psychological health in a trauma-exposed sample. *Mindfulness, 6*(5), 1033–1041. http://doi.org/10.1007/s12671-014-0351-x

Shapiro, S. L., & Carlson, L. E. (2009). *The Art and Science of Mindfulness: Integrating Mindfulness into Psychology and the Helping Professions*. Washington, DC: American Psychological Association.

Shapiro, S. L., Carlson, L. E., Astin, J. A., & Freedman, B. (2006). Mechanisms of mindfulness. *Journal of Clinical Psychology, 62*(3), 373–386. http://doi.org/10.1002/jclp.20237

Shonin, E., Van Gordon, W., & Griffiths, M.D. (2014). Do mindfulness-based therapies have a role in the treatment of psychosis? *Australian & New Zealand Journal of Psychiatry, 48*(2), 124–127. http://doi.org/10.1177/0004867413511268

Siegel, D. J. (1999). *The Developing Mind: How Relationships and the Brain Interact to Shape Who We Are*. Guilford Press.

Siegel, D. J., & Bryson, T. (2011). *The Whole-Brain Child: 12 Revolutionary Strategies to Nurture Your Child's Developing Mind*. Delacorte Press.

Singer, T., & Klimecki, O. M. (2014). Empathy and compassion. *Current Biology, 24*(18), R875–R878. http://doi.org/10.1016/j.cub.2014.06.054

Spinazzola, J., Hodgdon, H., Liang, L.-J., Ford, J. D., Layne, C. M., Pynoos, R., Briggs, E. C., Stolbach, B., & Kisiel, C. (2014). Unseen wounds: The contribution of psychological maltreatment to child and adolescent mental health and risk outcomes. *Psychological Trauma: Theory, Research, Practice, and Policy, 6*(Suppl 1), S18–S28. http://doi.org/10.1037/a0037766

Sprang, G., Ford, J., Kerig, P., & Bride, B. (2019). Defining secondary traumatic stress and developing targeted assessments and interventions: Lessons learned from research and leading experts. *Traumatology, 25*(2), 72–81. http://doi.org/10.1037/trm0000180

Stanley, B., & Brown, G. K. (2012). Safety planning intervention: A brief intervention to mitigate suicide risk. *Cognitive and Behavioral Practice, 19*(2), 256–264. http://doi.org/10.1016/j.cbpra.2011.01.001

Stanley, B., Brown, G. K., Brenner, L. A., Galfalvy, H. C., Currier, G. W., Knox, K. L., Chaudhury, S. R., Bush, A. L., & Green, K. L. (2018). Comparison of the safety planning intervention with follow-up vs usual care of suicidal patients treated in the emergency department. *JAMA Psychiatry, 75*(9), 894–900. http://doi.org/10.1001/jamapsychiatry.2018.1776

Steele, K. (2018, October 12–13). *Challenges in Treating Structural Dissociation: A Practical, Integrative Approach* [Presentation]. Durham, NC, United States.

Steele, K., Boon, S., & van der Hart, O. (2017). *Treating Trauma-Related Dissociation: A Practical, Integrative Approach*. New York: W. W. Norton & Company.

Steil, R., & Ehlers, A. (2000). Dysfunctional meaning of posttraumatic intrusions in chronic PTSD. *Behaviour Research and Therapy, 38*(6), 537–558. http://doi.org/10.1016/s0005-7967(99)00069-8

Strand, M., & Stige, S. H. (2021). Combining mindfulness and compassion in the treatment of complex trauma—A theoretical exploration. *European Journal of Trauma & Dissociation, 5*(3), 100217. http://doi.org/10.1016/j.ejtd.2021.100217

Strodl, E. & Wylie, L. (2020). Childhood trauma and disordered eating: Exploring the role of alexithymia and beliefs about emotions. *Appetite, 154*, 104802.

Sumantry, D. & Stewart, K. E. (2021). Meditation, mindfulness, and attention: A meta-analysis. *Mindfulness, 12*, 1332–1349. http://doi.org/10.1007/s12671-021-01593-w

TEND Academy. (2020, April). *Managing media exposure during COVID-19*. http://tendtoolkit.com/managing-media-exposure

The Clinical and Affective Neuroscience Laboratory. (n.d.). *Meditation Safety Toolbox*. http://sites.brown.edu/britton/resources/meditation-safety-toolbox.

Treleaven, D. A. (2018). *Trauma-Sensitive Mindfulness: Practices for Safe and Transformative Healing*. New York: W. W. Norton & Company.

VanderKooi, L. (1997). Buddhist teachers' experience with extreme mental states in western meditators. *Journal of Transpersonal Psychology, 29*(1), 31–46.

van Dernoot Lipsky, L. & Burk C. (2009). *Trauma Stewardship: An Everyday Guide to Caring for Self While Caring for Others*. Oakland, CA: Berrett-Koehler Publishers.

Visser, R. M., Lau-Zhu, A., Henson, R. N., & Holmes, E. A. (2018). Multiple memory systems, multiple time points: How science can inform treatment to control the expression of unwanted emotional memories. *Philosophical Transactions of the Royal Society B: Biological Sciences, 373*(1742), 20170209. http://doi.org/10.1098/rstb.2017.0209

Walker, L. E. (1979). *The Battered Woman*. New York: Harper & Row.

Waters, F., Ling, I., Azimi, S., & Blom, J. D. (2024). Sleep-related hallucinations. *Sleep Medicine Clinics, 19*(1), 143–157. http://doi.org/10.1016/j.jsmc.2023.10.008

Williams, D. R. (2018). Stress and the mental health of populations of color: Advancing our understanding of race-related stressors. *Journal of Health and Social Behavior, 59*(4), 466–485. http://doi.org/10.1177/0022146518814251

Woods, S., Rockman, P., & Collins, E. (2019). *Mindfulness-Based Cognitive Therapy: Embodied Presence and Inquiry in Practice*. Oakland, CA: New Harbinger Publications.

Zerubavel, N., & Messman-Moore, T. L. (2015). Staying present: Incorporating mindfulness into therapy for dissociation. *Mindfulness, 6*(2), 303–314. http://doi.org/10.1007/s12671-013-0261-3

Zerubavel, N., & Wright, M. O. (2012). The dilemma of the wounded healer. *Psychotherapy, 49*(4), 482–491. http://doi.org/10.1037/a0027824

Zhu, J., Wekerle, C., Lanius, R., & Frewen, P. (2019). Trauma- and stressor-related history and symptoms predict distress experienced during a brief mindfulness meditation sitting: Moving toward trauma-informed care in mindfulness-based therapy. *Mindfulness, 10*(10), 1985–1996. http://doi.org/10.1007/s12671-019-01173-z

Index

A

abandonment: BPD and avoidance of, 15, 17; fear of, 10, 22, 167, 172; psychological adaptation, 19, 22

ABBT (acceptance-based behavioral therapy), 43

absorption, 106

acceptance, 25, 32, 42–43; accommodation, 21; allowing emotional experiencing, 141, 172; attention regulation, 100–101, 104; body awareness, 126, 133; changes in perspective, 33, 97, 160, 162–163, 167–168, 172–173; emotion regulation, 136, 139, 141, 143, 146, 153; informal exposure, 57; radical acceptance, 26, 160, 162–163, 167, 172–173; in therapeutic relationship, 37, 54, 71, 78, 85

acceptance and commitment therapy (ACT), 43, 161–162

acceptance-based behavioral therapy (ABBT), 43

ADHD (attention-deficit/hyperactivity disorder), 101, 105

adverse childhood experiences (ACEs) investigation, 121

alexithymia, 54, 120–121, 137, 141

allowing emotional experiencing, 61, 71, 141, 153, 156–157, 172

anchoring: anchoring the end, 73; auditory anchors, 67, 190; landscape phase, 68; psychosis and, 46; safety-enhancing strategies, 189–190; somatosensory anchors, 67, 190; stillness practices, 123; teaching in preparatory sessions, 67; visual anchors, 67, 190

Anderson, T., 67

anhedonia, 28, 33, 142, 170

ANS. See autonomic nervous system

anticipation of threatening experiences, 50, 105

antidote practices, 157, 176, 179–180, 191

anxiety and anxiety disorders, 12–13, 22, 28, 42, 142; about interoceptive experience, 126–130; body awareness, 118, 126–132; changes in perspective, 162–163, 168; concentration problems, 105; cultural variation, 54; disturbances during meditation, 79–80, 82–83; emotion regulation and dysregulation, 137, 142–143, 147; meditation-related, 80; suppression, 137; therapists' reactions, 71; worry and, 106, 111

appraisal techniques for emotion regulation, 144–152; cognitive flexibility, 148–150; dialectical thinking, 151–152; kōan, 147–148, 150; mindfulness of thoughts, 148; nonevaluative awareness, 146–150; reappraisal, 150

attachment styles, 9–10, 118–119

attention regulation, 1, 29, 44, 100–115; attention practices, 107–109; attitude toward mindfulness practice, 104; body awareness and, 116; changes in perspective and, 159; disturbances related to, 105–107; effectiveness of meditation, 97; emotion regulation and, 135–136; identifying arousal cues and triggers, 51; improving, 25; inquiry process, 109–114; meditation and, 101–103; purpose or intent of mindfulness practice, 103; relationship to mindfulness and trauma, 100–101; switching, 101; in trauma, 104–105

attention-deficit/hyperactivity disorder (ADHD), 101, 105

auditory anchors, 67, 190

autonomic nervous system (ANS): attention regulation, 104; body awareness, 117–118, 126; freeze, fight, or flight response, 50–52; hyperarousal, 31, 51, 75–76; mindfulness and control over, 42; parasympathetic nervous system, 30, 50, 75, 118, 126, 164, 189;

prolonged anticipatory states and, 50; PTSD, 27; safety-enhancing strategies, 190; self-soothing skills, 76; sympathetic nervous system, 27, 50–51, 75–76, 104, 118; unconscious, automatic sensitivity to triggers, 50

autopilot, 25, 90, 94, 101–103, 105, 145

avoidance: body awareness, 120–121; containment versus, 55–56, 72; CPTSD, 17; emotion education, 54; emotion regulation, 136–137, 143, 153, 155; informal exposure, 56; intrusions and, 78; PTSD, 13–14; purpose of, 55; reduced, 61, 70; rumination, 29; stage model, 39

B

backdraft, 165–166, 176, 179, 191

behavioral domain of adaptation, 27; PTSD, 19; symptoms and sequelae, 18

betrayal: betrayal blindness, 9; betrayal trauma theory, 8–9; body betrayal, 120; freeze, fight, or flight response, 8; institutional betrayal, 173; physical health and, 121; social betrayal, 7–8; traumatic amnesia, 8

biological domain of adaptation, 27; PTSD, 19; symptoms and sequelae, 18

biphasic rollercoaster, 50–51

bipolar disorder, 101

body awareness, 1, 29, 44, 116–134; attachment style and, 118; attention regulation and, 116; changes in perspective and, 159, 168; conscious awareness of sensory stimuli, 116–117; considerations for work with trauma survivors, 122; disturbances related to, 119–122; effectiveness of meditation, 97; emotion regulation and, 117, 135–136, 140, 146, 156; emotionally neglectful caregivers and, 118; hypersensitivity and hyposensitivity, 117–118; identifying arousal cues and triggers, 51; instructions for, 125–130; interoception, 117, 126–130; mindfulness and, 25; movement practices, 124–125; past-present discernment, 130–133; relationship to mindfulness and trauma, 116–117; safety-enhancing strategies, 66, 73, 190–191; sensation words, 125; stillness practices, 123–124; in trauma, 117–119

body image distortions, 120–121, 174

body scan, 25, 46, 62, 97; attention regulation, 108–109; body awareness, 122–123, 126; changes in perspective, 178; self-compassionate, 178

borderline personality disorder (BPD): body awareness and, 116; disorganized attachment and, 10; dissociation and, 14–15; distinguishing from PTSD and CPTSD, 15–17; emotion regulation and, 143; features of, 15–16; fight response, 15; relative likelihood of trauma type, 16

Brach, Tara, 173

Britton, Willoughby, 47, 63–64

building awareness layer, of inquiry process, 93–95

burnout, 182–186

C

case conceptualization, 1–2, 24–34, 44; body awareness and, 126; change in perspective and, 168; connecting to treatment, 32–33; dangers of not considering, 47; defined, 25; emotion regulation and, 138, 148, 157; integrating mindfulness to facilitate awareness, 26–27; physiological dysregulation, 29–30; preparatory skills review, 67; process-based approach, 41; psychological adaptation to trauma, 13, 17; strategy and technique choices, 96; transdiagnostic framework, 27–29; trauma-informed framework and mindset, 26–27; trauma-sensitive principles, 35, 37; why and how of mindfulness, 25–26; window of tolerance, 30–32

CBTs (cognitive behavioral therapies), 29, 42, 55, 57, 101, 136, 168

CE-CERT (Components for Enhancing Clinician Experience & Reducing Trauma) model, 186, 189

Center for Victims of Torture, 185

central nervous system (CNS), 117

challenging balance, 76

changes in perspective, vii, 1, 25–26, 29, 44, 159–180; acceptance practices, 33; attention regulation and, 159; body awareness and, 116, 126, 159; disturbances related to, 166–167; effectiveness of meditation, 97; emotion regulation and, 135, 159; informal exposure, 57; mindset, 161–163, 172–176; relation to self and others, 163–165, 176–180; relationship to mindfulness and trauma, 159–160; safety-enhancing strategies, 190–191; thoughts, 160–161, 169–172; in trauma, 165–166; when to focus on, 168

Cheetah House, 63, 76, 80

Chödrön, Pema, 153

choice points, 29, 88, 133, 145

choiceless awareness (open monitoring), 77, 92, 102, 107, 169, 171–173, 175

CNS (central nervous system), 117

cognitive behavioral therapies (CBTs), 29, 42, 55, 57, 101, 136, 168

cognitive defusion: change in perspective, 97, 160–161, 169–172; defined, 25–26, 160; disturbances in relatedness, 167; mindfulness of thoughts, 172; noting practice, 170; pivoting away from mindfulness, 47; powerlessness and the internalization of stigma, 166; working with difficulty, 172–173

cognitive domain of adaptation, 27; PTSD, 19; symptoms and sequelae, 18

cognitive flexibility, 25, 136, 138, 146, 148–150, 158, 168

cognitive fusion, 160

cognitive grounding, 73–74

cognitive processing therapy (CPT), 29, 40–41, 57, 164

common humanity, 86, 176, 179–180

compassion: attention regulation, 100, 104; changes in perspective, 97; empathic strain, 183; mindfulness principles and therapeutic relationship, 37, 54, 71, 78, 85, 165; for others, 163–165, 179–180, 188; for others' hardships, 179; shifting from empathy (with) to compassion (for), 183, 188; therapist self-compassion, 4, 190–192. See also self-compassion

compassion fatigue (empathic strain), 182–183, 185–186

complex PTSD (CPTSD), 13–14; complex trauma and, 10; dissociation and, 14; distinguishing from PTSD and BPD, 15–17; emotion regulation and, 143; features of, 14, 16; relative likelihood of trauma type, 16; stage model, 39

complex trauma, 9–10; CPTSD, 13; defined, 9; development of attachment and emotional bonds, 9–10; hyperarousal and hypoarousal, 19; physiological and emotion dysregulation, 10; PTSD-D, 14; trauma adaptation, 20

Components for Enhancing Clinician Experience & Reducing Trauma (CE-CERT) model, 186, 189

concentration: practices involving, 62, 97, 103–104, 107–108, 116–117; problems with, 19, 105, 109

containment, 55–56, 72–73, 75, 188–189

control and power schema, 20

Cookie Thief, The (Cox), 150

countertransference, 37

Courtois, C. A., 14–15

covert trauma. See insidious trauma

Cox, Valerie, 150

CPT (cognitive processing therapy), 29, 40–41, 57, 164

CPTSD. See complex PTSD

Crane, R., 94

cultural diversity and variation: adaptation and, 37; anxiety, 54; cultural traumas, 38; harm in failing to acknowledge, 38; intersectionality, 37–38, 184; nonordinary states of consciousness, 62–63; therapists' reactions to trauma, 184; understanding of emotion, 54

D

DARVO pattern, 12

DBT (dialectical behavior therapy), 39–40, 43, 126, 146, 151, 161

decentering: body awareness and, 117, 159; changes in perspective, 160–161, 165–166,

169–172, 175; containment, 56; context and mindfulness, 47; titration strategies, 57

defectiveness, 22, 166

depersonalization: dissociation, 14, 121; during meditation, 61, 81–82

depression, 22, 28, 42, 142; changes in perspective, 162–164; concentration problems, 19, 105; overlap with PTSD, 28; rumination and, 106, 113–114; suppression, 137

derealization: dissociation, 14, 121; during meditation, 81–82

detachment, 11, 14, 53, 105, 142, 154; changes in perspective, 160; context and mindfulness, 47; CPTSD, 17; dissociation, 121–122; informal exposure, 57; metaphor, 58

Diagnostic and Statistical Manual of Mental Disorders (DSM-5), 6, 11, 13

dialectical behavior therapy (DBT), 39–40, 43, 126, 146, 151, 161

dialectical thinking, 146, 151–152, 158

disorganized (fearful-avoidant) attachment style, 10

disruptions during practice, 87

dissociation and dissociative disorders, 12, 19, 22, 28, 57, 67–68, 106–107; absorption, 106; betrayal trauma theory, 9; body awareness, 120–122, 130; BPD, 15; changes in perspective, 167; concentration problems, 105; CPTSD, 14, 143; emotion regulation, 141, 153–155; features of, 14; freeze response, 118; hyperarousal and hypoarousal, 52, 82, 105; during meditation, 79, 81–82; PTSD, 13, 143; window of tolerance, 30–31

double self, 167

doublethink, 167

DSM-5 (*Diagnostic and Statistical Manual of Mental Disorders*), 6, 11, 13

dual awareness, 42, 72–74, 78–79

E

eating disorders, 13, 28, 174; body awareness, 116, 120–121; emotion regulation, 144; stage model, 40; window of tolerance, 50–51

elongated inhalations and exhalations, 75, 191

emotion dysregulation. See physiological and emotion dysregulation

emotion education, 54–55

emotion regulation, 25, 135–158; appraisal techniques, 138–139, 144–152; aspects of, 139–141; attention regulation and, 135; autopilot, 145; body awareness and, 135; bottom-up and top-down processes, 137; choice points, 145; defined, 137; disturbances related to, 142–144; effectiveness of meditation, 97; emotion-varying emotion regulation, 144–145, 155–158; exposure techniques, 33, 139, 144–145, 152–155; informal exposure, 136, 139, 153; relationship to mindfulness and trauma, 136; safety and, 36; in trauma, 142. See also physiological and emotion dysregulation

emotional deprivation, 22

emotional domain of adaptation, 27; PTSD, 19; symptoms and sequelae, 18

emotion-varying emotion regulation, 144–145, 155–158; gratitude practice, 158; inviting and experiencing positive emotion, 156–158; mindfulness of emotion with naturally occurring positive emotion, 156

empathic strain (compassion fatigue), 182–183, 185–186

empowerment, 1–2, 4, 32, 35–37, 67, 90; attention regulation, 108; defined, 36; emotion regulation, 140; expanding the window of tolerance, 53–54, 57; informed consent, 36–37

end of practice, orientation to the upcoming transition of, 92–93

equanimity, 85, 161, 172, 175–176, 178, 191

esteem schema, 20

experiential acceptance, 43, 126, 163

exposure techniques for emotion regulation, 139, 144–145, 152–155; Looking at a Glass Jar, 154–155; mindfulness of emotion, 153; working with difficulty, 153

extinction, 139

F

failure, 22, 113–114, 151
Farb, N. A. S., 67
fawning, 21–22, 58, 167
fearful-avoidant (disorganized) attachment style, 10
five-minute breathing space, 107–109
flashbacks: dissociation, 14; gaze-related practices, 90; past-present discernment, 130–131; PTSD, ix, 13; safety-enhancing strategies, 61, 64, 67–73, 77; window of tolerance, 51, 55
focused attention, 81, 102–103, 105–106, 111
Ford, J. D., 14–15
formal exposure (memory processing), 56–58, 153
formal mindfulness practice. See meditation
freedom, 173
freeze, fight, or flight response, ix, 8, 14–15, 31, 55; attention regulation, 104; autonomic nervous system, 50–52; BPD, 15; CPTSD, 14; dissociation, 14; safety-enhancing strategies, 72–73

G

gaslighting, 12, 106
gaze-related practices, 90
gentle stretching, 75, 124–125
gratitude for the exception to the rule, 152
gratitude practice, 158
grounding, 42, 46, 73–74, 80; attention regulation, 107; body awareness, 122; changes in perspective, 161; cognitive, 73–74; safety enhancement, 65–67, 73–74, 78–80, 82–83; sensory, 65–66, 73–74, 83; therapists' reactions to trauma, 190–191; titration strategies, 57; window of tolerance, 53, 57

H

hallucinations, during meditation, 61, 63, 69, 81–83
heart-mindfulness, 104
Herman, Judith, 13–14
historical traumas, 38, 127
hoarding disorder, 28
Hölzel, Britta, 25, 97
hyperarousal and hypoarousal, 30–31, 47; attention regulation, 105, 109; body awareness, 122, 126; downregulating hyperarousal, 75, 80, 82, 190; emotion regulation, 143; rating arousal, 66–67; upregulating hypoarousal, 75–76, 80, 82, 190; window of tolerance, 31, 50–52
hypersensitivity (hypervigilance) and hyposensitivity (underactivity), 14, 29–30, 70, 82, 168; body awareness, 117–119, 121, 126; BPD, 15; informed consent, 64; PTSD, 29, 104–105

I

ICD-11 (*International Statistical Classification of Diseases and Related Health Problems*, 11th ed.), 14
identity, disturbances in, ix, 7, 9–10, 15, 21–22, 166–167
imagery practices, 67, 75, 92, 175; CBT, 101; compassion and loving-kindness, 164; decentering, 170; equanimity, 175–176; Tetris, 189
impulsivity, 15, 137, 145
informal exposure, 55–57, 123, 136, 139, 153; defined, 56–57; formal exposure versus, 57; strategies for, 57
informal mindfulness (off the cushion practice), 1, 60, 69–70, 76
informed consent, 2, 36–37, 43, 63–64, 188
inquiry process, 4, 26, 30, 52, 93–96, 109–114, 127, 148, 156; building awareness, 93–95; defined, 93; disruptions during practice, 87; following mindfulness of a raisin, 109–110; following mindfulness of breath, 111–112; home practice review, 113–114; insight and generalization, 93, 96; noting practice, 170–171; pacing, 92; tenderness and self-compassion, 177; tracking and contextualizing, 93, 95–96
insidious (covert) trauma, 10–12, 184; defined, 10; list of, 11; psychological maltreatment, 11–12; traumatic invalidation, 12

insight and generalization layer, of inquiry process, 96
interconnectedness, 158, 178, 180
internal reference, lack of, 167
International Statistical Classification of Diseases and Related Health Problems, 11th ed. (ICD-11), 14
interpersonal domain of adaptation, 27; PTSD, 19; symptoms and sequelae, 18
interpersonal trauma, 7–8; context and level of attachment, 8; defined, 7; lasting impact of, 7–8
intimacy schema, 20
invitational language, 36, 91
Iyadurai, L., 189

K

Kabat-Zinn, Jon, viii, 25, 100
Klimecki, O. M., 183
kōan, 58, 62, 97; Cookie Thief, The, 150; Muddy Road, 174; Story of Maybe, The, 147–148

L

landscape (slow start-up) phase, 67–69, 82
language of *we*, 86
Lindahl, J. R., 62–63, 81
Looking at a Glass Jar, 154–155
loving-kindness meditation (LKM; metta), 164–165, 175, 178–180
low-impact debriefing, 127, 187–188

M

Magyari, Trish, 66, 70, 123
Mathieu, F., 187
MBCT (mindfulness-based cognitive therapy), 42–43, 64, 93–94, 108, 126, 161, 170
MBSR (mindfulness-based stress reduction), ix, 42–43, 101–102
means restriction, 46
Meditating in Safety, 76
meditation (formal mindfulness practice): adverse experiences, 61–64, 69–84; attention regulation and, 101–103; choiceless awareness, 102; emotion regulation and, 138; focused attention, 102–103; meditation-based therapies, 43; metacognition, 103; preparation sessions, 64–69; shifting out of autopilot, 103
Meditation Safety Toolbox (Britton), 63
memory processing (formal exposure), 56–58, 153
mental labeling (noting practice), 101, 170–171
metacognition, 25, 92, 103, 160, 163
metaphor and analogy, 169–170, 176, 180
metta (loving-kindness meditation [LKM]), 164–165, 175, 178–180
Miller, Brian, 189
mind wandering, 91–92, 95, 107, 114
mindfulness: attitude toward, 104; choosing strategies and techniques, 96–97; client choice, 32; context versus technique, 1; contraindications for, 46–48; defined, viii, 25, 100; guidance for integrating into sessions, 85–87; inquiry process, 93–96; intentional approach to integration of, 1–2; mechanisms of, 25–26; mindset of, 32; misconceptions about, 24, 26; personal experience and practice of, 33, 54; processing trauma-related experiences/themes, 30; providing instruction in, 87–93; purpose or intent of, 24–25, 103; role of in healing trauma, viii, 1; safety, emphasis on, 2, 33; trauma-sensitive principles, 2
mindfulness of a raisin, 107–110
mindfulness of a rock, 107–108
mindfulness of body part, 123
mindfulness of breath, 107–108, 111–112, 123, 126–130
mindfulness of emotion, 33, 57, 153–154, 156–158, 171
mindfulness of thoughts, 148, 172–173
mindfulness-based cognitive therapy (MBCT), 42–43, 64, 93–94, 108, 126, 161, 170
mindfulness-based stress reduction (MBSR), ix, 42–43, 101–102
mindset, changes in perspective related to, 161–163, 172–176; equanimity, 161, 175–176; radical acceptance, 162–163, 172–173; values, 161–162; values clarification, 173–175
mistrust, 19, 22, 37, 88, 167–168, 183

movement practices, 66, 76, 123–125, 130
Muddy Road, 174
muscle activation, 75–76

N

National Child Traumatic Stress Network (NCTSN), 185
nonevaluative awareness, 145–150, 152
nonjudgment, 22, 25, 27, 32; attention regulation, 100–101, 113; body awareness, 117, 123; changes in perspective, 160–161, 166, 169–171, 173; emotion regulation, 136, 141, 143, 145–147; guidance for integrating mindfulness into sessions, 85, 91–92; safety-enhancing strategies, 71, 78, 83; in therapeutic relationship, 37; window of tolerance, 53–54, 57
nonordinary states of consciousness (NSC), 62–63
nonreactivity, 25, 57, 83, 88–89, 92; attention regulation, 102; body awareness, 126; changes in perspective, 161, 169–171, 175; emotion regulation, 136, 139, 143
noting practice (mental labeling), 101, 170–171

O

observer self, 53, 163
obsessive-compulsive disorder, 13, 28
ocean waves on a stormy day, 170
off the cushion practice (informal mindfulness), 1, 60, 69–70, 76
open monitoring (choiceless awareness), 77, 92, 102, 107, 169, 171–173, 175
organizing technique, 74
orienting to surrounding environment and context, 73
other-directedness, 167
overwhelm, 31; acute, 47; awareness of signs of, 55; body awareness, 122–123; containment, 55–56; dissociation and, 14; distress versus, 56; emotion regulation, 154; meditation-related, 69, 79–81; psychological safety, 45; therapists' reactions to trauma, 189. See also safety-enhancing strategies; window of tolerance

P

pacing: of trauma narrative, 58, 79; of treatment and sessions, 36, 92
past-present discernment, 73, 130–133, 154
PE (prolonged exposure), 40, 57, 188
perceptual disturbances, 69, 81–83
perfectionism and unrealistic standards, 21–22, 191
peripheral nervous system (PNS), 117
Perls, Fritz, 101
perpetrator strategies, 55, 154
physiological and emotion dysregulation, 10; BPD, 15–16, 143; contraindications for mindfulness, 47; CPTSD, 15, 143; defined, 137; diagnostic comorbidity, 28; effective learning and, 45; emotion regulation, 137, 142; meditation-related, 69, 79–81; PTSD, 14, 143; trauma and, 29–30, 33. See also safety-enhancing strategies; window of tolerance
PNS (peripheral nervous system), 117
post-traumatic stress disorder (PTSD): attention regulation, 104; concentration problems, 105; dissociative subtype, 14; distinguishing from CPTSD and BPD, 15–17; emotion regulation, 142–143; features of, 13, 16; loving-kindness meditation, 164; mindfulness and, 22; overlap with depression, 28; psychological adaptation to, 27; relative likelihood of trauma type, 16; secondary traumatic stress, 183; stage model, 39; SUDs and, 39; trauma not synonymous with, 10, 12; variants of, 10
posture, 65, 76, 89–90, 124, 189
powerlessness, 166
preparation sessions, for safety enhancement in meditation, 64; landscape phase, 68–69; practice modifications, 65–66; skills acquisition in, 66–67
present participles, 91
present-moment awareness, 70, 73, 78–79, 104, 116, 122, 130, 141
process-based approach, 40–42. See also attention regulation; body awareness; changes in perspective; emotion regulation

Professional Quality of Life: Health Worker (ProQol-H) assessment, 185
progressive muscle release, 75, 124, 126
prolonged exposure (PE), 40, 57, 188
protocol-based approaches, 41–42
providing choices, 90–91
psychodynamic approaches, 42–43
psychological adaptation to trauma, 17–22; domains of, 17–19, 27; examples of, 21–22; identity and interpersonal relatedness, 21–22; individual, unique constellation of adaptations, 19; integrating mindfulness into therapy, 19; meaning-making and, 19–22; Psychological Adaptation Model, 19; schemas, 19–22; symptoms versus sign of intrinsic pathology, 26–27
psychosis, 46, 63
PTSD. See post-traumatic stress disorder

Q

questioning perceptions of reality, 20–22
quickened breathing, 75

R

radical acceptance, 26, 160, 162–163, 167, 172–173
RAIN practice, 173
reappraisal, 38, 136, 138–139, 146, 150
reconsolidation, 139
reducing emotional intensity, 72–73, 80, 190; anchoring the end, 73; containment, 72; dual awareness, 73
Reducing Secondary Traumatic Stress (Miller), 189
relatedness, 21–22, 167
relation to self and others, changes in perspective related to, 163–165, 176–180; compassion and loving-kindness, 164–165; compassion for others, 179–180; interconnectedness, 180; self-compassion, 176–179; self-referential thinking, 163–164
resourcing, 53–54, 64–66, 76, 190–191
responding to painful emotions, 76–77, 80; resourcing, 76; restorative activities, 76; self-compassion, 77; self-soothing, 76–77

responsiveness in self-care, 88–89
restorative activities, 76, 190
Rothschild, Babette, 63, 79, 119
rumination, 13, 23, 29, 105–106, 137; attention regulation, 101–106, 113–114; body awareness, 120; CE-CERT model, 189; changes in perspective, 33, 161, 163, 166, 168, 172–173; eating disorders, 120; emotion regulation, 137–138, 143, 149; feeling "stuck" in the past, 25; inquiry process, 113–114; worry versus, 106

S

safety, 35–36; acute safety risk as contraindication for mindfulness, 46; basis for, 35; contextual factors, 37; emphasis on, 2, 33, 35, 42; expansion of window of tolerance, 54; pacing of treatment, 36; psychological safety, 45; stage model, 38–40
safety schema, 20
safety-enhancing strategies, 36, 42, 60–84; informed consent, 63–64; meditation-related adverse experiences, 61–63, 69–84; preparation sessions, 64–69; therapists' reactions to trauma, 189–192
schemas, 19–22; accommodation, 20–21; assimilation, 20–21; associated with childhood maltreatment, 22; development of, 19–20; list of, 20; overaccommodation, 21; polyvictimization and revictimization, 21; revision of, 20; strengthening or challenging, 19–20; variation in effects on belief system, 20
Secondary Traumatic Stress Consortium, 185
secondary traumatic stress (STS), 182–186, 189
self-blame, 20, 25, 27; allowing emotional experiencing, 141; attention regulation, 104, 106; changes in perspective, 165, 167, 174; cognitive fusion, 160; organizing technique, 74; reappraisal, 138
self-care, 53, 88, 156; changes in perspective, 160, 174, 177; somatic awareness, 119; therapists' reactions to trauma, 189, 191–192; working definition of, 124
self-compassion, 22, 29, 97; body awareness, 123; changes in perspective, 33, 164,

166–168, 176–179; emotion regulation, 136, 141, 152–153; expanding window of tolerance, 55, 57; safety-enhancing strategies, 66, 69, 77; therapists' reactions to trauma, 4, 190–192
self-compassionate body scan, 178
self-criticism, 69, 104, 149, 164, 170, 177
self-doubt and not trusting oneself, 21, 166
self-injury, 15, 70, 142
self–other differentiation, 184
self-referential thinking, 163–164
self-regulating touch, 75
self-sacrifice, 22
self-soothing, 12, 15, 55–56, 76–77, 143–144, 164, 167, 190
sensory grounding, 65–66, 73–74, 83
shame, 12–13, 16, 22, 27, 42; attention regulation, 113; body awareness, 120–121, 123; changes in perspective, 164, 166, 168, 170–171; emotion regulation, 142–143, 153–155; metaphor, 58; safety-enhancing strategies, 69, 74, 76, 81; suicide ideation and, 83; window of tolerance, 30, 51, 55–56
Shapiro, S. L., 103–104
shifting of the body, 65
Shonin, E., 46
SI. See suicide ideation
Siegel, Daniel, 31
Singer, T., 183
sleep disorders, 21, 104
slow start-up (landscape) phase, 67–69, 82
social isolation, 22
somatic awareness, 119, 173
somatosensory anchors, 67, 190
stage model, 38–40; controversy surrounding, 39; reappraisal of traumatic memories, 38; stabilization and safety, 38–40; trauma processing, 38–39
starting small technique, 76
Steele, K., 73
stigma, internalized, 166
stillness practices, 66, 122–124
Story of Maybe, The, 147–148
STS (secondary traumatic stress), 182–186, 189
stuck points, 29, 165

subjugation, 22, 167
substance use disorders (SUDs), 28; body awareness, 116; emotion regulation, 137, 143–144; PTSD and, 39–40; suppression, 137
suicide ideation (SI), 28, 41; acute safety risk as contraindication for mindfulness, 46–47; meditation-related, 69, 83–84
suppression, 23, 91, 137; body awareness, 117–120; containment, 55; emotion education, 54–55; emotion regulation, 136–137, 143–144, 155, 157; window of tolerance, 30
sustained attention practices, 102, 107–109, 111, 114
switching (intentional shifting of awareness), 90, 101–102, 108
sympathetic nervous system, 30–31
systemic traumas, 38

T

TEND Academy, 186
tenderness, 57, 77, 93, 153, 164, 173, 177–178
Tetris, 189
therapeutic relationship: quality of, 37; safety and, 54; therapist and client dialogue during meditation, 65; traumagenic relational dynamics, 37
therapists' reactions to trauma, 182–192; burnout, 182–186; education regarding, 185; empathic strain, 182–183, 185–186; frequency, depth, and pervasiveness of exposure, 186–188; mindfulness practices, 190–192; responding to indirect exposure, 188–190; safety-enhancing strategies, 190–191; secondary traumatic stress, 182–186, 189; self-awareness, 185; self-monitoring, 185; trauma stewardship, 183; warning sign identification, 185
thoughts, changes in perspective related to, 160–161, 169–172; cognitive defusion, 171–172; decentering, 169–171
titration strategies, 66, 78–79; beginning by talking about what happened after the trauma, 79; creating a present-moment sensation, 79; Looking at a Glass Jar,

154–155; pacing the trauma narrative, 79; pendulation, 66; shorter practice periods, 66; small pauses to integrate movement, 66; structured breaks for resourcing, 66
tonglen, 62, 179–180
tracking and contextualizing layer, of inquiry process, 95–96
transference, 37
trauma: defined, 6; diagnostic comorbidity, 28; linking mindfulness with, 22–23; patterns of traumatic stress, 12–17; physiological and emotion dysregulation, 29–30; prevalence of, 6; psychological adaptation to, 17–22; spectrum of, 6–12; trauma within a trauma, 7
trauma-focused therapy, 40–41
trauma-informed therapy, 40–41
trauma-related intrusions during meditation, 69–79; describing emotions, 71–72; downregulating hyperarousal, 75; dual awareness, 72–73; generalization, 77; grounding techniques, 73–74; pivoting, 71, 77–78; recognizing, 71; reducing emotional intensity, 72–73; responding to painful emotions, 76–77; titration strategies, 78–79; upregulating hypoarousal, 75–76
trauma-sensitive principles, 2, 35–38; contextual factors, 37–38; empowerment, 36–37; safety, 35–36; therapeutic relationship, 37; traumagenic relational dynamics, 37
trauma-sensitive starting sequences, 66
treatment planning, 35–48; contraindications for mindfulness, 46–48; integrating mindfulness into plan, 44–46; mindfulness-based interventions, 42–43; protocol-based versus process-based approaches, 41–42; stage model, 38–40; trauma-informed versus trauma-focused therapies, 40–41; trauma-sensitive principles, 35–38

tree with deep roots, 176
Treleaven, David, 30, 38, 63, 66, 71, 76
trust schema, 20

V

vagus nerve activation, 75
values: changes in perspective and, 161–162, 173–175; clarification of, 173–175
VanderKooi, L., 62
varieties of contemplative experiences (VCE) study, 80
visual anchors, 67, 190
visual imagery. See imagery practices
visualization, 62; avoiding and disrupting, 188; disrupting consolidation of visual elements of memory, 189
vulnerability to harm, 22, 183

W

walking meditation, 25, 124, 130
Walsh, Erin, 72
weighted blankets, 75
willingness, 26, 141, 162, 179, 191
window of tolerance, 30–32; acute overwhelm as contraindication for mindfulness, 47; defined, 30–31, 51; expanding, 31–32, 50–59; explaining psychobiology of trauma response, 53; foundation of self-regulation through resourcing, 53; hyperarousal and hypoarousal, 31, 50–52; individual differences in, 31, 52; mindfulness and, 51–53; rating arousal, 66–67
working with difficulty, 33, 54, 57, 153–154, 172–173
working with discomfort, 88
worry: attention regulation, 7, 101, 103–106; body awareness, 116, 126–127; changes in perspective, 161, 166, 168, 170; cultural variation, 54; inquiry process, 111–112

Noga Zerubavel, PhD, is a licensed psychologist, cofounder of Arise Psychological Wellness and Consulting, and medical assistant professor in the department of psychiatry and behavioral sciences at Duke University Medical Center. She is former director of the Stress, Trauma, and Recovery Treatment (START) clinic at Duke, where she led a trauma consultation team and supervised psychiatry residents, clinical psychology interns, and fellows in trauma-informed psychotherapy. Zerubavel led mindfulness-based cognitive therapy (MBCT) groups at Duke from 2014-2020, and supervised psychiatry and psychology learners in providing MBCT. She is an active clinician, trainer, supervisor, and consultant.

Terri Messman, PhD, is professor of psychology and distinguished scholar at Miami University. She was an O'Toole Family Endowed Professor from 2013-2018, director of clinical training for the American Psychological Association (APA)-accredited clinical psychology PhD program, and interim deputy Title IX (sexual assault) coordinator. Her research program focuses on trauma and interpersonal violence, mindfulness and self-compassion, and emotion dysregulation. She is a licensed psychologist and certified yoga instructor.

Foreword writer **Jeffrey Brantley, MD**, is professor emeritus in the department of psychiatry and human behavior at Duke University Medical Center. He is founder and former director of the Mindfulness Based Stress Reduction (MBSR) Program at Duke Integrative Medicine. He is author of several books, including *Calming Your Anxious Mind*.

Real change *is* possible

For more than fifty years, New Harbinger has published proven-effective self-help books and pioneering workbooks to help readers of all ages and backgrounds improve mental health and well-being, and achieve lasting personal growth. In addition, our spirituality books offer profound guidance for deepening awareness and cultivating healing, self-discovery, and fulfillment.

Founded by psychologist Matthew McKay and Patrick Fanning, New Harbinger is proud to be an independent, employee-owned company. Our books reflect our core values of integrity, innovation, commitment, sustainability, compassion, and trust. Written by leaders in the field and recommended by therapists worldwide, New Harbinger books are practical, accessible, and provide real tools for real change.

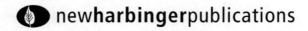

CLINICIANS CLUB

newharbingerpublications

Join the New Harbinger Clinicians Club—Exclusively for Mental Health Professionals

In our ongoing dedication to supporting you and your essential work with clients, we created the **New Harbinger Clinicians Club**—an entirely free membership club for mental health professionals.

Join and receive these exclusive club member benefits:

- **A special welcome gift**
- **35% off all professional books**
- **Free client resources for your practice**—such as worksheets, exercises, and audio downloads
- **Free e-books throughout the year**
- **Access to private sales**
- **A subscription to our *Quick Tips for Therapists* email program,** new book release alerts, and e-newsletter
- **Free e-booklets of the most popular *Quick Tips for Therapists***
- **Surveys on book topics you'd like to see us publish,** and resources you're looking for to better serve your clients

Join the New Harbinger Clinicians Club today at

newharbinger.com/clinicians-club

MORE BOOKS from NEW HARBINGER PUBLICATIONS

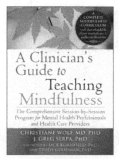

A CLINICIAN'S GUIDE TO TEACHING MINDFULNESS

The Comprehensive Session-by-Session Program for Mental Health Professionals and Health Care Providers

978-1626251397 / US $64.95

TREATING ADULT CHILDREN OF EMOTIONALLY IMMATURE PARENTS

A Clinician's Guide

978-1648483592 / US $49.95

TRAUMA-FOCUSED ACT

A Practitioner's Guide to Working with Mind, Body, and Emotion Using Acceptance and Commitment Therapy

978-1684038213 / US $64.95
CONTEXT PRESS
An Imprint of New Harbinger Publications

ACT-INFORMED EXPOSURE FOR ANXIETY

Creating Effective, Innovative, and Values-Based Exposures Using Acceptance and Commitment Therapy

978-1648480812 / US $64.95
CONTEXT PRESS
An Imprint of New Harbinger Publications

THE MINDFULNESS AND ACCEPTANCE WORKBOOK FOR ANXIETY, THIRD EDITION

A Guide to Breaking Free from Anxiety, Phobias, and Worry Using Acceptance and Commitment Therapy

978-1648484476 / US $25.95

THE DIALECTICAL BEHAVIOR THERAPY SKILLS WORKBOOK FOR CPTSD

Heal from Complex Post-Traumatic Stress Disorder, Find Emotional Balance, and Take Back Your Life

978-1648483103 / US $26.95

newharbingerpublications
1-800-748-6273 / newharbinger.com
(VISA, MC, AMEX / prices subject to change without notice)
Follow Us

QUICK TIPS for THERAPISTS

Written by leading clinicians, Quick Tips for Therapists are free e-mails, sent twice a month, to help enhance your client sessions.

Visit **newharbinger.com/quicktips** to sign up today!

Did you know there are **free tools** you can download for this book?

Free tools are things like **worksheets**, **guided meditation exercises**, and **more** that will help you get the most out of your book.

You can download free tools for this book—whether you bought or borrowed it, in any format, from any source—from the New Harbinger website. All you need is a NewHarbinger.com account. Just use the URL provided in this book to view the free tools that are available for it. Then, click on the "download" button for the free tool you want, and follow the prompts that appear to log in to your NewHarbinger.com account and download the material.

You can also save the free tools for this book to your **Free Tools Library** so you can access them again anytime, just by logging in to your account! Just look for this button on the book's free tools page.

+ Save this to my free tools library

If you need help accessing or downloading free tools, visit **newharbinger.com/faq** or contact us at customerservice@newharbinger.com.